T0333131

PENGUIN BOOKS
Ulysses Unbound

Terence Killeen is Research Scholar at the James Joyce Centre, Dublin. He has published in the *James Joyce Quarterly*, the *James Joyce Literary Supplement* and the *Joyce Studies Annual*. A former journalist with *The Irish Times*, he continues to write on Joyce-related matters for the newspaper. He is a former trustee of the International James Joyce Foundation. His most recent publication is an essay on Joyce's early 'A Portrait of the Artist' in the volume *Joyce's Non-Fiction Writings*. He has taught *Finnegans Wake* for many years at seminars at the Dublin James Joyce Summer School and the Trieste Joyce Summer School. He has also lectured at both schools, at the James Joyce Centre, at Trinity College, Dublin, at various International and North American James Joyce symposiums and at the Irish Cultural Centre in Paris.

Colm Tóibín's most recent novel is *The Magician*.

TERENCE KILLEEN

Ulysses Unbound

A Reader's Companion to
James Joyce's Ulysses

NEW EDITION

PENGUIN BOOKS

PENGUIN BOOKS

UK | USA | Canada | Ireland | Australia
India | New Zealand | South Africa

Penguin Books is part of the Penguin Random House group of companies
whose addresses can be found at global.penguinrandomhouse.com

First published by Wordwell Ltd in association with the National Library of Ireland 2004
Reissued 2005, 2014
New edition published in Penguin Books 2022
005

Set in 9.25/12.5pt Sabon LT Std
Typeset by Jouve (UK), Milton Keynes
Printed and bound in Great Britain by Clays Ltd, Elcograf S.p.A.

The authorized representative in the EEA is Penguin Random House Ireland,
Morrison Chambers, 32 Nassau Street, Dublin D02 YH68

A CIP catalogue record for this book is available from the British Library

ISBN: 978-0-141-99976-0

www.greenpenguin.co.uk

In memory of
NOREEN
and of
MICHAEL GRODEN

For ELIZABETH *and* ANNA

Contents

CONTENTS

Foreword: Killeen's Joyce

The ideal reader is someone who, without consulting any criticism or works of expurgation, picks up a book and slowly becomes engrossed, the attention held by the style or the plot or by something harder to define that has to do with the prospect of further pleasure in the pages ahead.

In the case of James Joyce's *Ulysses*, however, the ideal reader comes in two guises. The first type is a student or scholar, someone who takes pleasure in the intricacies and complexities of the text, who enjoys working on sources and annotations or connecting Joyce's book to literary theory or to aspects of Joyce's own life.

The second type of reader is someone who comes innocently to the book, becoming slowly intrigued by the shifts in tone and style, the heightened language, the jokes and parodies, or, again, something harder to define that has to do with the underlying rhythms in the prose and the way the book seems to contain, in energies hidden and on display, an astonishing and rich response to life.

Terence Killeen's '*Ulysses*' *Unbound* is a bridge between these two readers, connecting the world of scholarship and literary exegesis to the world of the ordinary reader coming to the book for the first time, or taking it up again having found one episode or other too dense and allusive, too textured and literary, too hard.

Joyce's book, as Killeen makes clear, has a close relationship to the idea of the common and the ordinary. '*Ulysses*', he writes, is 'a marvellously democratic book'. Killeen's impulse, then, is to take this idea seriously and create a commentary on *Ulysses* that opens the book for anyone to read. He writes clearly; his companion to *Ulysses* makes the book easier to follow without simplifying anything. His book is not his own insistent interpretation of *Ulysses*; rather, it is a guide for others that is systematic and supremely helpful.

Each reader will have different moments when '*Ulysses*' *Unbound* becomes essential. Anthony Burgess described the 'Oxen of the Sun' episode in *Ulysses* as the one he would have most like to have written:

> It is an author's chapter, a dazzling and authoritative display of what English can do. Moreover, it is a fulfilment of every author's egotistical desire not merely to *add* to English literature but to *enclose* what is actually there.

This episode is also, Killeen writes, 'by general agreement the most difficult episode'. The problem, for an unprepared reader, is that 'Oxen of the Sun' is written in a parody of style, but the styles shift as the narrative proceeds. Trying to work out what is actually happening in this episode, and then trying to appreciate the various styles, is an intense experience. It is one moment in the book where it might help to be a professor of English rhetoric or a polyglot like Anthony Burgess.

This is when *'Ulysses' Unbound* comes to our aid most practically and succinctly. In twenty pages, Killeen sets out with great precision how the text of 'Oxen of the Sun' works, what it does. He begins by outlining 'the course of the "action", as if there were no stylistic screen between reader and events narrated'. Then he deals with the style: 'The episode is written as a succession of parodies of passages of English prose, tracing its development from Latin and Anglo-Saxon up to the late nineteenth century.' He then outlines, citing page numbers, the thirty-one parodies.

While he works in detail, glossing words and phrases, working his way through some passages line by line, he also has a view of the entire work which makes clear to us what we should look out for. He notes that the Sirens episode – the eleventh out of eighteen – 'takes on a different tonality: things that had been very serious begin to seem merely occasions for fun.' And then he continues: 'If *Ulysses* is about anything, it is about this change of tone, more than it is about paternity, or androgyny, or colonialism, or Irish freedom, or many another thematic word one could summon up.' He refers to this change as 'a kind of liberation, a liberation into style'.

For the reader, any reader, this response to the novel allows us to savour sentences and tones that might previously have seemed intimidating or too performative. It nudges us to note the changes in style from the very beginning. But Killeen's noting the shift in tone also encourages us to take lightly what we once took seriously, to see the response to life, as exemplified in the book, as fluid, as open to possibility, and indeed pleasure, as any reader of the book must be.

Colm Tóibín, 2022

Preface

This book offers access to James Joyce's *Ulysses* on a number of levels. On the most basic level, each episode is summarised; this is followed by an account of the Homeric parallels that underpin the narrative. Next there is a discussion of the style of the episode, followed by a broader discussion, under the neutral rubric 'Commentary', of some of the issues that the episode raises. The distinction between 'Style' and 'Commentary' is obviously rather artificial; nonetheless in this book style is foregrounded so clearly, attention is drawn to it so markedly, that there are good grounds for devoting a separate section to it.

These sections are followed by notes on some of the principal personages and events mentioned in the text, followed in their turn by a select glossary of foreign language words and phrases. The notes are by no means intended to be comprehensive; that is too large a task for a work of this scope. But it is hoped that they provide interesting information, especially about the real people on whom many of the characters in *Ulysses* are based. The recently published *Annotations to James Joyce's 'Ulysses'*, by Sam Slote, Marc A. Mamigonian and John Turner (see Bibliography), provides the most comprehensive and reliable annotations for the book available.

Again, to provide glosses for all the strange words used in *Ulysses* is beyond the purview of this work. But the 'Select glossary' does help with one of the most obvious barriers: the large number of expressions in languages other than English that are used throughout. Stephen in particular is much given to such terminology, and many readers might welcome help with some of his very recondite locutions.

The line numbers used in the notes and glossary are keyed to the line numbers in the edition of *Ulysses* edited by Hans Walter Gabler (The Bodley Head, London, 1986; revised edition 1993). Although controversial when published (see Epilogue), this remains the best and most reliable text available.

One peculiarity of this work is that it does not feature a broad overall introduction, setting out themes and theories. I have preferred to follow the more natural course, whereby one first reads the book, and then attempts an overall view. Even at that, the 'overall view', when it comes in a concluding essay, is not very overall; one thing that the last few episodes of *Ulysses* seem to inculcate is a suspicion of totalising views and grand interpretations.

An unhelpful way to approach *Ulysses*, I believe, is to start with a word, be it 'paternity', 'androgyny', 'différance' or 'colonialism', or many another, and to use this as a master key to unlock the entire book. Very often such an approach works only by focusing on one part of this vast work, and ignoring evidence which contradicts, or at least questions, it from another part. So the concluding essay is more a set of probes, a discussion of possible approaches, than it is a key to all Joycean mythologies.

Despite this eschewing of introductory material, some basic facts should be spelt out. *Ulysses*, like Gaul, is divided into three parts, the first consisting of three episodes ('episodes' is the term that Joyce consistently used in English, rather than 'chapters'), the second of twelve episodes, and the third of three again. The entire book covers a period of some nineteen hours, from 8 a.m. on Thursday, 16 June 1904 to around 3 a.m. the next day. The three parts, and the eighteen episodes, correspond to the structure of Homer's *Odyssey*. The detailed correspondences are given in the discussion of each episode, but the first part concerns Stephen Dedalus and corresponds to the story of Odysseus's son, Telemachus, which begins *The Odyssey*. The second part, by far the longest, introduces us to the book's Ulysses, Leopold Bloom, who enters on the scene relatively late in the work, just as Odysseus does in Homer (actually in Book 5). (The name 'Ulysses', incidentally, is the Romanised version of the Greek 'Odysseus'.) This part corresponds to the actual adventures of Odysseus in Homer's epic. The third part concerns Bloom's rather dilatory return, with Stephen, to his home, corresponding to the similar 'Nostos' or return to Odysseus's home, Ithaca, in *The Odyssey*.

Each episode was given a Homeric title by Joyce, although these do not appear in the book itself. These titles reflect the major setting or personages of the part of *The Odyssey* being exploited at that point: Episode 6, Bloom's visit to Glasnevin cemetery, is called 'Hades' because that is the name of the land of the dead which Odysseus visits at the corresponding point in *The Odyssey*, Episode 11 is called 'Sirens' because it corresponds to the point in *The Odyssey* where Odysseus has to resist the enchanting songs of the sea maidens, the Sirens, who lure sailors to their doom.

Although Joyce decided not to use these titles in the work itself, and was reluctant to make them publicly known, they have by now become the standard names for each episode. They are not difficult to remember and they are used for convenience throughout this work.

The first substantial critical work devoted to *Ulysses* was Stuart Gilbert's *James Joyce's 'Ulysses'* (1930). This included a plan or 'schema' of the book, supplied by Joyce to Gilbert. (A version of it had already been given to Valery Larbaud, the most influential French champion of Joyce's work.) This schema lists the Homeric correspondences; but we also learn from it that each episode has its own specific narrative technique, its own specific symbol, its own art. Many have a particular colour and organ of the body assigned to them. The reasons for all this will be discussed later. (The schema's authority is slightly compromised by the fact that much earlier, in 1920, Joyce had sent the Italian critic Carlo Linati a schema which differs markedly in some respects from the later one, while agreeing on the main outlines.)

Joyce's reasons for preparing and distributing this schema were complex: he wanted to promote awareness of the book, but he also did not want to give too much away. There may be some significance in the fact that he ultimately seems to have decided that no great harm would be done by distributing the schema to selected individuals, with the likelihood that it would then become more widely known: it may indicate that ultimately, the inner core of the book is not there. The Gilbert schema is not 'the key' to *Ulysses*, but it does provide a structure which clarifies some important aspects of the book. It is reproduced on pages 326–7 of this work and is discussed in some detail in what follows.

∗

I am grateful to the National Library of Ireland and its former Director, Brendan Ó Donoghue, for providing the opportunity to write this work, which had been gestating, in some shape or form, for many years. Some of the ideas in the concluding essay go back to conversations with John Banville when we were both working on the sub-editors' desk of *The Irish Press* in the 1970s. Along the way, many other intellectual debts have been incurred; no great surprise will be occasioned if I single out, as nearly every Joycean does at some point, Fritz Senn. Catherine Fahy and Luca Crispi, of the National Library, have been very supportive throughout. Although I deliberately do not refer much to Joyce criticism in the course of this work, I am indebted to all the works listed in the bibliography, even, or maybe especially, the ones I disagree with.

I am also grateful to my employers, *The Irish Times*, for providing a period of sabbatical leave that made the writing of this work possible. My wife, Noreen O'Donohue, greatly assisted this project through much wise counsel.

June 2004
Revised 2022

Preface to the Penguin Edition, 2022

For this Penguin edition of the book, I have added an Epilogue, '*Ulysses* at 100', which reflects on the history of *Ulysses*'s reception in the century since it was published. I have added a passage in the 'Styles' section of the 'Oxen of the Sun' episode to deal with an issue that has arisen in recent years. I have also clarified somewhat the musical structure of the 'Sirens' episode in the light of some new (and old) information and have provided new information, based on recent scholarship, on the real-life origins of Leopold and Molly Bloom. I have also, of course, substantially updated the Bibliography.

I am grateful to Colm Tóibín for contributing a new foreword to this work and for his persistent and powerful advocacy of '*Ulysses*' *Unbound*.

Preface to the Penguin edition, 2012

Life of James Joyce

James Augustine Joyce was born on 2 February 1882, at 41 Brighton Square West, Rathgar, Dublin. His father was John Stanislaus Joyce, a Corkman, who at the time of Joyce's birth was working in the office of the collector of rates for Dublin. His mother was Mary Jane Murray, a member of a petty bourgeois Dublin family. James Joyce was the oldest surviving child (a boy named John was born in 1881 but did not live). Altogether John Joyce and May Murray had ten children who survived infancy, four boys and six girls. Five other children did not survive infancy.

At the age of six (an exceptionally early age) Joyce was sent as a boarder to Clongowes Wood College, Co. Kildare. His experiences there are recorded in *A Portrait of the Artist as a Young Man*. While Joyce was still at Clongowes, the downfall of Parnell occurred in 1891; this event permanently coloured Joyce's view of Irish politics and also deeply affected his father, a committed Parnellite. That same year, Joyce's sojourn in Clongowes was terminated; John Stanislaus Joyce had started on the long career of financial mismanagement that would finally destroy his family. The Joyces moved from Bray, where they lived at the time of the Parnell debacle, first to Blackrock and then to the north inner city of Dublin, where they went through an astonishing number of changes of address, each one more impoverished than the preceding. James was educated briefly by the Christian Brothers (this experience goes unmentioned in his work), but was then enabled to attend Belvedere College through the good offices of Father John Conmee, the former rector of Clongowes. At Belvedere, Joyce underwent a spiritual crisis, occasioned by his precocious experiences with prostitutes and his subsequent drastic repentance. However, the return to the bosom of the Church was short-lived; soon after Joyce discovered the artistic vocation which was to remain with him for the rest of his life and which made religion redundant.

John Stanislaus Joyce had lost his job in the rate collector's office in 1892; from then on he subsisted on a meagre pension and occasional odd jobs. However, on leaving Belvedere with an excellent academic record, James was still able to attend University College Dublin in 1898. He was an extremely confident young man, impervious to the attitudes of others towards him, reticent, but at times very witty. Under the influence of drink, which he took up rather belatedly after leaving college, but very enthusiastically, his behaviour could be raucous and uninhibited. He made some very close friends at college, in particular J. F. Byrne (Cranly in *A Portrait*), though all of Joyce's close male friendships show a pattern of gradual cooling, sometimes exacerbated by a sense of betrayal and suspicion.

Joyce's academic performance at college was less impressive than at school: he was bored with the official curriculum on offer and instead pursued particular interests of his own, such as Henrik Ibsen, virtually unknown both to the professors and the students. However, he graduated with a Bachelor of Arts in 1902. He then determined on pursuing a medical career, apparently with the idea that he could combine it with writing. Joyce's attendance at the medical lectures was desultory, however, and he was also angered when the authorities declined to offer him any tutoring work in his degree subjects. He decided, a trifle irrationally, that he would fare better at medical school in Paris than in Dublin and determined to go there. This decision was of course a first step in the myth of enforced exile that Joyce was always to cherish thereafter.

He departed for Paris on 1 December 1902. Not surprisingly, his medical studies were scanty, but, insofar as his straitened circumstances permitted, he explored the intellectual, artistic and other delights of Paris (his French was already fluent, though perhaps not fluent enough for understanding technical medical lectures). However, he was more than happy to come home for Christmas in the best Irish tradition when his parents made a special effort to fund his return.

Back in Dublin, he made a new acquaintance (he and Byrne had by now fallen out): this was Oliver St John Gogarty, a far more successful medical student than was Joyce. Gogarty's wit and bawdry appealed to Joyce and superficially the two were on friendly terms. Joyce returned to Paris on 23 January, having remained nearly a month in

Dublin, and continued to pursue his rather desultory studies and to write some verse. He also had some difficult but not entirely unfriendly meetings with John Synge. However, his time in Paris was abruptly cut short by the shocking news that his mother was very ill, indeed dying, as his father informed him in a telegram.

Joyce returned to Dublin on 13 April 1903, to find his mother slowly dying of liver cancer. She died on 13 August, worn out, as Joyce saw it, by the rigours of the life she had been forced to lead. He regarded her as a victim, and, as he later told Nora Barnacle, he 'cursed the system that had made her a victim'.

The family circumstances, which had been bad enough while May Murray was alive, became dire after her death. Joyce's own life was as disorganised as that of Stephen Dedalus in *Ulysses*. Nevertheless, his artistic progress continued: he embarked on a subjective essay about himself that was the germ of both *Stephen Hero* and *A Portrait of the Artist as a Young Man*. He had also written a series of 'epiphanies', brief glimpses of Dublin life or of his own aesthetic life that were also to undergo considerable expansion in later works.

He tried out various occupations including singing (he had inherited his father's fine tenor voice), and teaching at a school in Dalkey, none of them with any great conviction. Finding life in his father's house impossible, he moved in briefly with Gogarty to the Martello tower in Sandycove, which Gogarty had rented. It was shortly before this, in June 1904, that the most important event in Joyce's life occurred: his meeting with Nora Barnacle, the young woman from Galway who had come to Dublin to work in Finn's Hotel in Nassau Street. The relationship between her and Joyce was still in its early stages when Joyce went to live in the tower but it is likely, as Richard Ellmann speculates, that this new element in his life made Joyce all the more hostile to Gogarty's cynicism. In any case, Joyce lasted in the tower just five nights: the nocturnal ravings of another guest, Samuel Chenevix Trench, and Gogarty's alarming response of firing off a gun allegedly to quieten Trench down, led to Joyce's precipitate departure in the middle of the night of 14 September 1904.

This drama seems to have been the final straw for Joyce. He determined to leave Ireland on a semi-permanent basis. In a daring act of commitment, he asked Nora to come with him and, even more daringly, she agreed. Joyce understood that there was a language teaching job available at the Berlitz School in Zürich, and on the strength of this belief he and Nora departed thither on 8 October 1904.

When they arrived in Zürich, it turned out that the hoped-for job did not exist; however, Joyce and Nora went on to Trieste, then in the Austro-Hungarian Empire, now in Italy. The job in Trieste proved equally illusory, but Joyce did obtain a real one in Pola, at the very bottom of the Istrian peninsula (it is now in Croatia). Throughout this tempestuous period, he continued to write: in addition to the ongoing autobiographical novel that he had begun in Dublin, he had written some stories (three of them had appeared in the magazine, *The Irish Homestead*) and in Pola he wrote more. These would eventually form the *Dubliners* collection.

Joyce's stay in Pola did not last long; a position became available in the Trieste Berlitz School, very fortunately as the Austrians had decided to expel all aliens from Pola, their main naval base. He moved to Trieste in March 1905 and remained there for most of the next ten years. His son Giorgio was born there on 27 July 1905. His brother Stanislaus joined him there in October and also took up a position at the Berlitz School.

Joyce now began to experience the difficulties with publishers that were to dog him for many years to come. He sent the *Dubliners* collection (minus 'The Dead', which was not yet written) to the London publisher Grant Richards and immediately encountered objections on grounds of decorum and possible libel. Thus began a long saga which would have strained the nerves of a more phlegmatic writer than Joyce: on him the effect was devastating. Allied to this cause of instability was Joyce's innate tendency to become bored with any fixed situation in which he found himself. It was this, more than a minor problem in the Berlitz school, that prompted him to leave Trieste with Nora and Giorgio in July 1906 and take up a job in a bank in Rome.

The period in Rome was not a happy one; Joyce did not like the job or the city, which he considered 'a cemetery'. The one productive result of his stay there was the story 'The Dead', written in a mood of greater tenderness for the country he had left than he had yet experienced. His unhappy Roman experience may have made home seem rather more attractive. Another interesting outcome of the Rome experience was an idea for an unwritten *Dubliners* story, to be called 'Ulysses'. Much more was later to be heard of this.

Joyce returned chastened to Trieste in March 1907. A daughter, Lucia Anna, was born on 26 July. His first volume, the collection of poems called *Chamber Music*, was published in May, but publication of *Dubliners* remained blocked.

In 1909 he made two return visits to Dublin: the first to see his family again and to show off his son Giorgio; the second to set up Dublin's first cinema, the Volta, in Mary Street. (The venture, which began well, was not ultimately a success; in this, as in much else, Joyce was ahead of his time.) The visit was marked by a crisis in his relations with Nora; a former friend, Vincent Cosgrave (Lynch in *A Portrait*), told Joyce that he had enjoyed Nora's favours at the time when Joyce and she were first going out together. Joyce, devastated, wrote accusatory letters to Nora. However, he was reassured by a closer friend, Byrne, and by Nora herself, that it was all a 'blasted lie'. In reaction to this trauma, and to a further contretemps at the start of his second visit, Joyce engaged in a correspondence with Nora that reached extraordinary heights and depths of emotional and erotic intensity.

While in Dublin, Joyce engaged in negotiations with the firm of Maunsel and Company, managed by George Roberts, for the publication of *Dubliners*. These negotiations dragged on for two more years, with Roberts, like Grant Richards before him, raising objections to many aspects of the collection. Joyce's last visit to Ireland, in 1912, was in connection with this planned publication. The encounter with Roberts on this occasion was a disaster; after many years of prevaricating, he definitively withdrew from the publication of *Dubliners* and the proofs of the collection (it had been set up in type) were pulped or, in Joyce's version, burned. On that note, Joyce left Ireland for good, dispatching a retaliatory blast, the poem 'Gas from a Burner', as his final response. Whatever one may think of his prolonged exile, it is hard not to feel sympathy for an author subjected to such treatment.

Back in Trieste, he and his family resumed the life they had taken up there. Joyce now had a position at the Revoltella Commercial

School, which eased very slightly the financial burden mainly caused by his spendthrift habits. He had jettisoned the first version of the autobiographical novel he had been writing for many years and had begun to rewrite it under the title *A Portrait of the Artist as a Young Man*. Towards the end of 1913, a breakthrough finally occurred in the *Dubliners* saga: Grant Richards, of whom Joyce had despaired, asked to see the manuscript again and in January 1914 finally agreed to publish it. At the same time Ezra Pound, the most influential Modernist propagandist, having heard about Joyce from Yeats, took an interest in his case. The tide had begun to turn.

Dubliners was published in June 1914, and none of the anticipated reactions ensued. Meanwhile the avant-garde magazine, *The Egoist*, was publishing *A Portrait* in instalments. Encouraged by these developments, Joyce towards the end of 1914 embarked on two more projects: the play *Exiles* and the novel *Ulysses*, which had been in his mind in some shape or form since 1907. These activities were interrupted, however, by the need for a hasty departure from Trieste in June 1915: after Italy entered the war, the situation in Trieste became more tense. The Joyces, as British subjects in an Austro-Hungarian city, were in a dangerous position. They could be interned by the Austrian authorities, as Joyce's brother Stanislaus had already been. With some difficulty, Joyce obtained permission from the authorities to go to neutral Switzerland.

He arrived in Zürich ('the first big city after the frontier') and the family remained there for the duration of the war. Despite the difficulties caused by the conflict, Joyce's reputation continued to grow; he began to attract patronage, something that he had always hoped for and frequently sought. His principal benefactor was Harriet Shaw Weaver, an Englishwoman who was associate editor of *The Egoist*. *A Portrait* was first published in New York in 1916 (an English edition was published by *The Egoist* in 1917). Miss Weaver (there is no other term by which to call her) began to make small donations, at this stage anonymously. Later, the amounts increased considerably, and the anonymity was dropped. In these circumstances, Joyce advanced well with the writing of *Ulysses*.

One or two circumstances did hamper his progress in Zürich: one was his involvement with a company called The English Players, dedicated to staging English-language plays in Switzerland. This in itself would not have hindered his work, but he became involved in acrimonious litigation with the British Consulate over an issue connected with the Players. At the same time, he had a mild liaison with a woman named Marthe Fleischmann. Both of these events, however, proved to have their uses in *Ulysses*: Joyce was not a writer to let material go to waste.

More productive than either of these events was Joyce's friendship with Frank Budgen, an English painter who had ended up in Zürich when war broke out. Budgen became Joyce's principal sounding board for ideas about *Ulysses* and their discussions led many years later to Budgen's important book, *James Joyce and the Making of 'Ulysses'*.

With the end of the war, Joyce decided to move back to Trieste, whither he returned in October 1919. However, the city was now a rather different place from the one he had left. It was a good deal quieter and, moreover, there was nobody as receptive as Budgen with whom to discuss *Ulysses*. Joyce's brother Stanislaus was no longer interested; he had greatly resented James's treatment of him over the years and was determined to forge a life of his own. Joyce regained his old position at the Higher Commercial School, soon to become the University of Trieste. But he remained most unhappy with his lot in Trieste; he thought about going to England or even to Ireland for the summer. In these circumstances, he was quick to take up a suggestion from Ezra Pound that he stop off in Paris for a few days *en route* to London. Joyce then decided on a permanent departure from Trieste: he resigned his position in the university (it soon went to Stanislaus) and the Joyce family departed Trieste for good on 4 July 1920.

Joyce arrived in Paris on 8 July ostensibly intending to remain just a week. However, he remained for some twenty years; Paris suited him. By now, he was becoming famous; excerpts from *Ulysses* were appearing in various little magazines, and a fine scandal was developing. Four issues of *The Little Review* in New York were confiscated and burned because they contained extracts from the novel. Ultimately there was an obscenity trial in the US; the magazine was banned from publishing any more extracts. This was in one sense a setback, but on the other hand all the publicity was making the unpublished book a huge *succès de scandale. Ulysses* was nearly finished, but it seemed impossible to publish it anywhere. In this situation, a young American, Sylvia Beach, who owned a bookshop, Shakespeare and Company, on the Paris Left Bank, undertook to publish it in France. The book was printed by the firm of Darantière in Dijon, and, after much trauma and agitation, published on 2 February (Joyce's birthday) 1922. Joyce had finally arrived.

Since *Ulysses* could not be legally sold in either Britain or the United States, and since it was also very expensive, Joyce's fame or notoriety did little to ease his financial situation. However, Miss Weaver, despite some doubts occasioned by Joyce's drinking habits, virtually took over his financial maintenance, settling enormous sums on him and almost impoverishing herself in the process.

Following publication of *Ulysses*, Joyce's life took on a more settled pattern: he lived in Paris, though every summer he and Nora would take off for long excursions, sometimes in France, sometimes as far afield as Austria or Denmark. He never returned to Italy. Joyce did live in London for several months in 1931, in order to establish residency there to enable him to marry Nora. This was a social convention that Joyce and Nora had long flouted, but for testamentary reasons they found it necessary to go through a civil ceremony in a London register office on 4 July that year. Although Joyce talked at the time of settling in London, the city did not really agree with him, and he was happy to return to Paris in September 1931.

In 1923, Joyce had embarked on a new work, ultimately to be called *Finnegans Wake*. The extreme obscurity and complexity of this undertaking very quickly aroused loud protests as extracts from it appeared, but with incredible determination Joyce persisted with it through sixteen long years of many difficulties until it finally appeared in 1939. (It should be added that the work also had its passionate supporters from the very start.) The relatively more settled framework in which Joyce began to write the work, which meant that the earlier parts of it were composed with comparative speed, was soon disrupted by a number of factors, some relatively trivial, some extremely serious.

One of these factors, which was in fact present from the very start but which worsened greatly as time went on, was the state of Joyce's eyes. These had always been bad; but from 1922 to 1930 he had to undergo eleven operations as his sight continued to deteriorate. He sometimes needed a magnifying glass to see the words he was writing. It was only when he was operated on by an eminent Swiss surgeon, Dr Alfred Vogt, in 1930 that the situation was somewhat stabilised, though his eyes continued to cause him difficulties for the rest of his life.

Another distraction from work on *Finnegans Wake* was Joyce's campaign on behalf of an Irish tenor, John Sullivan, whom Joyce first heard sing in Paris in late 1929. Joyce engaged in propaganda on behalf of this singer with a vehemence that astonished his friends: but it is evident that Joyce saw the treatment of Sullivan, who claimed he was prevented by an 'Italian ring' from singing in the world's major opera houses, as analogous to his own experiences of censorship and neglect by officialdom. Joyce's efforts on Sullivan's behalf were astonishingly energetic, but only partially successful; he had met the singer at a time when his voice was beginning to lose its quality.

But by far the greatest burden on Joyce's life in those years was the ongoing mental illness of his daughter, Lucia. She began to show signs of disturbance from about 1930 onwards, soon after giving up what had seemed a promising career as a dancer. Gradually her behaviour became sometimes violent and always unpredictable in the extreme. A visit by her to Ireland was particularly traumatic for all those involved. As her condition worsened, Joyce became more and more absorbed in her plight, doing his utmost to save her from permanent committal to a mental institution. In this he ultimately failed, but Joyce's increasingly frantic efforts on her behalf (especially in view of the relative indifference of her mother to her case and the very hard-line and negative attitude taken by her brother) take on a Lear-like, tragic intensity. While Lucia's illness casts a major shadow over his last years, it also reveals depths of love and devotion in his nature which might not otherwise be apparent. And not all developments in his family were bad ones: although his father died on 31 December 1931, unvisited by James for almost twenty years, a son, Stephen James, was born to Giorgio and his wife, Helen Kastor Fleischman, a wealthy American divorcee, on 15 February 1932. Joyce was powerfully affected by this near-coincidence of his father's death and the birth of a grandson; it led to his finest poem, 'Ecce Puer'.

As with so many other people, the prospects of another European conflagration weighed heavily on the Joyces as 1939 advanced. Even the publication, at last, of *Finnegans Wake* in May of that year was overshadowed, much to Joyce's annoyance. On the declaration of war on 3 September 1939, Joyce managed to move Lucia from a clinic at Ivry, near Paris, to one at La Baule, in Brittany, further away from danger. Meanwhile, Giorgio and his wife were separating: Helen was going through a severe nervous breakdown (she recovered her health only after her return to America and her divorce from Giorgio). In this very uncertain situation, James and Nora Joyce accepted an invitation from their friend, Maria Jolas, to join her in the village of Saint-Gérand-le-Puy, near Vichy. They arrived there with Giorgio on 24 December 1939 (Stephen Joyce was already there, having been sent there out of harm's way in November). When the German invasion began in May 1940, following the false calm of the first few months of the war, Joyce and Nora realised that it would not be safe to remain in Saint-Gérand, of which they were tired in any case. After much difficulty, they succeeded in obtaining permission to leave France for Zürich in neutral Switzerland. This was the city where the Joyces had sat out the previous war, and where Joyce had first arrived with Nora at the start of his continental odyssey many years before – and, indeed, where they had first made love.

After a difficult journey from France, they reached Zürich on 17 December 1940. Joyce planned to have Lucia join them there as soon as possible; he had already obtained permission for her to leave France. But before that could happen, he was taken violently ill with stomach pains on the night of 10 January 1941. He was suffering from a perforated duodenal ulcer; he had been getting severe stomach pains for several months, if not years, previously, but was happy to accept the view of a French doctor who put them down to nerves and he chose not to alter his opinion even when they worsened. An operation was carried out at the Red Cross Hospital, which at first seemed successful. However, Joyce's condition weakened over the following days, and he died at 2.15 a.m. on 13 January 1941. He was buried in the Fluntern cemetery overlooking the city, where he still lies.

Commentary on
Episodes of *Ulysses*

I

[1 · Telemachus]

Time: 8 a.m. Thursday 16 June 1904
Location: Martello Tower, Sandycove, Co. Dublin;
Forty-Foot Bathing Place

SUMMARY

Malachi Mulligan, a medical student, appears at the top of the Martello tower in Sandycove, Co. Dublin, holding a shaving bowl, and launches into a parody of the consecration of the Mass (the turning of bread and wine into the body and blood of Christ), using the shaving bowl and its contents as a mock chalice for the consecration of the wine. Stephen Dedalus, a would-be writer and currently a teacher, who also lives in the tower, soon joins him. Stephen watches as Mulligan completes the parody. It is clear that there is friction between them: the first thing we learn about Dedalus is that he is 'displeased and sleepy'. Almost immediately we find out why: another young man is staying as a guest in the tower, an Englishman, known only as Haines, a friend of Mulligan's. Stephen quietly objects to the presence in the tower of Haines, who was raving in his sleep all the previous night in a manner that Stephen finds disturbing. There is a strong contrast between the manners of the two young men: Mulligan is all bluster and bravado; Stephen is reticent to the point of rudeness, refusing any sociability. It is as if as the exaggerated exuberance of Mulligan's manner is an equal and opposite reaction to the exaggerated reticence of Stephen's. Mulligan more or less ignores Stephen's complaint, turning to the sea and praising it with mock-Homeric epithets: 'snotgreen'; 'scrotumtightening'. Mulligan mockingly holds up his shaving mirror to Stephen's gaze. Stephen, pointing to it, bitterly declares it to be a symbol of Irish art: 'The cracked lookingglass of a servant'.

The problem with Haines (later in the conversation Stephen, quite characteristically, says 'let him stay') is only the ostensible cause of their disaffection. As the ensuing difficult conversation between them makes clear, it has its roots in events prior to the novel's opening: the death of Stephen's mother and what Stephen takes to be Mulligan's disrespectful attitude to him over that death. As they discuss this issue (Stephen has relaxed his guard at least to the point of telling Mulligan what the matter is), Mulligan again comments on Stephen's mother's death in a way that worsens still further the 'gaping wounds' in Stephen's heart.

Nothing is resolved by the quarrel; Mulligan goes down to the living room and Stephen is left alone on the roof of the tower. Here he has an intense imaginary encounter with his mother's spirit, and tries to shake off the burden of guilt he feels over her death (he apparently refused to kneel and pray for her as she lay on her deathbed). Descending, he joins Mulligan and Haines for breakfast, a meal at which the two Irishmen take pleasure in baffling and teasing their guest (an ardent Hibernophile) with their almost impenetrable and highly oblique conversational exchanges. An old woman comes to deliver the milk; she is duly mocked by Mulligan and silently scorned by Stephen, who sees her as a figure of subjected Ireland. (He sees everything as a figure of something else.) She is ardently admired by Haines, however, who is pleased to see her as a type of the Irish peasantry and talks in Irish to her. After her departure, Mulligan and Stephen engage in further repartee. In the course of this it emerges that Stephen rarely washes, having a phobia about water; however, he consoles himself with the observation that 'All Ireland is washed by the gulfstream.' This remark greatly tickles Haines, but when Stephen inquires if he might make money by it, Haines is instantly on his guard. Mulligan sees Haines as a potential source of funds (both he and Stephen are chronically short of money) and he is annoyed that Stephen has ruined a chance to extract some cash from their English visitor.

After breakfast, Mulligan, accompanied by Stephen and Haines, goes down to the Forty Foot Bathing Place for his morning swim, singing a self-composed ditty, 'The Ballad of Joking Jesus', en route. As they go along, Haines attempts to engage Stephen in some philosophical conversation. In response to Haines's remark that Stephen seems to be free to make his own choices, the would-be poet declares that he is 'a servant of two masters', the British Empire and the Roman Catholic church. A third master, probably his own muse, wants him for odd jobs. Haines reacts calmly to the remark about the British Empire, opining that 'history is to blame' for Britain's oppression of Ireland. Stephen, meanwhile, probably in reaction to Haines's comment and to his own mention of the Roman Catholic church, has drifted off into an elaborate fantasy glorifying the power of the church and associating Mulligan with some of the routed heresiarchs. Stephen appears to identify himself with the church in this instance.

At the bathing place, he hears two men discussing the man who had drowned nine days previously: they expect his body to be found today when the tide comes in at about 1 p.m.

Stephen has locked the door of the tower behind them and takes the key with him. Before he leaves for his teaching job, however, Mulligan asks him for the key, ostensibly to keep his clothes flat while he swims. Stephen has foreseen this request: he believes the key is his, that he paid the rent, but he nonetheless hands it over without complaint and departs with bitterness in his heart, expressed in a single unspoken word: 'Usurper'.

CORRESPONDENCES

The Odyssey begins on the Greek island of Ithaca, the home of Odysseus (Ulysses). He has been missing since the end of the Trojan War, many years previously, and in his absence, a gang of arrogant suitors for the hand of Penelope, his wife, has taken over the royal palace. The boldest of the suitors is Antinous. Odysseus's son, Telemachus, is displaced, usurped, and ignored, able only to watch helplessly as his father's goods are laid waste. The goddess Pallas Athena, the constant supporter of Odysseus, visits Telemachus, disguised at first as Mentes, an old friend of the family, and then as old Mentor, the rather ineffectual guardian of Odysseus's houses and stables. She advises Telemachus to leave Ithaca and go in quest of his father on the Greek mainland. In the Gilbert schema, Stephen is Telemachus, Mulligan is Antinous and the milkwoman is Mentor (although Stephen's response to her is much more ambiguous than is Telemachus's to Mentor).

Another system of correspondences is already in play, and this is specifically alluded to, unlike the Homeric parallels. Haines at one point remarks that the tower and its setting remind him of Elsinore, the setting of Shakespeare's *Hamlet*, and this is a clue to the analogy between Stephen and Prince Hamlet, the heir displaced by his usurping uncle, Claudius, who has murdered Hamlet's father and married his mother. Haines foreshadows this important motif with his remarks about the father/son relationship in *Hamlet*: he links it explicitly to the theological father and son. The *Hamlet* parallel will run through the book in tandem with the Homeric one.

STYLE

The episode is written in what Joyce himself called 'the initial style', a style that, with variants and interruptions, holds good up to about midway through the book. The technique of this episode is called in the Gilbert schema 'narrative (young)', and there is a remarkable sense of freshness and clarity to the physical descriptions. The time is early morning and the style has a corresponding sharpness of outline; the famous opening sentence: 'Stately, plump Buck Mulligan came from the stairhead, bearing a bowl of lather on which a mirror and a razor lay crossed' leaves nothing in shade or unclear; with its carefully chosen adjectives, the physical image of Mulligan is immediately present before us. The second sentence instantly reinforces this by telling us what Mulligan is wearing.

A cool, detached narrative voice seems, therefore, to be in control of the action. Very soon, however, we realize that there are complications with this scenario: the first hint comes with the insertion of the single word 'Chrysostomos' after the detached narrative description of Mulligan's 'even white teeth glistening here and there with gold points'. Once the reader has figured out that 'chrysostomos' is Greek for 'golden-mouthed' (and is thus an appropriate term to apply to Mulligan's mouth as described, as well as being a term used for particularly eloquent Greek orators), the question arises as to where this strange comment comes from.

The answer can only be that it emanates from the mind of Stephen, that it is Stephen's internal mental comment on the sight of Mulligan's teeth, rendered without any intermediary forms such as 'he thought', 'he felt', etc., and even without any distinguishing typographical device such as italics. Thus we are introduced to the aspect of *Ulysses* that probably caused the greatest stir on its initial appearance (apart from its sexual frankness, of course): the 'interior monologue' or 'stream of consciousness'. This method whereby the feelings and thoughts of characters are conveyed with unprecedented immediacy, apparently just rendered directly on the page as they occur, is indeed one of the dominant features of the book in the first ten episodes, growing increasingly complex in its deployment as the novel goes on; even in the later episodes it persists, although overlaid with many other techniques.

This episode also introduces a stylistic aspect of Stephen's consciousness that is pervasive: his extraordinary powers of visualisation. We first encounter this in the scene he summons up after Mulligan speaks of giving Haines 'a ragging worse than they gave Clive Kempthorpe'. Stephen instantly conjures up this event, which occurred in Oxford and which he could not have attended; so vivid is his depiction, however, that it is exactly as if Stephen had been a witness, if not a participant. The addition of the passage about the deaf gardener, oblivious to what is going on in Kempthorpe's room, is a typical Dedalus flourish and converts the little scene into a strange epiphany. Stephen has entirely annexed the event, made it his own in his imagination. It is significant that his next remark shows a relenting in his anger with Haines; it is as if the imaginary evocation has sufficed to dissipate a real problem (which has not thereby gone away). Stephen's imaginative powers have worked again, as they do throughout the book.

COMMENTARY

In addition to the formal correspondences noted above, a more immediately obvious symbolism is operative throughout this first episode. It is clear, as Jeri Johnson points out in her notes to the Oxford University Press edition, even in the opening sentence: Mulligan emerges *bearing* a bowl of lather on which a mirror and a razor lay *crossed*: the words 'bearing' and 'crossed' suggest a more lofty and dignified action than that ostensibly being described. Mulligan proceeds in this first page to parody explicitly the actions of the priest in the Mass, from the opening *introit* to the consecration of the bread and wine into the body and blood of Christ, the central moment of the Mass. But this explicit parody is merely the outward form and visible substance of an implicit parallel with the Mass that operates throughout the episode: the description of the breakfast which Mulligan serves up to Stephen and Haines is heavy with sacramental overtones, down to the two rays of light from the slit windows of the tower, doubling as candles on an altar. Mulligan's shedding of his dressing-gown is given a similarly sacerdotal, indeed Christ-like, emphasis – and the appearance of an actual priest at the end of the episode merely serves to underscore a motif that has been operative throughout.

The Mass that Mulligan celebrates for Haines and at which Stephen is server (he fetches the breakfast items from the locker at Mulligan's bidding, and he explicitly links Mulligan's bowl of lather to the boat of incense he carried as an altar server at Clongowes) is just one aspect of the episode's overall burden: servility. The dominant, privileged consciousness throughout is that of Stephen, although he is not the main actor: his is the only consciousness to which we are given direct access. This consciousness is acutely aware of its oppression. Although Haines is mocked, he is also being entertained, because he has money. Mulligan is putting on a show for his benefit (the Mass as spectacle); Stephen is encouraged to join in the entertainment and to some extent he does so, while occasionally kicking over the traces ('Would I make money by it?').

The symbolic, historical and mythic resonances of the episode come to a head in the scene with the milkwoman. We have already noted the Homeric parallel: the old milkwoman as the mortal form of the goddess Athena. In the Irish tradition of visionary poetry called the aisling, Ireland often appears to the poet as an old woman only to reveal herself at the end as the young, beautiful, ideal Erin. This tradition is highly relevant to the scene being enacted here: Haines is the English conqueror, Mulligan is, as Stephen reflects, Ireland's 'gay betrayer', the traitor figure who is a constant presence in Irish history and legend; Stephen is the dispossessed, usurped poet, the server of a servant, abandoned by his muse and by his country.

So at the very outset, *Ulysses* inscribes itself in a long Irish literary tradition: the positions being taken up carry an enormous cultural and historical baggage with them. Stephen's parting mental shot at Mulligan as he leaves for his teaching job, 'Usurper', condenses into one word the entire burden of a history and the symbolic structures it has generated (as well, of course, as referring to both *The Odyssey* and *Hamlet* scenarios).

Importantly, none of this historical symbolism has to be forced on to the text. The characters themselves are well aware of their historical and cultural situation and enunciate it clearly. Stephen turns everything into allegory; Mulligan turns everything into parody. With such temperaments, there is no need for the reader to look for overtones; they do the interpreting for us, over and over again.

BIOGRAPHICAL/HISTORICAL

Line 1. *Buck Mulligan*: based on Oliver St John Gogarty (1878–1957), who had become friendly with Joyce in 1903. Gogarty later became a surgeon and a notable writer in his own right. The portrait of him as a young man presented in *Ulysses*, although later much resented by Gogarty, appears to have been largely accurate. Gogarty seems to have thought of the tower as a centre for the Hellenisation (and hence civilisation) of Ireland, just as Mulligan does in *Ulysses*, and wanted to enlist Joyce in the cause. But relations between the two swiftly soured.

11. *Stephen Dedalus*: based on James Joyce himself. His earlier story had already been told in *A Portrait of the Artist as a Young Man*, which had ended with the young Stephen heading off to the continent in a spirit of exultation and redemptive artistic destiny. At the start of *Ulysses*, as we have just seen, he is back, defeated, lost, embittered.

Joyce did indeed live in the Martello tower in Sandycove, Co. Dublin, from 9–15 September 1904. However, not everything about his situation there in reality corresponds to this fictional portrayal. Joyce, for instance, had met Nora Barnacle by the time he came to stay in the tower, and indeed had met her by 16 June, the day on which *Ulysses* is set. This does not feature in the book.

49.   *Haines*: based on Samuel Chenevix Trench, an English-reared and educated member of an old and distinguished Anglo-Irish family, who was a guest of Gogarty's at the tower at the same time that Joyce was staying there. Trench had passionately embraced the Irish Revival, even changing his first name to Dermot, in a manner that disgusted Joyce.

77.   *Algy*: Algernon Charles Swinburne, poet (1837–1909). The line Mulligan quotes comes from *The Triumph of Time*.

128.   *Connolly Norman*: (1853–1908), superintendent of the Richmond Lunatic Asylum. A distinguished Irish alienist.

159.   *Cranly*: Stephen's closest friend in *A Portrait*. By the time of *Ulysses*, they appear to have fallen out. Based on J. F. Byrne.

257.   *Royce*: Edward William Royce, a popular English comic actor of the 1880s.

367.   *the weird sisters*: Elizabeth and Lily Yeats, sisters of W. B. Yeats, who printed and published their brother's works and other writers from the Dun Emer Press (later the Cuala Press) in Dundrum, Dublin.

SELECT GLOSSARY

Line 5.   *Introibo ad altare Dei*: Latin, from Psalms 43:4: 'I will go unto the altar of God'. These were the opening words of the Tridentine (Latin) Mass, spoken by the priest as he approached the altar.

78.   *Epi oinopa ponton*: Homeric Greek, 'upon the wine-dark sea'; the standard epithet in Homer for the sea.

80.   *Thalatta! Thalatta!*: Attic Greek, 'The sea! The sea!'
             The cry of the ten thousand Greek warriors after
             making their way out of Persia and reaching the
             Bosphorus, as reported by the historian Xenophon in
             his *Anabasis*.

176, 544.   *Omphalos*: Greek, 'navel'. Mulligan at line 544 calls
             the tower the omphalos, linking it to the oracle of
             Delphi, known as the omphalos because it was seen as
             the navel of the earth and the centre of prophecy in
             ancient Greece. So the term has a mystic as well as a
             literal meaning.

276–7.   *Liliata rutilantium* ... : Latin, 'May the lily-bedecked
             throng of shining confessors surround you: may the
             choir of rejoicing virgins receive you.' One of the
             prayers for the dying in the Catholic sacrament of
             Extreme Unction. It becomes the anthem of Stephen's
             guilt and remorse over the death of his mother.

481.   Agenbite of inwit: Middle English, 'remorse of
             conscience'. The title of a medieval tract. Another
             catchphrase of Stephen's.

651.   *Et unam sanctam catholicam et apostolicam
             ecclesiam*: Latin: 'and one holy Catholic and Apostolic
             Church'. From the *Apostles' Creed*.

665.   *Zut! Nom de Dieu!*: French, 'Damn it! In the name of
             God!'

708.   *Übermensch*: German, 'Superman'. From Nietzsche's
             Thus Spake Zarathustra.

I
[2 · Nestor]

Time: 10 a.m.
Location: a private school in Dalkey

SUMMARY

Stephen is in the classroom, teaching a class of roughly 11-year-olds. He is initially teaching a history lesson and while doing so he feels acutely his alienation from his pupils, children of well-off families in the area. He is also conscious of his lack of control over them, a situation highlighted when a boy whom he has asked to recite some of *Lycidas* blatantly reads it out from a book propped under his satchel. Stephen is mentally very withdrawn from his surroundings, brooding on history and its infinite thwarted possibilities. However, he does touch obliquely on his personal traumas when, towards the end of the class, he asks the boys an odd riddle, the answer to which is 'The fox burying his grandmother under a hollybush'.

After the class ends, one boy, Sargent, stays behind with some extra maths work he has been assigned. Sargent's weakness and timidity remind Stephen of his own childhood. Sargent, too, has been loved by a mother, perhaps 'The only true thing in life?'. But, preoccupied with his own mother's death, Stephen is unable to share any of his fellow feelings with his young pupil.

Stephen then goes to the study of the headmaster, his employer, Mr Garret Deasy – as we have already learned in 'Telemachus', Stephen is to be paid today, marking his third month in the school. He is duly paid and is also given a less welcome commission by Deasy: to endeavour to have a letter which Deasy has written on the perils of foot-and-mouth disease published in two newspapers. Stephen accepts this task with a reasonably good grace, however. He and Deasy, a unionist, engage in an apparently rather pointless dialogue about money, Irish history, and foot-and-mouth disease, from which the most salient elements to emerge are Deasy's virulent anti-Semitism and distinct misogyny. (Characteristically, Mrs O'Shea, the lover of Parnell, is blamed by Deasy for his downfall, and compared to Helen of Troy, the first direct reference to Homer's world in the novel.) Most of the time, the two are at cross-purposes: remarks by Stephen, such as his famous declaration that 'History is a nightmare from which I am trying to awake' or that God is 'A shout in the street', fall on deaf ears.

Stephen leaves the school with a final piece of anti-Semitic invective from Deasy ringing in his ears.

CORRESPONDENCES

In Book 3 of *The Odyssey*, Telemachus, having left Ithaca in quest of his father Odysseus, goes to the Greek mainland and approaches old Nestor, 'the master charioteer', for help. Nestor can only recount how he and Odysseus took different courses on their way home at the end of the Trojan war. Nestor also tells Telemachus something of the history of the war's end and advises him to call on Menelaus, brother of Agamemnon and husband of Helen, for more information. Nestor's son Pisistratus brings Telemachus to the court of his father and later guides him to the court of Menelaus. In the Gilbert schema, Nestor is Deasy, Pisistratus is Sargent, and Helen, seen as the cause of the Trojan War, is Mrs O'Shea. (This last correspondence is an important indication that these analogies can refer to a person who is merely mentioned in the text, not necessarily a character in it.)

STYLE

The style of the episode is continuous with that of the preceding one: by now we may have become more accustomed to the 'interior monologue' method, and, in fact, in this episode we spend more time in Stephen's head and he is even more detached from the outside world than he was in 'Telemachus'. The technique is referred to in the Gilbert schema as 'Catechism (personal)': this refers to Stephen's questioning of the pupils at the start of the episode and to the subsequent interrogation Deasy subjects him to during their conversation in the study. A particularly amusing example of the style's effects of condensation and foreshortening occurs in the rendering of Stephen's hasty perusal of Deasy's letter to the press. This is given in short, jerky, disconnected phrases: 'Our cattle trade. The way of all our old industries . . .' just as the letter would be read by someone who is merely skimming through it rather than reading it line by line. The reader of the novel is already learning to supply the connections, just as will be required when following the thinking of Leopold Bloom later.

COMMENTARY

The first episode situated Stephen at a very precise historical conjuncture, linking this historical positioning closely to his personal guilt and remorse over his mother's death. This second episode sees Stephen gradually deepening and intensifying his engagement with history – not as an abstraction but as a living, changing, almost ungraspable entity. At the beginning of the episode, Stephen's dialogue with history is almost entirely internal. The formal questions he asks the boys lead him into a meditation on what the book will later call 'the irreparability of the past': what has actually happened is 'not to be thought away'; asking what would have ensued if Julius Caesar had not been knifed to death (the great 'what ifs' of history) brings us into a world of speculation, of possibility, but in the world out there, a world which Stephen here fully acknowledges, those possibilities have been ousted by the realisation of one possibility only. 'The world that was not/Comes to pass', as Joyce writes in a very different context many years later.

This and Stephen's subsequent thoughts on the origin of historical events remain rather abstract, far removed (as Stephen is painfully aware) from the reality of the noisy, disorderly classroom in which he is engaging in these abstruse meditations. For the boys, 'history was a tale like any other too often heard, their land a pawnshop'.

In his dialogue with Sargent, and in the fellow-feeling Sargent evokes in him, Stephen is humanised to a degree we have not encountered before. This prepares us and him for the startling immediacy of his encounter with the living reality of history in his conversation with Deasy. In this exchange, Stephen experiences history as messy and real. Deasy is a mass of prejudices and many of his statements are factually wrong: that, however, is what history is like when it ceases to be an abstraction, 'a tale like any other too often heard', and instead becomes palpable and real. Stephen engages fully with that reality, including its violence: 'The lodge of Diamond in Armagh the splendid behung with corpses of papishes.'

It matters little that Stephen's conversation with Deasy barely qualifies as a conversation: on the one side are groundless assertions and total confidence; on the other are extreme reticence and beautifully judged interjections: a fine example occurs when Deasy denounces the Jews as having 'sinned against the light' and Stephen gently murmurs: 'Who has not?'

Just after that subtle question, Stephen declares: 'History is a nightmare from which I am trying to awake.' It is clear, however, that he must first live the nightmare before he can awake from it, and much of the book consists precisely in this process. He remains a 'learner', as he says himself.

The experience of history as presented in 'Nestor' is the exact antithesis of Haines's vacuous comment to Stephen in the preceding episode, apropos of Britain's role in Ireland, that 'history is to blame'. In Haines's version, history is an impersonal force, operating independently of any human agency or responsibility, and the human agents involved are absolved of any guilt for what may have occurred. 'History', in this reading, itself stands outside history, operating as a nineteenth-century substitute for God; it is a convenient cop-out for the actions of real historical agents. Stephen, and in his own way Deasy also, reject this view, insisting on the reality of genuine historical personae, people like you and me. 'History' is not some remote entity back in the past, which can be conveniently blamed for any small bother that may have occurred over the years; it is all around us, living and changing and being enacted in front of our eyes.

In Stephen's exchanges with Deasy, contrasting visions of history are at work: for Deasy, it all moves to 'one great goal, the manifestation of God', but for Stephen, God is a ' shout in the street', always already manifest within history and everywhere throughout it. Anything, in Stephen's view, can be an expression of God's presence in the world: a shout in the street, the murmuring of a name. (This is the basis of Joyce's theory of epiphany. It is the task of the artist to make this underlying numinous reality manifest.) For Deasy, history is goal-directed, marching on to one great apocalypse, when the son of God will eventually arrive to judge the living and the dead. For Stephen, if one will pardon the phrase, it is always apocalypse now, occurring over and over. Essentially he rejects a goal-oriented view of historical development in favour of a cyclical one, a worldview that *Ulysses* will underscore again and again.

Deasy's persona raises quite acutely an issue concerning the Homeric parallels, one that has also come up in connection with the milkwoman. In Homer, both these figures (Athena, Nestor) are unequivocally benevolent and helpful to Telemachus (Nestor is not actually much help, but his intentions are good). In *Ulysses*, their attitudes are much more ambiguous: 'Is this old wisdom?' Stephen asks himself as Deasy lectures him about the iniquities of the Jews, and the answer would seem to be 'Surely not'. And again, towards the end of the episode, Stephen asks himself: 'here what will you learn more?', the question seeming to be purely rhetorical and inviting the answer 'Nothing'.

Any such ambivalence on the part of two such characters would be intolerable in Homer, whose characters are either totally benevolent or totally malevolent. Joyce's complicating of the issue is part of the book's burden of modernity: the signals are always mixed, and can be read in different ways. To take an instance: though Stephen rejects Deasy's version and vision of history, he does not necessarily reject Deasy himself. In fact, Deasy's isolation, and the genuinely good intentions behind his foot-and-mouth campaign, do awaken Stephen's sympathies to a certain degree. (The kind of revulsion that Deasy's anti-Semitism would now occasion was far less pronounced in the early twentieth century.) Stephen's efforts to place Deasy's letter in two journals (successful in at least one case) are probably the most constructive things he does all day.

BIOGRAPHICAL/HISTORICAL

Line 1.   *Cochrane*: none of the names of the boys mentioned
            appears to correspond with a real pupil at the Clifton
            School, Dalkey, when Joyce taught there for a few

weeks in 1904. But it is likely that their personalities are based on those of actual pupils.

19. *Pyrrhus*: (318–272 BC). Leader of the Tarentines (in southern Italy) in their campaign against the Romans. Although he won some battles, the victories were so costly in terms of men and arms that he lost the war. He died in Argos when struck by a tile thrown by a woman from a housetop.

131. *Mr Deasy*: based on Francis Irwin, an Ulster Scot who was headmaster of the Clifton School when Joyce taught there. Deasy is also at least partly modelled on another Ulsterman, whom Joyce knew in Trieste: Henry Blackwood Price. Joyce transfers some of Price's genuinely distinguished Ulster ancestry to Deasy, and he also transfers to him Price's preoccupation with eradicating foot-and-mouth disease in Ireland. (Price becomes Deasy's cousin in the episode.) Just like Stephen, Joyce actually did take up Price's foot-and-mouth campaign on his last visit to Ireland in 1912, writing an article in the *Freeman's Journal* and forwarding Price's letters to a member of parliament about the issue: in this unexpected way, art is here echoing life.

As has been mentioned, many of Deasy's historical assertions are false or deeply confused: a 'French Celt' did not make the remark about the sun never setting on the British empire; while the orange lodges did have an anti-union and pro-Ulster nationalist bias at their inception, they soon developed into their traditional role as the fiercest possible defenders of the union; and Sir John Blackwood was *against* the Union, not for it – although his son was a unionist. Similarly, Deasy has the story of Dermot MacMurrough and O'Rourke, prince of Breffni, the wrong way round: it was O'Rourke's wife who eloped with MacMurrough, so MacMurrough was the 'leman'. Having been deposed as king of Leinster, he turned to the Normans for help.

158. *Averroes, Moses Maimonides*: Averroes (1126–98), Spanish-Arabian philosopher and physician. Moses Maimonides (1135–1204), Jewish philosopher.

256. *Curran*: Constantine P. Curran, a friend of Joyce. Appears in *A Portrait* under the name Donovan.

256. *McCann*: based on Francis Sheehy Skeffington, another friend. Appears in *A Portrait*.

256. *Fred Ryan*: journalist, economist, editor of the magazine *Dana*, which published a poem by Joyce but refused his autobiographical essay *A Portrait of the Artist*.

257. *Temple*: based on John Ellwood, another friend. A character in *A Portrait*.

257. *Russell*: George William Russell (AE), (1867–1935), leading Irish mystic and social reformer.

257. *Cousins*: James H. Cousins, a theosophist and friend of Joyce.

257–8. *Bob Reynolds*: unidentified.

258. *Keohler*: Thomas G. Keohler, minor poet and mystic.

258. *Mrs MacKernan*: Joyce's landlady at 60 Shelbourne Road in 1904.

SELECT GLOSSARY

Line 165. *Amor matris*: Latin, 'love of a mother'. It can mean either a mother's love for her child (subjective genitive) or a child's love for a mother (objective genitive).

282. *Per vias rectas*: Latin, 'by straight roads'.

I
[3 · Proteus]

Time: 11 a.m.
Location: Sandymount Strand

SUMMARY

Stephen has travelled from Dalkey to Sandymount Strand, apparently with the intention of calling on his uncle and aunt who live nearby. He may have it in mind to ask them for a place to stay for the night (at the end of the first episode, he had declared to himself, in reference to the tower: 'I will not sleep here tonight. Home also I cannot go.'). In any case, he does not go to their house in Strasburg Terrace. Instead he walks along the strand and engages in the most intense introspection that we have encountered thus far.

The episode begins very abruptly with an intense meditation on Aristotle's theories of space and vision. As part of this meditation, Stephen closes his eyes to find out how he can fare in the dark. As he moves along, eyes shut, he wonders: 'Am I walking into eternity along Sandymount strand?' Having opened his eyes, and found that the outside world is still there, he is distracted by the sight of two women coming down the strand from Leahy's Terrace. Instantly Stephen concocts a fantasy about the pair, giving them names and occupations based on very scanty evidence. This is the same procedure that we saw at work in the Clive Kempthorpe scene in the first episode: Stephen will create an imaginary scenario around anything that catches his fancy, and it will seem as real as anything else in the novel—as it does in this case.

From this Stephen moves on to imagining the welcome he will receive if he does call on his uncle and aunt: this passage is so vivid that a reader could easily think it is part of the action of the episode, rather than just occurring in Stephen's head.

Incited by the impoverished scene he has just evoked, Stephen reflects bitterly on the 'houses of decay' inhabited by his uncle, his own father and by 'all' in Dublin; he moves from this to even more bitter self-reproach and thence to memories of his time in Paris and to memories of Kevin Egan, the exiled Fenian who had befriended him there. He self-mockingly remembers his plans to be a cultural missionary to Europe in the wake of the Irish saints and scholars. (Self-mockery is a trait that was notably absent from the Stephen of *A Portrait*.)

He has come nearer the edge of the sea and now begins to turn back. As he does so his attention is caught first by the body of a dead dog and then by a live dog, described with remarkable concentration and attention to detail. In between these two perceptions, Stephen engages in more self-reproach, this time over his hypothetical failure to rescue a drowning man. The dog's owners come into view, and these are instantly, and without warrant, transformed into an Elizabethan criminal and his female accomplice.

This culminates very powerfully in a vision of a woman's encounter with her 'demon lover' (Coleridge, not Joyce), a 'pale vampire' (Joyce, not Coleridge) that comes 'through storm' over the sea: this seems to be the climax of the episode and leads Stephen to compose four lines of verse, though characteristically these are not communicated to us until much later in the novel and in a context that puts their import in question. But the episode – and the opening Telemachiad – close on a vision of the body of a drowned man, mentioned already in the first episode, and also alluded to in the second, surfacing from the deep, bearing all the physical evidence of a sea-change. The sea has yielded up this drowned body and Stephen realises his links to the dead who have gone before him: 'Dead breaths I living breathe, tread dead dust, devour a urinous offal from all dead.'

CORRESPONDENCES

In Book 4 of *The Odyssey*, Telemachus has arrived at the court of Menelaus while the wedding feast of Menelaus's son, Megapenthus, is being celebrated. Menelaus tells Telemachus of his own return from Troy, and of how he was becalmed on the island of Pharos. Menelaus was obliged to trap the old man of the sea, Proteus, and learn from him how to make his way home. Proteus was a shape-shifter, who altered his form at will, and Menelaus had to hold on to him doggedly through all his changes of appearance until he finally appeared in his true form, and imparted his wisdom to the impatient Greek. Menelaus learned from Proteus that Odysseus was himself becalmed on the nymph Calypso's island, under her spell – the first concrete news

Telemachus has had of him. In *Ulysses*, Proteus is 'primal matter', with which Stephen struggles, Menelaus is Kevin Egan, the person who receives and talks to Stephen on his 'mission' to the Continent (it seems safe to assume that Egan's wife, who has abandoned him, corresponds to Helen, the fickle wife of Menelaus), and Megapenthus is the male cocklepicker, the dog's owner, whose imagined sexual relationship with his female companion echoes that of Megapenthus and his bride-to-be.

STYLE

The style of the episode is continuous with that of the previous two, but it is characterized by a far greater degree of interiority. The technique is called in the Gilbert schema 'monologue (male)' and we experience it from the very start: 'Ineluctable modality of the visible' plunges us abruptly into Stephen's consciousness; it is as if we have been brought into his mind midway through an extended meditation, and we suddenly start to eavesdrop on him. The narrative voice that provided reasonably coherent connections hitherto is here much more faint and occasional; the ground is taken from under the reader's feet much as Stephen's footing is unsure on the beach at Sandymount: 'If I had land under my feet.' The transitions in Stephen's interior monologue are very sudden and hard to follow. Even the conventional unit of the paragraph does not necessarily guarantee coherence: Stephen's thought is capable of sudden turns that can, at least ostensibly, disrupt such a self-contained structure. Thus in one paragraph he goes from meditations on the decay of his family's fortunes to summoning up the ghosts of Dean Swift and Joachim of Flora to a strange vision of a eucharistic celebration. His thoughts are dense with literary echoes, Latin quotations and medieval philosophy.

Here and there the narrative voice provides the clarity we have become accustomed to: one paragraph reassuringly begins: 'The grainy sand had gone from under his feet.' But, even in such a paragraph, this voice is becoming increasingly infected by the character it is ostensibly describing: the account of Stephen's progress along the strand goes on to mention the pebbles that his feet encounter, and suddenly thrown in is 'that on the unnumbered pebbles beats', a partial misquotation from *King Lear*, that can only have come from Stephen's own word-haunted consciousness. In this instance, and unlike the 'Chrysostomos' case cited previously, the narrative voice has been hijacked, taken over by the character narrated, in the midst of a sentence that began as quasi-objective description. So the distinction between the two, never really watertight, is becoming more and more tenuous.

Ultimately, the reader has to struggle with the shifting style much as Menelaus has to engage with the shape-changing Proteus in order to learn the truth from him. And this struggle, too, will have its rewards.

COMMENTARY

In the Gilbert schema, Proteus corresponds to 'primal matter': the episode depicts Stephen's struggle with space and time, his attempts to wrest some knowledge or revelation from the intractable foundations of the phenomenal world around him. Hence the sense of struggle and effort that the episode conveys; as noted above, it is also a struggle for the reader. Hence, too, the lightning transitions already mentioned: the 'subject matter', or 'theme' of the episode changes shape just as rapidly and unpredictably as Proteus himself. Stephen's meditation moves almost seamlessly through several literary modes: it is partly reminiscence, e.g. of his time in Paris, of his schooldays; partly fiction (fictions within a fiction), e.g. the imagined visit to his uncle's house, the scene in medieval Dublin; partly confession (youthful vainglory, sexual obsessions, etc.); partly theology; and partly quasi-philosophy.

Importantly, whatever Stephen learns in the course of this tortuous episode, whatever he undergoes, does nothing to assuage his personal problems: his guilt over the death of his mother, his sense of alienation and estrangement from the world around him, the reader's general sense that he is just as trapped in Dublin as any of the characters of *Dubliners*, remain as intense at the end of 'Proteus' as at the beginning.

Any benefit Stephen gains from his struggles operates at another level, the level of vision and prophecy, not of self-healing. This reward, if reward is what it is, begins with the strongest moment of Stephen's meditation, his vision of a strange impending sexual encounter: 'He comes, pale vampire, through storm his eyes, his bat sails bloodying the sun, mouth to her mouth's kiss.' Crucially, this vision follows Stephen's focus on the passing female cockle-picker and his intense (if entirely gratuitous) rendering of her inner life. This, as the Gilbert schema has shown, is Joyce's rendering of the bride of Megapenthus, son of Menelaus, and it is as if this heightened sexualisation (with its strong lunar imagery) has liberated Stephen into a greater power of vision.

The vision of the pale vampire is one of a number of proleptic moments in the episode, moments that point forward, in a strange way, to the encounter with the unsuspecting Leopold Bloom that is the ultimate telos, or goal, of the book. Another such is Stephen's memory of his dream the previous night, a dream of a 'street of harlots' and a man who invites him into an unspecified dwelling. The traditional function of dreams as prophecy is being exploited here, since this dream points forward (to allow ourselves one forbidden glimpse into the future) to the climactic 'Circe' episode and the later parts of the book.

The two epiphanies that end the episode – the vision of the body of the drowned man being yielded up by the sea, and the actual sight of a ship sailing into Dublin port – bring no revelations in their wake (and they are preceded by a passage in which the moon is no longer a creative source but rather another weary element in the weary Creation groaning for its deliverance from daily toil). But they both offer tantalizing hints (which is all *Ulysses* ever gives us anyway) of both cyclical reincarnation ('God becomes man becomes fish becomes barnacle goose becomes featherbed mountain') and of homecoming and return ('a threemaster . . . homing, upstream, silently moving, a silent ship.'). We remember that *The Odyssey* is all about the return of a mariner.

Through the apparently arbitrary twists and turns of this episode, the reader may in these closing pages begin to glimpse a movement, 'an actuality of the possible as possible' going on. From the appearance of the cockle-pickers to the end, the sense of something being accomplished, a vision being fulfilled, does begin to gather strength, though it is far easier to report this sensation than it is to describe it, still less account for it. Nonetheless, the feeling that by the end Stephen has got somewhere, even if such a place is hard to name, is perhaps both his ultimate reward and the reader's.

Dense and difficult though this episode is, it also contains some memorable and powerful passages. Stephen's powers of evocation are finely shown in the portrait of the old patriot Kevin Egan in Parisian exile: 'They have forgotten Kevin Egan, not he them. Remembering thee, O Sion.' Even more striking is his vision of the life of Viking Dublin: 'Galleys of the Lochlanns ran here to beach.' Stephen's imagination makes history actual; he inhabits it and lives it with just as much reality as he lives his actual life. Indeed, he makes no distinction between the two. While one may never warm to him as a character, the intensity of his lived and remembered and projected experience in this episode will stay with a reader long after the more recondite reflections are forgotten.

Stephen has indeed walked into eternity along Sandymount Strand.

BIOGRAPHICAL/HISTORICAL

Line 4. *he*: Aristotle. The previous phrases are heavily
         Aristotelian.

61.   *aunt Sara's*: based on Joyce's aunt, Josephine Giltrap
         Murray. She was one of the few rocks of sense and
         sound advice in the turbulent world of the Joyce
         children, despite having a number of children of
         her own.

76.   *nuncle Richie*: based on William Murray, a brother of
         Joyce's mother, May, and aunt Josephine's husband.
         The family did not live in Strasburg Terrace, Irishtown,
         but rather in Fairview; Joyce transports them there to
         give Stephen a pretext for being on Sandymount
         Strand. William Murray, like the Richie Goulding who

is his persona in *Ulysses*, was a cost-drawer for a firm of solicitors, only recently defunct, called Collis and Ward. Again like Richie, he was fond of opera. He was loathed by Joyce's father, John Stanislaus, and there is no doubt that the epithets about him that Stephen places in the mouth of his father ('the drunken little costdrawer', etc.) are drawn from life.

108.   *Joachim Abbas*: Father Joachim of Floris (*c.* 1145– *c.* 1202), an Italian Franciscan mystic.

112.   *Foxy Campbell*: nickname for Father Richard Campbell S.J., who taught Joyce at Belvedere College. He was also known as 'lanternjaws'. He is mentioned in *A Portrait*, chapter 4.

144.   *Pico della Mirandola*: (1463–94), leading Italian humanist, philosopher and scholar.

163–4.   *Patrice ... Kevin Egan*: Kevin Egan is based on Joseph Casey, an elderly former Fenian whom Joyce had met in Paris on his first visit there in 1903. He had been allegedly involved in rescuing two Fenian leaders from a Manchester police van in September 1867, in the course of which a police sergeant was left dead. He was arrested and jailed in Clerkenwell prison, London, and the explosion at the prison in December 1867, which killed a number of people, was due to a failed attempt by the Fenians to rescue him and his leader, Colonel Richard Burke. Casey was virtually in exile in Paris, where he worked as a typesetter, and his bitterness at what he saw as his abandonment by his former associates (and by his wife) is fully reflected in the text. Patrice is his French-born son.

227.   *Arthur Griffith*: (1872–1922), leading Irish statesman, founder of Sinn Féin.

230–31.   *M. Drumont*: Edouard Drumont, (1844–1917), anti-Semitic and nationalist French journalist.

233.   *M. Millevoye*: Lucien Millevoye (1850–1918), minor French politician and lover of Maud Gonne.

241.   *head centre*: James Stephens (1824–1901), leader of the Fenians. He did indeed escape dramatically from British custody in 1867.

247.   *colonel Richard Burke*: a leading Fenian, also a prisoner in Clerkenwell at the time of the explosion.

287.   Louis Veuillot: French journalist and critic.

313–14.   *The Bruce's brother*: Edward Bruce (d. 1318), younger brother of Robert the Bruce. He invaded Ireland in 1314, but was himself murdered by the Irish.

314.   *Thomas Fitzgerald*: Silken Thomas (1513–37). Led a rebellion against the English and was executed at Tyburn.

314.   *Perkin Warbeck*: a Yorkist pretender to the throne of England, supported by some of the Anglo-Irish lords.

315–16.   *Lambert Simnel*: Another pretender to the English throne, was crowned king of England in Dublin in 1487. His rebellion also failed.

318.   *Guido*: Guido Cavalcanti, Italian poet. The courtiers who mocked him did so when he was visiting a graveyard; hence Guido's retort that they were in their own house.

SELECT GLOSSARY

Lines 6–7. *maestro di color che sanno*: Italian, 'master of those who know'. Dante's description of Aristotle (the 'he' referred to in the sentence).

13, 15.   *Nacheinander . . . nebeneinander*: German, 'one after another . . . side by side'.

18.   Los *demiurgos*: Los the demiurge. Los is the creator figure in William Blake's symbolic system and 'demiurge' is Plato's name for the creator of the material world.

26.   *Basta!*: Italian, 'Enough!'

30.   *Frauenzimmer*: German, 'a slovenly woman'.

48.	*lex eterna*: Latin, 'eternal law'.
51.	Contransmagnificandjewbangtantiality: a compound word including 'consubstantiality', 'transubstantiality', 'magnificent', 'magnify' and 'Jew'.
54.	*omophorion*: Greek, the special form of stole worn by bishops.
82.	*Duces Tecum*: Latin, 'Bring with you', the title of certain legal writs.
83.	Wilde's *Requiescat*: Latin, 'May she rest'; Oscar Wilde's poem on the death of his sister.
99–100.	*All'erta! ... aria di sortita*: *All'erta*, Italian, 'Beware, look out!', an aria from Verdi's *Il Trovatore*. It is Ferrando's *aria di sortita* (the song on which he enters) in the opera.
113–14.	*Descende, calve ... decalveris*: Latin, 'Get down, bald one, lest you be made even balder.'
131–2.	*O si, certo*: Italian, 'Oh yes, certainly.'
144.	mahamanvantara: Hindu, 'great year', a span of some 4,320 million years.
161–2.	*Qui vous a mis ... le pigeon, Joseph*: French, 'Who has put you in this deplorable condition?/ It's the pigeon, Joseph.'
165.	*lait chaud*: French, 'warm milk'.
166.	*lapin*: French, 'rabbit'.
166.	*gros lots*: French, first prize in a lottery.
167.	*La Vie de Jésus*: French, 'The Life of Jesus'.
169–72.	*C'est ... oui*: French, 'It's hilarious, you know. Me, I'm a socialist. I don't believe in the existence of God. Don't tell my father. – He believes? – My father, yes.'
173.	*Schluss*: German, 'enough'.
176.	*Paysayenn*: As the letters P. C. N. would be pronounced in French.
176–7.	*Physiques ... naturelles*: French, 'physics, chemistry and biology'.

177.   *mou en civet*: French, a stew made of cattle lungs.

179.   *boul' Mich'*: Slang French for the Boulevard St Michel, Paris.

182–3. *Lui, c'est moi*: French, 'he is I.'

187.   *Encore deux minutes*: French, 'still two minutes left'.

187.   *Fermé*: French, 'closed.'

194.   *Euge! Euge!*: Latin, 'Well done! Well done!'

196.   *Comment?*: French, 'What?'

196–7. *Le Tutu*: French, the title of a weekly magazine; literally, a short ballet skirt.

197.   *Pantalon Blanc et Culotte Rouge*: French, again apparently another magazine title; literally, 'White Underclothes and Red Breeches'.

214.   *chaussons*: French, 'puff pastry'.

214.   *pus*: French, 'pus, a yellow liquid', in this case custard.

214.   *flan breton*: French, a Breton-style custard tart.

215.   *conquistadores*, Spanish, 'conquerors', but also French slang, 'lady-killers'.

218–19. *Un demi setier!*: French, 'a half-glass'.

220–21. *Il est irlandais . . . Ah oui!*: French, 'He is Irish. Dutch? Not cheese. Two Irishmen, us, Ireland, you know? Ah, yes!'

224.   *slainte!*: Irish, 'your health!'

232–3. *Vieille ogresse . . . dents jaunes*: French, 'Old ogress . . . yellow teeth.'

233.   *la Patrie*: French, *The Fatherland*, name of a paper founded by Millevoye.

234.   *froeken*: Swedish, 'a single woman'.

234.   *bonne à tout faire*: French, 'maid of all work' (with a double entendre).

235–6. *Moi faire . . . tous les messieurs*: French: 'I do . . . all the gentlemen.'

252.   *rue de la Goutte-d'Or*: French, 'Street of the Golden Drop'.

254.   *rue Gît-le-Cœur*: French, literally, 'Street Here Lies the Heart', or 'Sacred to the Memory of the Heart'.

257.   *Mon fils*: French, 'my son'.

287.   *Un coche ensablé*: French, 'A coach mired in sand.'

311.   *Terribilia meditans*: Latin, 'meditating on terrible things'.

321.   *Natürlich*: German, 'naturally'.

381–4.   *White ... kiss*: Elizabethan rogues' slang: 'fambles' means hands; 'gan', mouth; 'quarrons', body; 'couch a hogshead': lie down and sleep; 'darkmans', night.

385.   *frate porcospino*: Italian, 'the porcupine (or prickly) monk'.

394.   *oinopa ponton*: Homeric Greek, 'the wine-dark sea'.

396–7.   *Omnis caro ad te veniet*: Latin, 'all flesh shall come to you.'

432.   *Piuttosto*: Italian, 'rather'.

439–40.   *Et vidit ... bona*: Latin, 'And God saw (the things that He had made) and they were exceeding good' (Genesis, 1:31).

447.   *nebeneinander*: See lines 13, 15.

448.   tripudium: Latin, a triple beat or stroke, a regular measure.

450.   *Tiens, quel petit pied!*: French, 'My, what a small foot!'

466.   *diebus ac noctibus ... ingemiscit*: Latin, 'by day and by night [the Creation] groans, suffering wrongs'.

483.   *Prix de Paris*: French, 'Prize of Paris' (the main event then in French horseracing). Already mentioned in the previous episode, line 302.

486–7.   *Lucifer ... occasum*: Latin, 'The morning star, I say, which knows no setting'. From the service for Holy Saturday, but of course Lucifer is also a name for Satan.

493.   *Già*: Italian, literally 'already', but here an expression of impatience.

II
[4 · Calypso]

St. George's Church, Dublin.

Time: 8 a.m.
Locations: Bloom's house at Number 7 Eccles Street, Dublin;
Dorset Street area

SUMMARY

Leopold Bloom, a 38-year-old advertisement canvasser, is preparing breakfast in the kitchen of his house at Number 7, Eccles Street. He decides he wants a pork kidney and leaves the house to buy it around the corner in Dlugacz's pork butchers in Dorset Street. Before going he checks whether his wife Molly, still in bed, wants anything special for breakfast. Receiving a negative answer, he sets off and makes his purchase. On the way to the butcher's he becomes absorbed in a long fantasy about journeying around the world in the track of the sun. He passes and greets Larry O'Rourke at the door of his pub at the corner of Eccles Street and Dorset Street. At Dlugacz's, who is an eager Zionist, he reads with interest a leaflet seeking participants in a model farm to be set up in Palestine, an early Zionist enterprise. Although Bloom has no intention of participating, he still feels that there is an 'idea behind it'. On the way back, he experiences a sudden, intense feeling of emptiness and depression; this coincides with, though it is hardly occasioned by, the overshadowing of the sun by a passing morning cloud—the same cloud, we realise, described in the same terms, that had passed over Stephen Dedalus just after his confrontation with Mulligan on the roof of the tower, and that had led on to Stephen's evocation of the ghost of his mother. In this mood, Bloom thinks of Palestine not as the hopeful place depicted in Dlugacz's leaflet, but rather as an exhausted, dead land: 'the grey sunken cunt of the world'. Bloom is rescued from this dismal reverie by the return of 'Quick warm sunlight', envisaged as a girl running to meet him.

Back in the house, he finds three items of mail awaiting him in the hall: one is a letter for him from his 15-year-old daughter Milly, working for the summer in a photographer's premises in Mullingar, and the others are a card for Molly from Milly and a letter for Molly from Hugh 'Blazes' Boylan, a concert promoter with whom, as we soon learn, she is having an affair. Bloom puts his kidney into the frying pan and then brings Molly's breakfast up to her. In response to his carefully casual question, Molly tells him that Boylan is calling that day, ostensibly to bring the programme for the concert performances which

Boylan is promoting and in which Molly (a professional singer) is to perform, and to rehearse the pieces. In the course of a desultory conversation, while he is engaged in giving her a complicated explanation of the term 'metempsychosis' (the transmigration of souls), which she has encountered in a book, Molly stops listening and starts to sniff the air. She has detected a 'smell of burn' from the kidney which Bloom has left to fry on the range. Bloom rescues the kidney and sits down to have his breakfast and to read Milly's letter. He notes with concern and with 'troubled affection' the mention by Milly of a 'young student' whom she has met in Mullingar, but feels passively unable to intervene. This young student is Bannon, mentioned in the first episode and Milly is the 'sweet young thing' he has met in Mullingar.

After breakfast, Bloom feels the need to empty his bowels. He goes to the outside privy (the house has an indoor one, but it is too far up the stairs to bother) and brings a copy of *Titbits* with him to read. While there his eye falls on the magazine's 'prize story', 'Matcham's Masterstroke', and it strikes him that it should be easy to write something similar and win a guinea. His opinion of the story may, however, be best expressed by the fact that he uses part of it to wipe himself.

Bloom is dressed in black because later in the day he is to attend the funeral of a friend, Paddy Dignam, who has died suddenly. Leaving the outside toilet, he hears the bells of the nearby St George's Church tolling the hour and he links the sound lugubriously to a dirge for Dignam: 'Heigho! Heigho!'

CORRESPONDENCES

In Book 5 of *The Odyssey*, we finally encounter the epic's hero, Odysseus. He has been on the island of the goddess and enchantress Calypso, for seven years, in thrall to her and (allegedly) compelled to lie with her every night. The goddess, we are told, had long ago 'ceased to please' and Odysseus is feeling his exile very acutely. Zeus, moved by the pleas of Athena, sends the messenger of the gods, Hermes, to command Calypso to release Odysseus and to recall him to his homeland. Odysseus does set off, having built a boat with Calypso's aid, but is soon shipwrecked through storms brought on by the angry god Poseidon. However, Athena intercedes, calming the storms and ensuring that Odysseus reaches land.

In the Gilbert schema, the picture of the nymph over Molly's bed (which Bloom alludes to and thinks about during his explanation of metempsychosis) corresponds to Calypso; Dlugacz the Zionist corresponds to the recall back to Ithaca that Odysseus receives from Hermes, and Zion itself, or Palestine, corresponds to Odysseus's homeland, Ithaca. Too obvious to mention, but crucial to an understanding of the book are, of course, Bloom as Odysseus (Ulysses), Molly as Penelope, the wife whose husband is missing, and Boylan as another version of Antinous, whom we have already seen reincarnated in Mulligan. Milly, interestingly enough, does not seem to have a parallel in the Homeric story.

STYLE

The style of the episode is broadly continuous with that of the preceding three: a detached narrative voice, interior monologue, great clarity and freshness in descriptions: the kidney Bloom purchases, for instance, is 'the moist tender gland' or when Molly is having breakfast, 'The sluggish cream wound curdling spirals through her tea'. The main difference is occasioned by the fact that, for much of the time, we are inhabiting a different consciousness from that of Stephen, the privileged bearer of interiority hitherto: the style (and this is a key Joycean procedure) adapts itself to the personality it is representing. Stephen's sensibility is represented in prose that is elaborate, ornate, highly allusive. To represent the workings of Bloom's mind, the style is clipped, condensed, fragmentary, often not forming complete sentences.

Bloom's mind scurries over the surface of things, and the style similarly hops from point to point, the reader's job often being to keep up with, or supply, the missing connections. This is not in general very difficult: when the text reads, for instance, 'Might manage a sketch. By Mr and Mrs L. M. Bloom. Invent a story for some proverb. Which?' the reader can 'translate' this as Bloom thinking (after reading the

Titbits story) that 'I (or we) might manage to write a sketch for *Titbits*. By Mr and Mrs L. M. Bloom. We might invent a story to illustrate some proverb. Which one?' This, of course, is a very plodding procedure, and the reader quickly grows quite adept at sinking into Bloom's mind, as it were, and following its sometimes surprising twists and turns. Indeed, it is the almost unprecedented immediacy of access to this mind that is one of the great achievements of the book, the one that most excited its first readers. Stephen's mind, although represented just as directly, is less accessible because of the literary overlay that it possesses; we really do feel we know Bloom in a way in which we know hardly any other character in fiction.

So the style of 'Calypso' is easier, not because it is any less complex than in the preceding episodes, but simply because Bloom's consciousness is easier of access than Stephen's. A different style is called for, and a different style is provided, something that Joyce can do virtually at will. But the basic narrative voice remains, at this point, recognisably the same.

COMMENTARY

'Mr Leopold Bloom ate with relish the inner organs of beasts and fowls.' The first thing we learn about the great Leopold Bloom is a sensual fact, to do with his sense of taste. The first thing we learned about Stephen Dedalus was a mental fact, to do with his state of mind: he was 'displeased' at having been kept awake for much of the night by Haines's ravings. It is hardly an accident, either, that the first emotion attributed to Stephen is one of displeasure, while the first emotion attributed to Bloom is one of pleasure, his liking for the inner organs of beasts and fowls.

From this point on, each episode of the book has a bodily organ ascribed to it (in the current case, naturally, the kidney). It is appropriate that the organs make their appearance simultaneously with Bloom, for one of the essential things about him is his sheer physicality (this is partly why the episode ends with Bloom's visit to the toilet, to reinforce the bodily dimension). So, although we find that Bloom's familial and social situation is complex and in some ways painful, there is an underlying solidity to his relationship with the world that is far removed from the tortured relationship Stephen has to external things. In 'Proteus', the previous episode, Stephen struggled with the material world, trying to wrest a secret from it. Bloom does not have to struggle; his relationship to the material world is fixed and comfortable; this is part of the intense reality that invests him as a character.

With 'Calypso', the book begins all over again, just as *The Odyssey* begins all over again in Book 5, with the appearance of Odysseus. We go back to the starting time of the first episode, 8 a.m. At the same time as Mulligan and Stephen are having their quarrel in the tower, Bloom is buying his kidney in Dlugacz's and lusting after the maidservant from the house next door, who is also in the shop. On the face of it, there is not much to connect the sensitive young aesthete in Sandycove with the serious shopper in Dorset street. But in fact their situations are not entirely dissimilar. Bloom, too, is displaced, usurped; in his case the position is perhaps even worse, for he is in his own home, internally displaced. Like Stephen, Bloom is passive in the face of this usurpation; he is not even prepared to intervene decisively in the case of Milly, although he does think of going to Mullingar to see her.

In *The Odyssey*, Odysseus is held in thrall by the nymph Calypso, being unable to leave her island, though there is a rich ambiguity about how unwilling his servitude may be; in *Ulysses*, Bloom is similarly in thrall, with Calypso figured as the nymph in the picture above his and Molly's bed. This seems to imply that Bloom's servitude is sexual; he is in thrall to a female image, or perhaps *the* female image. This is exemplified in his lust for the 'nextdoor girl' at Dlugacz's counter and in the strange passage that follows in which women are assimilated to the cattle in the cattle market where Bloom once worked (perhaps Bloom's revenge for his own subjugation). There are several references to witchery and entrapment in the episode: 'the laughing witch' of the *Titbits* story, for instance, and Bloom avoids 'the loose cellarflap' in the street, waiting to entrap him. The fact that Bloom tries to use the image of the nymph above the bed in his attempted explanation to Molly of metempsychosis does hint at possibilities of transformation in this situation that the novel will later explore.

If Bloom is in thrall to a female image, his wife is certainly not having any of it; she has transferred her desires, if not her affections, to a more satisfactory male partner. In this, of course, Molly is very unlike her parallel, Penelope, who remains famously faithful to Odysseus throughout his wanderings, and one of the issues of the book is how, or whether, Molly does fulfill Penelope's role.

An important element in the episode is the Zionist issue. Bloom, an Irish Jew, or a Jewish Irishman, is at a considerable remove from the Zionist fervour that was sweeping Europe at this time; nonetheless his racial origin does also distance him in significant ways from the actual Irish world he is living in. This distance will matter increasingly as the book goes on. Here, the leaflet at Dlugacz's does recall Bloom to the source of his race and history. It is a recall he rejects, much as Stephen rejects the recall of the milkwoman to his own history and race in the first episode, but nonetheless the idea stays with him. His sudden powerful vision of Palestine as the dead land, exhausted and unable to bear more, indicates that for Bloom, at least, there is no going back; Palestine is not Ithaca for him, whatever it may be for others. He is rescued from that horrifying vision by the return of sunlight, figured as 'a girl with gold hair on the wind' and corresponding to Leucothea, the 'slender-ankled' sea goddess who intervenes to rescue Odysseus from Poseidon before Athena arrives.

Another crucial aspect of the book is figured in Bloom's reference to Ponchielli's *Dance of the Hours*. This ballet item from Amilcare Ponchielli's opera *La Gioconda* enacts the passing of the hours of the day through dancers dressed appropriately in a sequence of costumes, as Bloom recalls, going from rosy pink for dawn to black for night. It is a reminder, as is Bloom's earlier vision of a day spent wandering in the east, the source of the sun, that *Ulysses* is a day book, that the day here is thought of as an epitome of human life, and that the novel will go through the entire sequence of the day, and of a life, in its progress, under the auspices of the daystar. Time's passing is similarly marked in the tolling of the bells of St George's Church, which concludes the episode.

As the book proceeds, certain elements that have been fore-shadowed in earlier episodes are picked up and developed. The reader may not always spot the connection (often the matter being referred back to happened many pages previously), so skilled readers build up a network of cross-references to help them steer through the book.

Two such significant thematic echoes in this episode have been mentioned in the summary: Milly's reference to a 'young student' links back to Bannon and to the 'sweet young thing' he had met in Mullingar, as narrated in the first episode; and the cloud which accompanies Bloom's depressing vision of the dead land is the same that had accompanied Stephen's struggle with his mother's ghost on the top of the tower.

There are also verbal echoes that work to tie up the various episodes with each other and keep the book unified: the first page of 'Calypso' contains references to a tower and 'green stones' (in this case the eyes of the cat, in 'Telemachus', an appropriately coloured stone set in Haines's cigarette case). In the first episode we heard about a black panther, here we encounter a cat; the first episode featured a milkwoman, this one mentions a milkman. The highly symbolic resonances of the opening episode have been cut down to size: from panther to cat, from highly symbolic milkwoman (who herself has something to do with Bloom's vision of the dead land) to the decidedly banal and real 'Hanlon's milkman'.

BIOGRAPHICAL/HISTORICAL

Line 1.   *Mr Leopold Bloom*: no definite source has been
            identified for Leopold Bloom. Joyce knew very few
            Jews in Dublin, but he knew many in Trieste, and
            Bloom probably has elements of Triestine friends such
            as Teodoro Mayer and Ettore Schmitz (Italo Svevo).
            Recently, the links between Bloom and Mr Alfred
            Hunter, the person on whom Joyce based his projected
            short story 'Ulysses', have been shown to have been
            stronger than originally thought: both Bloom and
            Hunter were advertisement canvassers and had wives

called Marion, both of whom were of foreign
origin – and both wives were rumoured to be unfaithful.
Another likely source is a Dubliner named Charles
Chance, who had as many occupations as the fictional
Bloom himself, and whose wife, like Bloom's, was a
concert singer. (Chance's link to Bloom is obscured by
the fact that he also appears in *Ulysses* under the name
C. P. McCoy.) Aspects of Bloom resemble Joyce himself;
some of Bloom's experiences echo those of Joyce.
Further than that it is probably not possible to go.

36. *Hanlon's milkman*: probably S. Hanlon, dairyman, 26
Lower Dorset Street.

45. *Buckley's*: John Buckley, victualler, 48 Dorset Street
Upper.

46. *Dlugacz's*: while quite a number of the butchers in
Dublin were of Eastern European or of German origin,
there was no Dlugacz among them: Joyce took the
name from a Triestine friend of his, an ardent Zionist
named Moses Dlugacz.

63. *old Tweedy*: Molly Bloom's father, Major (or more
likely Sergeant-Major) Brian Cooper Tweedy. Partly
based on a Major (or Sergeant-Major) Powell, whom
Joyce and his father knew in Dublin and whose
daughters are also mentioned in *Ulysses*.

69. *Plasto's*: John Plasto, hatter, 1 Great Brunswick (now
Pearse) Street.

105. *Larry O'Rourke's*: publican, 74 Dorset Street Upper,
on the corner of Eccles Street.

108. *M'Auley's*: Thomas McAuley, publican, 39 Dorset
Street Lower.

119. *Dignam*: the fictional Paddy Dignam lived at 9
Newbridge Avenue, Sandymount.

128. *Adam Findlaters*: Adam S. Findlater, owner of a
leading Dublin grocery chain.

128. *Dan Tallons*. Daniel Tallon, grocer, wine merchant,
with two stores.

148.   *Denny's sausages*: Henry Denny and Son, meat-
        product manufacturers, originally based in Limerick.

148.   *Woods*: an R. Woods is listed in *Thom's Directory* for
        1904 as living at 8 Eccles Street, next door to the
        (fictional) Blooms. Number 7 is listed as vacant.

156.   *Moses Montefiore*: (1784–1885), leading Jewish
        philanthropist.

205.   *Citron*: J. Citron, 17 St Kevin's Parade, a neighbour of
        Bloom when he lived in Lombard Street West. The 'J.'
        in *Thom's* for 1904 is apparently a misprint for 'I.' (for
        Israel).

205.   *Mastiansky*: apparently based on P. Masliansky, a
        grocer at 16 St Kevin's Parade.

209.   *Moisel*: M. Moisel lived at 20 Arbutus Place in 1904.

224.   *Cassidy's*: James Cassidy, publican, 71 Dorset Street
        Upper.

234.   *Sandow's*: Eugene Sandow (Frederick Muller, 1867–
        1925), a famous turn-of-the-century strongman. He
        appeared in Dublin in 1898.

236.   *Towers*, *Battersby*, *North*, *MacArthur*: Dublin
        auctioneers.

244.   *Mrs Marion Bloom*: Molly Bloom, Bloom's wife. Her
        original, if any, is unclear. As with Leopold Bloom, the
        Hunter connection may also be more relevant than
        originally thought: as well as being called Marion, Mrs
        Hunter was also rumoured, probably groundlessly, to
        be unfaithful to her husband, and, like Molly, Marion
        Hunter was foreign. A daughter of a friend of Joyce's
        father, Mat Dillon, who was considered a Spanish
        type, may also be involved. However, much of the style
        of Molly's thinking (if not the content) came from
        Nora Joyce; her letters are nearly as punctuation free
        as Molly's monologue and Molly's pithy expressions
        and pungent comments owe much to Nora's
        temperament. The character of Molly Bloom is Joyce's
        greatest tribute to his wife.

312.   *Boylan*: Hugh 'Blazes' Boylan, Molly's lover, is also of dubious origin. He may be partly based on a horse dealer called James Daly who had premises at Island Bridge and partly on another horse dealer called Ted Keogh.

314.   *J. C. Doyle*: a leading baritone.

361.   *Kearney*: Joseph Kearney, book and music seller, 14 Capel Street.

417.   *Mrs Thornton*: midwife, 19A Denzille Street. She delivered several of the Joyce children.

488.   *Drago's*: hairdresser, 17 Dawson Street.

491.   *O'Brien*: J. P. O'Brien was superintendent of the Tara Street Baths. There is no record that he was involved in the escape of James Stephens from Richmond Gaol, though Stephens had two very close associates named O'Brien: William Smith O'Brien and James F. X. O'Brien.

502–03.   *Mr Philip Beaufoy*: a real person who contributed stories to *Titbits*.

522.   *Roberts*: possibly George Roberts, later manager of Maunsel and Company, publishers.

522.   *Gretta Conroy*: a central character in 'The Dead', in *Dubliners*.

526.   *May's band*: run by May and Co., music sellers and teachers, 130 St Stephen's Green West.

SELECT GLOSSARY

Line 314.   *Là ci darem*: Italian, a duet from Mozart's *Don Giovanni*: '*Là ci darem la mano*', 'then we'll go hand in hand'.

327.   *Voglio e non vorrei*: Italian, 'I want to and I would not like to'. A line from the duet, misquoted by Bloom; it in fact goes '*vorrei e non vorrei*' ('I would like to and I wouldn't like to').

II
[5 · Lotus-Eaters]

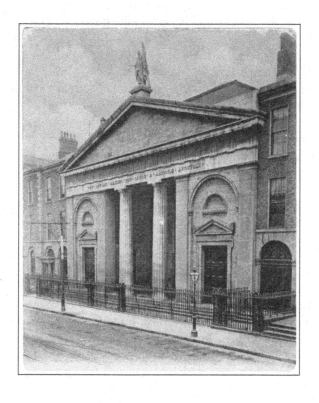

Time: 10 a.m.
Location: Westland Row area of city

SUMMARY

Mr Bloom, having purchased the *Freeman's Journal*, has crossed the Liffey and is now on the south side of the city. Having probably crossed on the ferry, he goes along Sir John Rogerson's Quay and up Lime Street to Westland Row. At Westland Row post office (then numbers 49–50) he hands in a card which he has previously surreptitiously transferred from the headband of his hat, where it is kept hidden, to his pocket and receives a letter. The letter, we immediately learn, is addressed not to him, but to Henry Flower Esq. It is easy to see that Bloom is engaged in a clandestine correspondence and that he is taking some precautions not to be observed.

He puts the letter in his pocket and leaves the post office. He attempts to open it inside his pocket but is suddenly interrupted by an acquaintance, C. P. McCoy. McCoy engages in desultory conversation about when and where he heard of the demise of Paddy Dignam; Bloom has been distracted by the sight of an elegant-looking woman about to mount an 'outsider' (a jaunting car) at the door of the Grosvenor Hotel. However, his hopes of catching a glimpse of the woman's silk stockings as she gets on to the car are thwarted by a tramcar which gets in the way at the crucial moment.

Meanwhile McCoy has changed tack and is talking about an imminent concert engagement which his wife, a singer like Molly, has secured. This alerts Bloom to the likelihood of a request for 'the loan' of a valise being proffered and he hastens to forestall such a demand by telling McCoy about his own wife's upcoming concert tour. (Bloom's mixed feelings about this tour, combined of pride in his wife's starring role and pain at the fact that Boylan is the tour manager, with all that implies, form one of the comic leitmotifs of the book.)

McCoy moves off but before going he asks Bloom to 'put down' his name at the funeral (this means informing the press that he was there even though he was not). He explains that he would go, but a drowning case in Sandycove might turn up. McCoy works as a coroner's assistant and is professionally engaged in these matters. (This drowning case is, of course, the one that Stephen Dedalus heard about at the end of the first episode.)

Left alone, Bloom is still worried that McCoy might be 'pimping after' him, as he puts it, so he lingers in apparent idleness for a while, studying the advertisements on the hoardings. Eventually reassured, he walks back down Westland Row, turns right into Brunswick (now Pearse) Street, past the horses at the cabstand, and then immediately right up Cumberland Street. Here he finally feels sufficiently safe and unobserved to open and peruse his letter.

The letter has a flower enclosed. It is (apparently) from a woman named Martha Clifford, with whom Bloom has engaged in a semi-erotic correspondence after she answered an ad he placed in *The Irish Times* for a 'smart lady typist to aid gentleman in literary work'. The letter is written in a wonderfully coy, cajoling style, veering between blandishments and threats ('if you do not I will punish you'). Its reading occasions in Bloom what the text describes as 'weak joy'.

Still reflecting on it, he moves on up Cumberland Street and enters St Andrew's Church (here referred to as All Hallows, which was the original name of the medieval monastery on which both St Andrew's and Trinity College now stand) by the back door. In the church, a Mass is being celebrated for a sodality, and Bloom disinterestedly observes. He understands little of the service, but is struck by the blind devotion of those involved. He makes sure to get out before any collection might be taken up. Leaving the church, he goes up to Sweny's the chemists in Lincoln Place, at the top of Westland Row, to order a skin lotion for Molly. While there he purchases a bar of lemon soap, which he carries around with him all day, and which we hear about every now and then. He plans to call back later in the day for the lotion, which the chemist is going to 'make up'.

On leaving the chemist's, Bloom is accosted by another acquaintance, Bantam Lyons, who eagerly snatches the *Freeman's Journal* from him in order to check the horses running in that day's Ascot Gold Cup race. Bloom, in order to get rid of him, tells him he can keep the paper, as he was just going to throw it away. At this, Lyons looks at him strangely, mutters enigmatically 'I'll risk it,' and dashes off.

Bloom then heads for the Leinster Street Turkish and Warm Baths at number 11, where he intends to have a bath prior to attending Dignam's funeral. It is also apparent that Bloom intends to masturbate in this bath, probably with Martha's letter as an aid: 'Also I think I. Yes I. Do it in the bath.' We leave him as he foresees 'his pale body' reclined in the bath at full, 'naked, in a womb of warmth', with his limp penis floating in the water, 'a languid floating flower'.

CORRESPONDENCES

In Book 9 of *The Odyssey*, following his shipwreck after his departure from Calypso's isle, Odysseus has found refuge on the island of Scheria, ruled over by King Alcinous. Having revealed his identity to Alcinous, he tells him of his adventures since his departure from Troy. Among these was his brief visit to the land of the lotus-eaters. Odysseus and his companions had landed there to take on water. The natives were friendly and gentle, and offered the three men of Odysseus's advance party leaves of the lotus flower to eat. However, when the three partook of that leaf, they fell into a total lethargy: they longed 'to stay forever, browsing on that native bloom, forgetful of their homeland'. Odysseus had to drive the three to the ships, to tie them, 'wailing', down, and to set off with all speed from that land lest more of his mariners should become infected.

In the Gilbert schema, almost all the groups in the episode correspond to the lotus-eaters: the cabhorses, the communicants, the soldiers that Bloom sees on the recruiting poster, the bather in the Dead Sea, the watchers of cricket.

STYLE

We have already been exposed to the workings of Bloom's consciousness in 'Calypso': this episode continues the exposure in a style which is largely continuous with that of the preceding episode. The 'technic' is defined as 'narcissism', but this seems to refer more to the tone of the episode than to any particular stylistic innovation. The permeability of inner and outer worlds, or rather the invasion of the latter by the former, that characterized 'Proteus', is far less evident in these early Bloom episodes. Bloom is a much more self-contained, reserved vessel than Stephen – we can generally be fairly confident of whether something is occurring in his mind or in the world out there; any scenes Bloom conjures up are instantly recognizable as scenes, not as part of the action.

One moment in which the episode amusingly echoes 'Nestor' is in the reading of Martha's letter: just as Stephen had hastily skimmed over Deasy's letter, giving us a truncated version of it, so Bloom, having read Martha's letter word for word, reads it again, interspersing in this reading names of flowers and plants that Martha's enclosure has brought to his mind: 'Angry tulips with you darling manflower punish your cactus' etc. Once again we are being given a brief lesson in how to negotiate the disconnections and interruptions that the rendering of modern consciousness entails.

COMMENTARY

'Lotus-Eaters' is one of the easiest episodes of *Ulysses* to comprehend. Once the basic analogy between Homer's lotus-eaters and Dublin's citizenry is grasped, almost everything falls into place. The world described is clearly continuous with that of *Dubliners* – the somnolent state of the lotus-eating city dwellers corresponds to the paralysis which is the famous leitmotif of Joyce's volume of short stories. It is not surprising that two characters from *Dubliners*, McCoy and Lyons, turn up in this episode, and that two others, Bob Doran and Hoppy Holohan, are mentioned.

Everything in the episode serves the same purpose: the early mention of the far east, with 'big lazy leaves to float about on', the bather in the Dead Sea, who does not even have to swim to stay afloat, the soldiers, 'hypnotised like' from the repetitive drill: these are instances, taken from the first two pages alone, and replicable over and over, of the stunned, numbed, bemused nature of the city that Bloom confronts. There has been much debate about the whole notion of Dublin and Joycean 'paralysis'; it is not the whole story and the city certainly possessed energies (largely linguistic) that are given their full due in *Ulysses*; nonetheless, the novel at this point wants to insist unambiguously (for once) on the somnolent, sleep-walking nature of Bloom's world. Everything seems to conspire to deaden the reality of experience.

Bloom himself is caught up in this lassitude; it is very hard to see his proposed masturbation (which does not happen anyway) as in any way a resistance or escape from the blighting condition that infects the episode. The final image of Bloom's penis portrays it as 'a languid floating flower', the very reverse of erect. Indeed, the correspondence with Martha, with its minimal, almost non-existent erotic frisson, looks much more like an evasion of sex (and, of course, an evasion of what is going on between Molly and Boylan) than like any true encounter with it. This point is important, because in the majority of the episodes that follow Bloom does indeed play the part of Odysseus and escape from or overcome the dangers that confront him: this episode, however, is not like that. At the same time, however, as observer and non-believer, Bloom at least possesses some detachment from the forces about him that does confer, perhaps, a certain immunity.

The most powerful evocation of lotus-eating, perhaps because it retains a certain power to shock, concerns the communicants in St Andrew's. Bloom is quite clear that the Mass, in this context, is indeed what Marx said it was: the opium of the people. With his detached, outsider's vision he sees the whole thing as an elaborate performance the constant repetition of which is designed, like the parade-ground drill, to numb and stun the congregation into blind obedience. His thoughts about the 'old fellow asleep near that confessionbox' really apply to all the communicants: 'Blind faith. Safe in the arms of kingdom come. Lulls all pain. Wake this time next year.' Clearly, the communion host is itself, in this context, a lotus leaf. The ones Bloom admires are not the communicants or the celebrant but the 'square-headed chaps' in Rome who 'work the whole show'.

Another striking evocation of the same syndrome is 'the drooping nags of the hazard', the horses at the cabstand in Brunswick street. Passing these, Bloom observes them chomping quietly on their 'gilded oats' and reflects that they 'get their feed all right and their doss'. He also observes that they are gelded and muses: 'Might be happy all the same that way.' There are curious analogies here with the world of Buck Mulligan in the opening episode, a gilded youth who is sowing some wild oats. The analogy might seem far-fetched were it not for the 'full buck eyes' of the horses that watch Bloom as he passes. (Their teeth also get mentioned, as do Mulligan's.) It is hard to believe that the repetition, in this context, of 'buck' can be accidental, and it does seem as if some sort of retrospective judgment is being passed on the apparently super-potent Mulligan and his world at this point.

The final, and very apt, instance of lotus-eating is the imagined cricket match: the endless repetition, 'over after over', is linked to the heavenly weather that Dublin is, unusually, experiencing. 'Heaven' here, however, seems to have mainly the value of 'unchanging', and Bloom does reflect, in what may be his farewell to the land of the lotus-eaters, that here on earth everything does change: 'Won't last.' This simple recognition is what the victims of the lotus are denied.

As already said, the overall purport of the episode is fairly evident: the depiction of Dublin as a contemporary land of the lotus-eaters. But Joyce is not content with a merely thematic treatment of this condition; the text itself is smothered in the names of flowers, which are strewn all over it as over a hearse. This may well strike the reader as excessive; is the point not sufficiently clear? However, *Ulysses* is not about making a point, of any kind. Joyce is interested in creating a total environment within each episode; for his intensely literary imagination, completely word-centred, the naming of many flowers, constant allusions to botany and chemistry (the 'arts' of the episode), are the ways to create this environment. The episode is not just about lotus-eating; the hope is that the reader will also experience the sense of being smothered in the deadening petals of the flower.

BIOGRAPHICAL/HISTORICAL

Line 2.   *Leask's*: H. M. Leask and Co, 14–15 Rogerson's Quay.
11.   *Bethel*: Hebrew, 'House of God'. The name of a
             Salvation Army Hall that Bloom passes in Lombard
             Street East.

11.   *Nichols'*: J. and C. Nichols, undertakers, 26–31 Lombard Street East. Still operating in that location.

12–13. *Corny Kelleher*: fictional undertaker employed by the real H. J. O'Neill's funeral establishment.

17–18. *Belfast and Oriental Tea Company*: 6 Westland Row.

20.   *Tom Kernan*: tea merchant. The central character in the story 'Grace', in *Dubliners*. Partly based on Ned Thornton, a neighbour of Joyce in North Richmond Street in the 1890s.

42.   *Vance*: Bloom's apparently fictional teacher in the High School.

70.   *Maud Gonne's letter*: a pamphlet was circulated in 1904, attributed to Maud Gonne, condemning the behaviour of British troops on the streets of Dublin at night. Curfew rules for soldiers had been relaxed in an effort to encourage recruitment for the Boer War. This is relevant to Stephen's later encounter with the soldiers in Nighttown.

82.   *M'Coy*: C. P. M'Coy is based on Charles Chance, a friend of Joyce's father who had nearly as many occupations as Lepold Bloom himself. He first appears in the story 'Grace' in *Dubliners*, where the whole business of the valise is explained much more coherently than in 'Lotus-Eaters'. As with Bloom, his wife was a concert singer, who performed under the name 'Marie Tallon'. As already mentioned, Chance is both C. P. M'Coy and Bloom; his identity as M'Coy tends to obscure his links with Bloom.

96.   *Holohan*: a real person, alluded to by Joyce in a letter to Nora (*Selected Letters*, ed. Richard Ellmann, Faber and Faber, 1975, p. 158). He is a character in the story 'A Mother', in *Dubliners*.

107.   *Bob Doran*: fictional; character in the story 'The Boarding House', in *Dubliners*.

108.   *Bantam Lyons*: fictional; character in 'Ivy Day in the Committee Room', in *Dubliners*.

108.   *Conway's*: public house, 31–32 Westland Row.

128.   *the Arch*: public house, 32 Henry Street.

180.   *Bob Cowley*: a 'spoiled priest', referred to as 'Father Cowley' later in the book. He is probably linked to the 'Father Keon' who appears in 'Ivy Day in the Committee Room', in *Dubliners*.

194–5.   *Mrs Bandmann Palmer*: Millicent Palmer (1865–1905), American actress.

197.   *Kate Bateman*: (1843–1917), celebrated English actress.

199.   *Ristori*: Adelaide Ristori (1822–1906), Italian actress.

200.   *Mosenthal*: Salomon Mosenthal (1821–77), author of the play on which *Leah* is based.

230.   *Meade's*: Michael Meade and Son, builders, 153–9 Great Brunswick Street.

304.   *Lord Iveagh*: the main director of Guinness's brewery.

306.   *Lord Ardilaun*: brother of Lord Iveagh. Whether the allegation about Lord Ardilaun's skin is true is unclear; it caused great indignation among early Irish reviewers of *Ulysses*.

322–3.   *the very reverend John Conmee S.J.*: (1847–1910), rector of Clongowes when Joyce was there, then prefect of studies at Belvedere in the early 1890s. He arranged for Joyce to go to Belvedere. He was superior of the residence of St Francis Xavier's Church, Gardiner Street from 1898 to 1904. He became Irish Provincial of the Jesuits in 1905.

325.   *Dr William J. Walsh D.D.*: Catholic Archbishop of Dublin, 1885–1921.

331.   *Martin Cunningham*: appears as a character in 'Grace', in *Dubliners*. Based on Matthew F. Kane, chief clerk of the crown solicitors' office in Dublin Castle. A friend of Joyce's father, he drowned in Dublin Bay in 1904.

378.   *the Invincibles*: the secret society that assassinated the new chief secretary for Ireland, Lord Frederick

Cavendish, and an undersecretary, Thomas Burke, in the Phoenix Park in May 1882.

379. *Carey*: James Carey (1845–83), a member of the Invincibles who turned queen's evidence against them and was later assassinated by them.

398. *Father Bernard Vaughan*: famous English Jesuit preacher (1847–1922).

460. *Prescott's dyeworks*: William T. C. Prescott, cleaners, with several branches in Dublin. Molly mentions the firm at the end of the book.

463. *Sweny's*: dispensing chemists, 1 Lincoln Place. Now a Joyce memorial location.

464–5. *Hamilton Long's*: apothecaries, with a branch at 107 Grafton Street.

560. *Captain Buller*: lived at Byron Lodge, Sutton. The mistaken alteration of his name to 'Culler' in the original Gabler edition of *Ulysses* became a *cause célèbre* during the textual controversy surrounding the edition.

SELECT GLOSSARY

Line 32. *dolce far niente*: Italian, literally 'sweet doing nothing', a stock phrase for idleness and inactivity.

135. *Esprit de corps*: French, 'fellow feeling'; another stock phrase for solidarity.

329. *Ecce Homo*: Latin, 'Behold the man'. Pontius Pilate's words when he presents Jesus to the people.

372. I.N.R.I.: Latin initials for *Iesus Nazareth Rex Iudaeorum*, 'Jesus of Nazareth King of the Jews'.

372. I.H.S.: Latin initials possibly standing for *Iesus Hominum Salvator*, 'Jesus the Saviour of Mankind', or *In Hoc Signo*, 'In this sign' (– thou shalt conquer). The initials derive from a Greek abbreviation of the name of Jesus.

397.   *Stabat Mater*: Latin, 'The mother was standing'; the title of a medieval hymn about Mary, adapted by Rossini, among others.

402.   *Quis est homo*: Latin, 'Who is the man?' or 'Who is there?'; the first words of the third stanza of the *Stabat Mater*.

477.   Aq. Dist. Fol. Laur. Te Virid.: Bloom reads some of the labels on the chemist's bottles. Aq. Dist.: distilled water. Fol. Laur.: Laurel leaves. Te [The] Virid.: green tea.

500.   *Peau d'Espagne*: French, 'Spanish skin': a skin lotion.

II
[6 · Hades]

Time: 11 a.m.
Locations: the route from Newbridge Avenue, Sandymount, to
Glasnevin Cemetery; Glasnevin Cemetery

SUMMARY

By now we have become accustomed to the abruptness of the episodes' openings: this one begins as abruptly as any: 'Martin Cunningham, first, poked his silkhatted head into the creaky carriage'. Paddy Dignam's funeral cortege is leaving 9 Newbridge Avenue *en route* to Glasnevin Cemetery. In the carriage with which we are concerned are Bloom, Martin Cunningham, Simon Dedalus (Stephen's father) and Jack Power. The carriage, as the text makes clear, goes via Tritonville Road, Irishtown Road, Ringsend Road into Brunswick (now Pearse) Street, thence into O'Connell Street and north to Glasnevin.

As they pass through Irishtown, Bloom observes 'a lithe young man, clad in mourning, a wide hat'. He points out Stephen (for it is he; this is Bloom's first glimpse of him this day, and the first explicit conjunction between the book's two narratives) to his father, Simon, who launches into a rant about the damage that Mulligan is doing to his son. Bloom listens in silent envy: his own son, Rudy, died a few weeks after he was born in 1893 and Bloom's sense of loss and regret over the missed opportunity is a constant companion throughout the day.

When the carriage nears the top of Brunswick Street and turns right into D'Olier Street, another passer-by is espied. This time Bloom does not point him out, in fact he shrinks back, since the person perceived is Blazes Boylan, 'airing his quiff', Molly's lover who, as Bloom knows, will be visiting the house at 4 p.m. for an assignation with Molly. The sight of Boylan leads on to discussion of the forthcoming concert tour, and Bloom again has the painful pleasure of discussing Molly's part in it.

A third figure is encountered as the carriage passes the 'huge-cloaked Liberator's form' in Sackville Street. This is Reuben J. Dodd, a solicitor and moneylender who is greatly resented by three of those in the carriage because of his reputation for lending money at extortionate rates. Bloom, far too prudent a person ever to be in debt to Dodd, attempts to show his solidarity with his companions by telling a disparaging story about Dodd. However, he makes a mess of the story (Bloom, unlike the others in the carriage, does not have an oral storyteller's gift) and it is completed by Martin Cunningham. The story involves the near-death by drowning of Dodd's son, and Dodd's grudging response to his rescue: he pays the rescuer two shillings and sixpence ('One and eightpence too much,' Mr Dedalus comments).

As the carriage toils up Rutland (now Parnell) Square West, the sight of another funeral, a child's, passing by leads the desultory conversation to different forms of death. Mr Power opines that a suicide is 'The greatest disgrace to have in the family'. At this, Martin Cunningham gets very embarrassed and attempts to soften the harshness of Power's remarks. Cunningham is aware, as Power is not, that Bloom's father, Rudolph, killed himself in the Queen's Hotel, Ennis, in 1886. Bloom, naturally, is painfully reminded of the episode, to which he had already discreetly alluded when mentioning he was going to Co. Clare on 'private business' (the anniversary of the death) later in the month.

The carriage turns into Berkeley Street and then swings left on to the North Circular Road and right at what was then Dunphy's corner. It passes the Brian Boroimhe public house along Phibsborough Road and thence left on Finglas Road to Glasnevin.

Having reached the cemetery, the mourners proceed to the mortuary chapel. Bloom listens to the funeral service with the same detachment and near incomprehension with which he listened to the Mass in the previous episode. The coffin is then brought from the chapel to Paddy Dignam's last resting place.

As the band of mourners ('Paltry funeral', Bloom thinks) follows along, one of their number, Paddy Dignam's former employer John Henry Menton, asks another, Ned Lambert, about Bloom, who is just behind. From this conversation we learn that Bloom's current profession is advertising canvasser, and we learn that his wife, Marion, sings professionally under her own name of Tweedy.

The appearance of the cemetery's superintendent, John O'Connell, sparks off in Bloom a long meditation on death and dying. This lasts until we reach the graveside, and the coffin is lowered into the earth. Bloom looks around the group of mourners, as one does, and spots a man in a mackintosh whom he does not recognize; he reacts as if he were in a country village and a stranger had appeared in the local pub, speculating furiously as to who the person might be. He is then approached by Joe Hynes, the newspaper reporter, who is checking on the names of the attendance. Through a misunderstanding, Hynes writes down the name 'M'Intosh'; thus is history transmitted.

After the burial, some of the group pass by the 'chief's' grave, that of Parnell, and speculate vaguely, hopelessly, about the possibility that he is not there at all, and that he might reappear. Bloom, however, has spied a large rat disappearing under a plinth; this leads to rather macabre reflections on the conditions of the bodies lying under the ground. Bloom emerges from this train of thought, however, to reflect: 'They are not going to get me this innings.'

The episode concludes with a passage of arms between Bloom and the solicitor, John Henry Menton. Bloom's would-be helpful, but possibly unwise, decision to point out a dinge in Menton's hat is met with a studied coldness that leaves him 'chapfallen' and resentful.

CORRESPONDENCES

In Book 10 of *The Odyssey*, Odysseus, still recounting to King Alcinous the story of his adventures, tells of arriving on the island of the enchantress Circe. Circe advises him to go down to the underworld, Hades, the land of the dead, to consult the shade of the prophet Tiresias before continuing on his voyage. In Book 11, Odysseus tells of his journey to Hades. The land has four rivers that have to be crossed, Styx, Acheron, Cocytus and Pyriphlegethon. The first shade he meets there is that of Elpenor, one of his men who has fallen to his death from the roof of Circe's hall. Odysseus remarks that Elpenor has got there before him, despite his swift journey in a 'black lugger'. He promises Elpenor a proper burial.

Odysseus next speaks with Tiresias, who tells him that it is the wrath of Poseidon, god of the sea and the earthquake, whose son's (Cyclops) eye Odysseus had blinded, that is preventing him from reaching Ithaca. Tiresias says that 'denial of yourself, restraint of shipmates' is the 'one narrow strait' that will bring him safely home. Specifically, he and his men must respect at all times the oxen of the sun god, Helios; otherwise disaster looms.

After speaking to Tiresias, Odysseus meets the shade of his mother,

Anticlea, who tells him how Penelope and Telemachus and his own father, Laertes, are faring. He then speaks with Agamemnon, the leader of the Greeks in the Trojan War, and learns of his death at the hands of his wife, Clytemnestra. He sees many famous shades, among them Sisyphus, condemned to roll his rock eternally up a hill and see it fall down again just before the summit. He meets Hercules, who tells him of his own descent into Hades while he was still alive, to tame Cerberus, the watchdog of the land of the dead. He also meets another Greek hero of the Trojan War, Ajax, who refuses to speak to him, because Odysseus, rather than he, was awarded the dead Achilles's armour.

In the Gilbert schema, the following correspondences are given. The four rivers: Dodder, Grand Canal, Liffey and Royal Canal. Sisyphus: Martin Cunningham ('Monday morning. Start afresh. Shoulder to the wheel.'). Cerberus: Father Coffey ('Belly on him like a poisoned pup.') Hades (the god who rules the underworld): John O'Connell. Hercules: Daniel O'Connell (only his body lies in Glasnevin; his heart is in Rome, just as the 'real' Hercules is not in Hades but instead is in heaven, feasting with the gods). Elpenor: Paddy Dignam. Agamemnon: Parnell ('A woman too brought Parnell low' – Mr Deasy). Ajax: Menton.

STYLE

The style of the episode does not vary from the tone already established. In this somewhat longer episode Bloom's meditations are more extended; we get to know his mind better and more corners are cut than heretofore. One example is the passage about the boy with the basket of grapes (lines 957–9) which condenses very drastically the story about the Greek sculptor Zeuxis (whom Bloom confuses with Apelles, whom he then confuses with Apollo) and the statue he made of a boy with a bunch of grapes. Zeuxis was displeased that the birds came down to peck the ultra-realistic grapes; he complained that if the boy had been equally well done, the birds should have been afraid to come down. This is in Bloom's rendering, but it is difficult indeed to decipher it without outside sources.

This is the first episode in which we see Bloom in society in an extended way. The difference between his mode of discourse and that of his companions is quite marked. For instance, Bloom's attempt to tell the story of the near-drowning of Reuben J. Dodd's son is hopeless: he gets the chronology confused, he doesn't specify which character he has in mind, he is frequently interrupted. Martin Cunningham steps in and tells the rest of the story in a couple of pithy, well-crafted sentences, using the kinds of expressions ('chiseller', 'piking it down the quay') that instantly register with the intended audience. Bloom does not possess this kind of ability: his expressions ('there was a girl in the case') are clichéd and entirely uninformative. In an oral culture, where story-telling ability is paramount, Bloom's essentially discursive mode is at a loss—and this is one of the principal factors that make him to some extent an exile in his own city.

Here and there in this episode, where the style has been fully established, some of the stylistic crossovers that we have seen in the 'Proteus' episode recur. The sentence: 'Mr Bloom walked unheeded along his grove by saddened angels, crosses, broken pillars, stone hopes praying with upcast eyes, old Ireland's hearts and hands.' begins as straight narration, but by its end it has strayed into something else. 'Old Ireland's hearts and hands' comes from a sentimental popular ditty by Richard F. Harvey. How, though, does it become attached to this piece of narration? Does it come as a memory or echo from Bloom's mind, the way 'Chrysostomos' comes from Stephen Dedalus's? (It is certainly a refrain Bloom might know.) Or is it a flourish from a narrative voice which is beginning to overstep the boundaries that have been traditionally assigned to the narrative voice in fiction? It is impossible, in this instance, to answer the question with certainty, and this narrative indeterminacy becomes increasingly an issue as the book goes on.

COMMENTARY

A descent to the land of the dead is a traditional feature of the epic mode, and, as has been mentioned, *Ulysses* is explicitly an epic. Such a descent occurs, as we have just seen, in *The Odyssey*, and it also forms the subject of Book 6 of Virgil's *Aeneid*. (It may not be an accident that

'Hades' is the sixth episode of *Ulysses*.) It is of course the basis of Dante's *Inferno*. So Bloom, the hero of this epic, is following in a long tradition in his visit to Glasnevin. The importance of the Homeric parallels varies somewhat from episode to episode; here, as can be seen from the number of them in the Gilbert schema, the correspondences are crucial. Both the larger picture and individual details are illuminated by the parallels: for instance, when Bloom reflects that Paddy Dignam 'Got here before us, dead as he is' he is echoing Odysseus's question to Elpenor as to how he could have arrived in Hades before his master.

Also relevant to this episode is a sense of epic geography. The parallel between the waterways of the Dodder, the Grand Canal, the Liffey and the Royal Canal and the four rivers of Hades means that Dublin itself is part of the Homeric world; in a parallel universe, Dublin and Hades are superimposed on each other. In this sense, the episode is continuous with the previous one, 'Lotus-Eaters'; we have moved from the land of somnolence and paralysis to the heart of darkness, the land of the dead.

In some strange way, however, the contact with the literal dead in this episode is vivifying: the people in it seem more alive than the torpid inhabitants of 'Lotus-Eaters'. In *The Odyssey*, the dead can speak and deliver their wisdom only when they have sipped the blood of the animal sacrifices Odysseus has brought with him; similarly here the juxtaposition of the living citizens of Dublin with their own actual dead is in some sense a redemptive exercise.

Bloom is conscious of the 'hosts of the dead' (to lift a phrase from the story of that name) lying around not as alien, other, frightening, but rather as continuous with, not very differentiated from, the people above ground: 'How many! All these here once walked round Dublin. Faithful departed. As you are now so once were we.' This last sentence is obviously spoken by the dead themselves and it stresses their continuity with, not their difference from, the living who have succeeded them. Here again the continuity is positive, to be welcomed, not evaded. It is significant that the Homeric correspondences listed promiscuously combine the living and the dead, though in Homer these are all inhabitants of the dead world: Martin Cunningham, Father Coffey, John O'Connell, Menton (living); Paddy Dignam, Parnell,

Daniel O'Connell (dead). It is as if the distinction is of no great importance – all here are inhabitants of Hades.

Bloom's attitude to this dead world is crucial to the resonances of this episode. The phrase 'heart of darkness' has existentialist overtones; certainly, if Stephen was the person undertaking this voyage, such overtones would be very relevant. Bloom, however, is a different matter. If, in 'Lotus-Eaters', his position was ambiguous – was he one of them or was he not? – here he is definitely detached from the world of the dead around him, observing it but not part of it. Bloom's attitude to the universe of death which he visits is curiously flat: he is not terrified or horrified by it and neither does he engage in any aspirational pieties or glossing over of its realities: 'Who passed away. Who departed this life. As if they did it of their own accord. Got the shove, all of them. Who kicked the bucket.' It is this literal-minded approach that saves him from absorption into the world of the dead.

He is by no means without compassion or tenderness: he is sorry for Dignam and for his son; thinking of all the dead who have passed through the mortuary chapel he evokes 'consumptive girls with little sparrows' breasts'. But he retains throughout his undeceived awareness of what this is all about: 'Once you are dead you are dead. That last day idea. Knocking them all up out of their graves. Come forth, Lazarus! And he came fifth and lost the job.'

Considering how closely the Homeric parallels are followed in this episode, it is striking that Odysseus's encounter with his mother is omitted; indeed, Bloom's dead mother is hardly ever referred to in the course of the book (she does give him the shrivelled potato he carries in his pocket as a talisman). So the obstacle or dangerous problem that the memory of his mother poses for Stephen hardly seems to exist at all for Bloom, another factor that makes the visit to the land of the dead so much less of a trial for him. His attitude to his father's suicide is again balanced: grieving but not self-accusatory – and it is perhaps his lack of this latter emotion that keeps Bloom safe through many a peril.

At the end Bloom leaves Glasnevin with a sense of relief: 'They are not going to get me this innings.' However, it never felt as if 'they' *were* going to 'get' him, either imaginatively or physically. Odysseus himself left hell in a hurry, frightened by the hosts of the dead that flocked around him. Whether the modern Odysseus gains any wisdom from the experience, as his ancient precursor did, is debatable; what is certain, however, is that he is not cowed. If anything, he seems fortified by the experience, though his final little clash with 'Ajax' Menton is a reminder that there is many a struggle to come.

As has been mentioned, this is the first episode in which we see Bloom in society in an extended way. It is also the first time we get a sense of what a group of representative Dubliners is like. One of the most striking aspects of their dialogue is its obliqueness; allusions are made, names are mentioned, to which the reader may or may not be privy, but no allowance is made for such gaps in readerly comprehension. We are plunged into this world as into a sea, and we may sink or swim in it. An instance is the reference to 'Fogarty' at line 454. This would be totally obscure were it not for knowledge about Fogarty and Tom Kernan imparted in the *Dubliners* story 'Grace'. Thanks to that story's background, we can infer that Kernan has run up such a large debt against Fogarty (a grocer) that he has put him out of business. (Similarly, far more information about C. P. McCoy and valises is provided in 'Grace' than is proferred in 'Lotus-Eaters'.) Frequently, however, both in these encounters and in many of Bloom's own reflections, no such safety net is available and the reader has to infer things that are never overtly stated, since they are so well-known to the people involved.

BIOGRAPHICAL/HISTORICAL

Line 1.   *Martin Cunningham*: as mentioned in the notes to the previous episode, he is based on Matthew Kane, chief clerk in the crown solicitor's office, Dublin Castle, and a close friend of Joyce's father. He died in a drowning accident in Dublin Bay in 1904, and James Joyce attended the funeral in Glasnevin. Many of the details of this episode are drawn from Joyce's experience of that funeral.

2.   *Mr Power*: based on a friend of Joyce's father called Tom Devin. Confusingly enough, he is also mentioned

in *Ulysses* under the name of Tom Devan. He was a Dublin Corporation official.

4.   *Simon*: Simon Dedalus, based, of course, on John Stanislaus Joyce (1849–1931), Joyce's father; best described by Stephen Dedalus in *A Portrait* as 'a medical student, an oarsman, a tenor, an amateur actor, a shouting politician, a small landlord, a small investor, a drinker, a good fellow, a storyteller, somebody's secretary, something in a distillery, a taxgatherer, a bankrupt, and at present a praiser of his own past.' His biography has been written by John Wyse Jackson and Peter Costello, *John Stanislaus Joyce*, Fourth Estate, 1997.

56.   *Richie Goulding*: Stephen's uncle, already evoked by him in Episode 3, 'Proteus'.

58.   *Ignatius Gallaher*: appears in the story 'A Little Cloud', in *Dubliners*. Based on Fred Gallaher, known to Joyce, who became a journalist of some notoriety first in Dublin, and then in London and Paris.

151.   *Dan Dawson*: Charles Dawson, Dublin merchant and politician, lord mayor in 1882 and 1883.

159.   *Crosbie and Alleyne's*: C. W. Alleyene, solicitor, 24 Dame Street. A Mr Alleyne, solicitor, is an unpleasant character in the story 'Counterparts', in *Dubliners*.

247.   *Crofton*: J. T. A. Crofton, worked with John Stanislaus Joyce in the rate collector's office in Fleet Street, Dublin. A 'decent Orangeman', he appears in the story 'Ivy Day in the Committee Room', in *Dubliners*, and also turns up in Episode 12, 'Cyclops' of *Ulysses*.

251.   *Reuben*: Reuben J. Dodd: solicitor, 34 Ormond Quay Upper; a member of Dublin City Council 1903–8. He was indeed a principal creditor of John Joyce, who had to mortgage several properties to him.

253.   *Elvery's Elephant house*: 46–47 Sackville (now O'Connell) Street, purveyors of sports goods. Its trademark was (and is) an elephant.

317.   *temperance hotel*: the Edinburgh Temperance Hotel,
56 Sackville Street Upper.

317.   *Falconer's railway guide*: John Falconer, printer, 53
Sackville Street Upper.

317.   *civil service college*: Maguire's Civil Service College,
51 Sackville Street Upper.

317.   *Gill's*: H. M. Gill and Son, booksellers, 50 Sackville
Street Upper.

318.   *catholic club*: Catholic Commercial Club, 42 Sackville
Street Upper.

318.   *industrious blind*: Richmond Institution for the
Industrious Blind, 41 Sackville Street Upper.

447.   *James M'Cann*: director of the Grand Canal Company.

454.   *Fogarty*: a grocer, he is a character in the story 'Grace',
in *Dubliners*.

568.   *John Henry Menton*: solicitor, 27 Bachelor's Walk.

595.   *Father Coffey*: the Revd Francis Coffey, curate in
charge and chaplain, 65 Dalymount.

609.   *Mervyn Browne*: probably the same person as the
character in the story 'The Dead', in *Dubliners*. A
Mervyn A. Browne is listed in *Thom's Directory* for
1904 as 'professor of music and organist'.

710.   *John O'Connell*: superintendent of Prospect Cemetery,
Glasnevin. Glasnevin Cemetery, of course, contains the
pantheon of Ireland's dead heroes. Parnell and Daniel
O'Connell are both referred to. However, Bloom is
somewhat over-confident about the grave of Robert
Emmet; it is possible he is buried in Glasnevin, but it is
by no means certain.

831.   *Mesias*: George R. Mesias, tailor, 5 Eden Quay.

950.   *alderman Hooper*: Alderman John Hooper, from
Cork. Father of Paddy Hooper, journalist on the
Freeman's Journal, mentioned in Episode 7,
'Aeolus'.

997.   *Mrs Sinico's funeral*: Mrs Sinico's death is the climax
of the story 'A Painful Case', in *Dubliners*. Her name

was based on that of a singing teacher Joyce studied
with in Trieste.

SELECT GLOSSARY

Line 49. *fidus Achates*: Latin, 'the faithful Achates': Aeneas's
friend and companion in Virgil's *Aeneid*.

238. '*Voglio e non vorrei*. No. *Vorrei e non*': Bloom corrects
the mistake he made in 'Calypso', replacing *'voglio'*
with *'vorrei'*.

239. *Mi trema un poco il*. Italian, 'My [heart] beats a little
[faster]'. From the *La ci darem* duet in *Don Giovanni*.
The word needed to complete the phrase is *cor*, Italian
for heart.

375–6. *Mater Misericordiae*: Latin, 'Mother of Mercy', the
largest Dublin hospital in 1904.

601. *Non intres … tuo, Domine*: Latin, 'Do not weigh up
[the deeds of] of your servant, Lord'; the opening
phrase of the funeral prayer that begins the absolution.

618. *Et ne nos … tentationem*: Latin, 'And lead us not into
temptation', towards the end of the Lord's Prayer.

628. *In paradisum*: Latin, 'Into paradise', the opening
words of the anthem as the coffin is being brought to
the grave. 'May the angels lead you into paradise.'

741–2. *Habeas corpus*: Latin, literally 'you may have the
body'. The legal term for an order to produce a
person, normally a prisoner, before a court.

794. *De mortuis nil nisi prius*: Bloom's misquotation of the
well-known Latin phrase *De mortuis nil nisi bonum*:
'Of the dead [say] nothing except good [things].' *Nisi
prius* is a legal term for a civil action tried before a
judge and jury; it means, literally, 'unless firstly'.
(Perhaps giving the dead priority in this context.)

II
[7 · Aeolus]

Time: 12 noon
Location: offices of the *Freeman's Journal* and *Evening Telegraph*,
4–8 Prince's Street North, right beside the GPO

SUMMARY

We are 'in the heart of the Hibernian metropolis', the area around Nelson's Pillar and the GPO. Bloom is in the offices of the *Freeman's Journal* and *Evening Telegraph,* trying to place an advertisement for a client in the papers. (Bloom's function as advertisement canvasser is to act as a middle-man: he persuades clients to place ads and is then paid commission by the paper for his efforts. It is essentially a form of travelling salesmanship.) He first obtains a copy of an ad previously placed by his client, Alexander Keyes, a grocer and wine merchant, and then proceeds with it to the printing foreman, Councillor Joseph Nannetti. Bloom explains the way Keyes wants his ad to appear, and the foreman agrees but adds a stipulation, as newspapers were entitled to do: that the ad has to run for three months, instead of the desired one. Bloom is somewhat taken aback at this, since Mr Keyes will require a good deal of persuading to agree to this condition. He decides to telephone Keyes (the Dublin telephone system was working well in 1904) from the office to sound him out about the stipulation.

He enters the *Evening Telegraph* office and finds Mr Dedalus, Ned Lambert, both of whom we have already met, and a Professor McHugh within. They are digesting with sarcasm and scorn the windy words of Dan Dawson, a local politician who the previous night had delivered a particularly flowery and empty speech at a meeting. After Bloom's arrival, they are joined by J. J. O'Molloy, a seedy barrister.

The editor of the *Evening Telegraph*, Myles Crawford, emerges from his inner sanctum, followed quickly by Lenehan, a small-time sports journalist who even in a city of cadgers is a noted practitioner of the art. Ned Lambert and Mr Dedalus depart to the pub; Bloom, 'seeing the coast clear', goes into the editor's office to telephone Keyes. He discovers that Keyes is in Dillon's auction room on Bachelor's Walk, around the corner, so he leaves the office to find him, followed by a trail of newspaper boys who imitate his walk. Soon after, as those remaining engage in a desultory discussion of Roman law, Stephen Dedalus enters, accompanied by Mr O'Madden Burke, a minor litterateur. Stephen is there to ask Crawford, the editor, to print Deasy's letter about foot-and-mouth. We discover from the editor's comments that Deasy, inclined to blame women for all the evil in the world, had marital troubles of his own. Crawford does promise to print the letter; he notices that the end of the letter page has been torn off, and wonders if Deasy was 'short-taken'. It is here, characteristically, that we are given the text of Stephen's poem, written at the end of 'Proteus':

> On swift sail flaming
> From storm and south
> He comes, pale vampire,
> Mouth to my mouth.

This poem, presented as Stephen's own, is largely taken from Douglas Hyde's *Lovesongs of Connacht*, a book which is referred to later in the library episode, Episode 9, 'Scylla and Charybdis'.

Following an encomium of Greek civilization from Professor McHugh, surreptitiously undercut by Lenehan, the editor's attention turns to Stephen: he urges him to write something for the paper, 'something with a bite in it.' 'Put us all into it, damn its soul. Father, Son and Holy Ghost and Jakes McCarthy.' He suggests that Stephen could become as famous as Ignatius Gallaher, an Irish journalist who had 'made it big' in Britain. He tells how Gallaher transformed a newspaper page into a map of the Invincibles' escape route in 1882 for the benefit of the *New York World*, thereby 'scooping' all the other newspapers of the planet. This is the future that Crawford seems to envisage for Stephen, who shows no inclination to concur in this vision of his destiny.

The conversation moves on to rhetoric; the editor bemoans the lack of current public speakers of the calibre of the great eighteenth-century orators. A couple of counter-examples are, however, given by McHugh and Molloy. One, a brief passage, concerns the Moses of Michaelangelo, the other, much more extensive, also has to do with Moses. It concerns the contempt in which the Jews were held during their bondage in Egypt, and how Moses, by keeping faith with the destiny of his people, brought them out of the land of bondage, and within sight of the Promised Land.

The main effect of this noble oratory is to prompt a mass exodus to the pub, led and inspired by Stephen. On the way over to Mooney's in Middle Abbey Street, he offers an alternative vision of his own to his listeners: it concerns two Dublin women, who take a special trip up Nelson's Pillar, and having finally reached the top, sit there casting plum stones down at the people below. Rather like the reader, his listeners are unsure exactly when this anecdote is over, but in any case the pub is now within view.

As they cross Sackville Street, Bloom reappears. He has already attempted to contact the editor by phone, but has now come around from Bachelor's Walk and seeks a word with Crawford. Keyes will give a two months' renewal of the ad, provided a bit of additional 'puffing' is done by the newspaper. (Ethics on these issues were somewhat looser in those days.) Perhaps unwisely, Bloom asks the editor what he should say to Keyes, and receives an unambiguous reply: 'He can kiss my royal Irish arse,' with which the editor moves on. Discomfited though he is, Bloom still notices Stephen Dedalus, and wonders (correctly, as it happens), if he is the 'moving spirit' of the pub expedition. Bloom's particular interest in Stephen is clear.

CORRESPONDENCES

In Book 10 of *The Odyssey*, Odysseus continues his narration to King Alcinous of his adventures ever since his departure from Troy. He and his men reach the island of Aeolia, home of Aeolus, whom Zeus has made 'warden of the winds'. The island is described as 'adrift upon the sea', hence a floating island. Aeolus also has the dubious distinction of having given his six daughters to his six sons in marriage. Aeolus initially helps Odysseus by confining all the winds in a bag which he gives him, except the west wind, which will speed Odysseus home. However, as Odysseus relates, 'the fair wind failed us when our prudence failed'. His men suspect that the tied bag contains gold; they open it while Odysseus is asleep and the released winds blow the ship back to Aeolia, where this time Aeolus refuses to help them, judging Odysseus 'a man the blessed gods detest'. Similarly, at the end of 'Aeolus', Bloom returns to Crawford and is rudely rebuffed.

In the Gilbert schema, Aeolus is Crawford, the editor; Incest (referring to Aeolus's children) is journalism; and the Floating Island (Aeolia) is the Press.

STYLE

The principal feature of the style of 'Aeolus' that distinguishes it from all the preceding episodes is the use of newspaper-type 'headlines' or, more strictly, cross-heads (not captions, as they are sometimes described) strewn throughout the text. These interrupt and complicate what is already a very diffuse and scattered narrative, as is evident from the summary attempted above.

In addition to this very obvious feature, the narrative style is more mannered, more self-conscious, than anything encountered hitherto: 'Grossbooted draymen rolled barrels dullthudding out of Prince's stores and bumped them up on the brewery float. On the brewery float bumped dullthudding barrels rolled by grossbooted draymen out of Prince's stores.' The second of these sentences tells us nothing that the first one has not already disclosed: it is clearly there for a different reason than the provision of narrative information.

In fact, this episode does mark a definite shift in focus from anything that has gone on previously. There is a move, to put it briefly, from content to form. The 'art' of the episode is rhetoric; hitherto the various 'arts' have been much more content-oriented: religion for 'Hades', economics for 'Calypso', etc. Here, though, the art has itself almost become a character in its own right, with a function all of its own.

Thus the episode features rhetorical devices of all kinds, many of them incorporated into the speech of the characters (largely, though not always—Lenehan is a particular exception—unbeknownst to them). Some of these devices, however, occur as parts of the narration, which they interrupt. Thus the two sentences adduced above are an instance of chiasmus, the inversion of the order of words in parallel clauses or sentences: the second sentence starts from the end of the preceding one and runs back through it again to its beginning. This is just a particularly overt instance of a procedure that is happening throughout. Bloom's reflection about the noise of the linotype machines in the caseroom, 'Hell of a racket they make,' is an instance of ana-strophe: the inversion of the natural order of words and phrases, especially for the sake of emphasis. 'They make a hell of a racket' would be the natural order. One could go on, but shall not: a little of this goes a long way. Enough has been said to indicate the oddness of reading a work of fiction that is also busily doing something else, something on the face of it rather unrelated to the traditional business of the novel.

As for the headlines, they come from a different impulse, although some of them also illustrate the rhetorical devices mentioned above. They were a late addition to the writing of the episode: Joyce inserted them on galley proofs, at a time when he was generally thickening and radicalising the text. Their presence seems due to a logic along these lines: this is an episode about a newspaper; however, it is not just about a newspaper, in some sense it *is* a newspaper; one of the most distinctive features of a newspaper is headlines; therefore this episode shall include headlines. I phrase the matter in this way to heighten, in a sense, the intrinsic absurdity of it. There *is* a certain logic to it, but it is a logic that, carried to its conclusion, will burst the form of the traditional novel and prove both a joyous and a disruptive experience for readers. Worth mentioning also (to employ some anastrophe) is the sheer fun of the exercise; returned from the land of the dead in 'Hades', the text seems set free to enjoy itself a little. The headlines are not just absurd as a device, they become increasingly ridiculous as they go on, although always retaining a certain fidelity to the form (alliteration, concision, etc.). Real newspaper headlines are themselves an area in which a certain sub-editorial licence is possible; it is not surprising that in this context, and with his gifts, Joyce would take a great deal more licence, at whatever cost to comprehension and readability.

COMMENTARY

'In the heart of the Hibernian metropolis' there is wind. The episode is dominated by windy words, and wind itself is mentioned almost immediately: 'They always build one door opposite another for the wind to.' Wind is the agent of instability, of shifting. It has here none of the destructive but ultimately renewing qualities that it possesses in, say, Shelley's 'Ode to the West Wind' or Yeats's 'In Memory of Eva Gore-Booth and Con Markievicz'. Here, it bloweth as it listeth, not destroying anything but not building anything either. 'Noble words coming,' Stephen thinks to himself, and there are many noble words, but all to little effect: after the most powerful piece of oratory in the episode, John F. Taylor's speech about Moses and the Promised Land, the company, rather than bursting into the tongue of the Gael, as the speech should in theory inspire them to do, forthwith decamps to a licensed premises. Rhetoric, whether legal or public, is meant to be kinetic, to move the listeners to do something. Here, it is entirely static, existing in a void remote from any action. Fine words are gone over, recalled, summoned up from a past in which they might once have had real effects; here they are merely rehearsed, savoured for their formal qualities, their content, if any, disregarded. Yes, these people are connoisseurs of oratory: they are easily able to tell the difference between the real qualities of Taylor's speech and the frothings of Dan Dawson. But this connoisseurship makes no difference to their actual situation: as the editor puts it: 'You and I are the fat in the fire. We haven't got the chance of a snowball in hell.'

The episode shows a keen awareness of the mechanics of newspaper production; the machines themselves are given voices of their own: 'Sllt. The nethermost deck of the first machine jogged forward its flyboard with sllt the first batch of quirefolded papers.' The mechanical nature of the process tends to isolate words from their human sources; they become autonomous products of a machine age, language that could not be more removed from living speech: 'WITH UNFEIGNED REGRET IT IS WE ANNOUNCE THE DISSOLUTION OF A MOST RESPECTED DUBLIN BURGESS'.

Presiding over this mechanical production is the editor, himself portrayed as a kind of weathercock, turning in the wind: 'a scarlet beaked face, crested by a comb of feathery hair'. One of the intrinsic qualities of journalism, and the reason why it is the appropriate home for a wind episode, is its ephemerality, not just in the obvious sense that it lasts only a day (*Ulysses*, too, lasts only a day), but in the more fundamental sense that it has no basis, that it is continually shifting, blowing with the zeitgeist (as has been empirically proven, newspapers that fail to do this, and that hold to or are identified with outmoded positions, do not last). Journalism is therefore aptly the 'floating island' that is Aeolia.

Bloom reflects: 'Funny the way those newspaper men veer about when they get wind of a new opening. Weathercocks.' This again is accurate: few journalists are ideologues; most are prepared to work for whatever publication offers the best or most convenient terms, along with a modicum of ethical standards. In this they are no different from most categories of worker, but the word-based nature of the profession can make it seem a little more strange. Also relevant – and accurate – here is the identification of the press with incest: more than most episodes, this one gives the impression of people existing in a cut-off world of their own, unaware of anything outside the confines of their own circle – and this despite ostensibly being the people with their fingers on the pulse of public opinion.

Lest all of this makes it sound as if journalism here is, as it were, getting a bad press, it should be stressed that newspapers provide Bloom's means of livelihood, so they can't be all bad; and that more importantly, *Ulysses*, as Declan Kiberd among others has argued, is itself modelled on a daily newspaper. The book's episodic structure, the huge and apparently unrelated array of materials it assembles, its intensive 'coverage' of the activities of just one day (as if there could be another *Ulysses* for every other day of the century, if someone had the genius and time to write them), all point to the fundamental importance of the newspaper model for this book. But this does not mean that the world of journalism is going to be treated any more gently than, for example, the world of the lotus-eaters.

A theme that animates the discussion in the newspaper office is empire, race and destiny. We hear much about the Roman empire, the Greeks, the Egyptians, the Jews, the British, the Irish. Certain parallels are made clear, particularly in the context of Taylor's speech: Irish, Jew and Greek, as subject races, are identified over against English, Egyptian and Roman, as imperialists. For all three subject races, however, a spiritual empire is being claimed instead. Both parties lay claim to an empire, only to a different kind of empire.

We hear from Professor McHugh about the 'empire of the spirit' of the Greeks; we hear in John F. Taylor's speech about the spiritual empires of the Jews and the Irish. By this logic, then, Bloom, the Irish Jew, or the Jewish Irishman, should be particularly honoured in his native land, given the affinity between the two races. But, as we will see later, this is far from being the case. The problem may be that he blurs the categories; a parallel that is fine in theory becomes troubling and threatening when presented in the form of a real blending. This may be a step too far, just as Bloom to some extent blurs the gender categories.

So the alleged identifications between Irish and Jew proposed in this episode remain theoretical and aspirational, caught up in its fatal windiness, and still cut off from any outside reality. Stephen's final 'Parable of the Plums' reduces the lofty vision of Moses overlooking the Promised Land to two Dublin women gazing down from Nelson's Pillar on the city below them and casting plum stones, rather than stone tables of the law, upon the people below them; odd and oblique as it may be, it voices a reality that is in refreshing contrast to the lofty but insubstantial pageants that have preoccupied many of the other characters.

Few people, if asked, would cite this episode as one of their favourites in *Ulysses*. It is very diffuse; characters come and go; Bloom and Stephen nearly meet, but do not; conversations seem to lead nowhere much. The interposed headlines, while amusing in themselves, are also off-putting for the reader, who has yet to become accustomed to the text's tendency to do this kind of thing from time to time. But the power and attraction of rhetoric as a mode should not be slighted; it is no accident that the only recording Joyce made from *Ulysses* was of Taylor's speech and the interspersed passages, and an exceptionally powerful recording it is. One has only to hear it to dismiss any suggestion that in this episode rhetoric, and the culture that valued it so highly, are merely being mocked. For a more extensive discussion of the Aeolus episode, see my essay on it in the *Cambridge Centenary Ulysses*, edited by Catherine Flynn (full details in Bibliography).

BIOGRAPHICAL/HISTORICAL

Line 25. *Red Murray*: Joyce's maternal uncle, John Murray, known as Red. He worked in the accounts department in the *Freeman's Journal*. John Stanislaus Joyce loathed him just as much as he loathed his brother William. Not only did the two brothers not get on with John Joyce, they did not get on with each other: they form the models for the estranged brothers Joe and Alphy in the story 'Clay', in *Dubliners*.

25. *Alexander Keyes*: listed in *Thom's Directory* under 'Grocers, etc.' at 5–6 Ballsbridge. He may have been manager of the Ballsbridge branch of a small grocery chain owned by Fagan Brothers.

28. *Ruttledge*: business manager of the *Freeman's Journal*

28. *Davy Stephens*: the 'prince of the Dublin news vendors'. He had a stall at Kingstown Harbour and engaged in repartee with King Edward VII on his visit in 1903. Here he is given some of the attributes of the god Hermes.

38. *William Brayden*: Brayden (1865–1933) of Oaklands, Sandymount, was a barrister and editor of the *Freeman's Journal* (1892–1916).

62. *His grace*: Dr William J. Walsh, Catholic archbishop of Dublin.

75. *Nannetti's*: Joseph Patrick Nannetti (1851–1915) was a master printer and politician of Italian descent. He was MP for the College Green division of Dublin from 1900 to 1906 and lord mayor of Dublin 1906–7. Bloom 'foresees' this latter honour in the course of the episode; Joyce, of course, when writing already knew it.

106. *Long John*: based on Long John Clancy, sub-sheriff of Dublin. He is given the surname Fanning in this book.

224. *Thom's*: Alexander Thom and Co., printers, 87–9 Abbey Street Middle.

237. *professor MacHugh*: based on Hugh MacNeill, a somewhat under-achieving classical scholar. He did for a time teach in Maynooth but he was not actually a professor – very often, in this book, titles can be misleading.

262. *Old Chatterton*: Hedges Eyre Chatterton (1820–1910), vice-chancellor of Ireland, a judge appointed to act for the lord chancellor in Ireland.

282. *J. J. O'Molloy*: down-at-heel barrister, apparently fictional.

300. *Lenehan*: a character in the story 'Two Gallants', in *Dubliners*. Based mainly on a friend of Joyce's father called Mick Hart, who spoke French, worked for a racing paper, composed doggerel, as Lenehan does, and gave frequently unreliable tips on horses.

304–5. *D. and T. Fitzgerald*: solicitors, 20 St Andrews Street.

307. *Gabriel Conroy*: central character in the story 'The Dead', in *Dubliners*.

337. *WETHERUP*: Probably W. Wetherup of 37 Gloucester Street Upper, who worked for a while with John Stanislaus Joyce in the rate collector's office.

348. *the sham squire*: Francis Higgins (1746–1802); married above his station as a solicitor's clerk by pretending to be a country gentleman. Eventually became owner of the *Freeman's Journal*. Betrayed Lord Edward Fitzgerald for a bribe of £1,000.

357. *Myles*: Myles Crawford, editor of the *Evening Telegraph*. Fictional, but partly based on Patrick Mead, in 1904 a sub-editor on the *Evening Telegraph*, who later became editor of the paper.

359. *North Cork militia*: this was a force, loyal to the crown, that fought the rebels in 1798. Earlier, members of the militia had been involved in an expeditionary force that failed to conquer the Ohio Valley in 1755. But, to say the least, the editor's history is both confused and confusing.

388–9.   *O. Madden*: Sceptre's jockey in the Gold Cup race that day.

455.   *the Oval*: public house at 78 Middle Abbey Street. Still there.

456.   *Jack Hall*: J. B. Hall, a well-known Dublin journalist of the day.

502.   *chief baron Palles*: Christopher Palles (1831–1920), lord chief baron of the Exchequer, i.e. chief judge in the court of Exchequer, a division of the High Court.

505.   *Mr O'Madden Burke*: based on a newspaperman called O'Leary Curtis; mentioned by name in Joyce's broadside, 'Gas from a Burner'.

541.   *Maximilian Karl O'Donnell*: Graf (or Count) von Tirconnell, Austrian-born son of an Irish Wild Goose, was an aide to the Emperor Franz Joseph of Austria. He did save the emperor's life from a Hungarian assailant.

622.   *Jakes M'Carthy*: a journalist on the *Freeman's Journal*.

639.   *Tim Kelly, or Kavanagh . . . Joe Brady*: All three were members of the Invincibles. Kavanagh was Michael Kavanagh.

640.   *Skin-the-Goat*: James Fitzharris, driver of a decoy cab to conceal the Invincibles' getaway. Later he minded stones for the corporation, like the Gumley mentioned in this episode, though Bloom thinks he may be the owner of the cabman's shelter he visits in Episode 16, 'Eumaeus'.

687.   *Tay Pay*: T. P. O'Connor, journalist and politician.

691.   *Chris Callinan*: a journalist, famous for his malapropisms.

700.   *Lady Dudley*: Rachel Gurney, wife of the lord lieutenant, the earl of Dudley.

707.   *Whiteside*: James Whiteside (1804–76), barrister noted for his eloquence.

707.   *Isaac Butt*: (1813–79), barrister and politician, leader of the Home Rule movement before Parnell.

707.   *O'Hagan*: Thomas O'Hagan (1812–85), barrister and jurist.

731.   *Flood*: Henry Flood (1746–1820), statesman and orator.

733.   *Harmsworth*: Alfred C. Harmsworth, Baron Northcliffe (1865–1922), born in Chapelizod, founder of the London *Daily Mail*, and the leading press baron of his day.

739.   *Dr Lucas*: Charles Lucas (1713–71), physician and patriot.

740.   *John Philpot Curran*: (1750–1817), barrister and orator.

741.   *Bushe K.C.*: Seymour Bushe (1835–1922), king's counsel.

743.   *Kendal Bushe*: Charles Kendal Bushe (1767–1843), jurist, orator and ally of Henry Grattan.

782.   *Professor Magennis*: William Magennis, professor of literature in University College Dublin in Joyce's time. He appears to have been well disposed to Joyce.

793.   *John F. Taylor*: (*c.* 1850–1902), barrister, orator and journalist. The speech attributed to him here is based on an actual oration he delivered in the circumstances described. It was reported in the *Freeman's Journal* at the time, and Yeats recalled it.

794.   *Mr Justice Fitzgibbon*: Gerald Fitzgibbon (1837–1909), an anti-Home Rule lord justice of appeal.

800.   *Tim Healy*: Timothy Michael Healy (1855–1931), leading opponent of Parnell, and later first governor general of Ireland.

800–01.   *the Trinity college estates commission*: essentially, a commission to enquire into how Trinity College could implement its obligations to the tenants of its lands as required under the new land acts, and at the same time maintain its income.

880–82.   *Hosts at Mullaghmast ... within his voice*: Stephen is thinking of Daniel O'Connell ('The tribune').

Mullaghmast (near Dublin, the site of a massacre by the English in 1577) and Tara were the scenes of two of O'Connell's monster meetings.

SELECT GLOSSARY

Line 206. hagadah: Hebrew, 'a telling'. Here, the ritual retelling of the story of the deliverance from Egypt on the first day of the feast of Passover in Jewish households.

207. Pessach: Hebrew, 'Passover'.

209. *alleluia*: the Latin and Greek form of the Hebrew *Hallelujah*, 'Praise the Lord.'

209. *Shema Israel Adonai Elohenu*: Hebrew, 'Hear, O Israel, the Lord our God.' Part of the chant during the Hagadah.

417. *Pardon, monsieur*: French, 'Pardon, sir.'

422. *anno Domini*: Latin, 'in the year of our Lord', hence 'years'.

468. *vous*: French, 'you'.

478. *Imperium romanum*: Latin, 'the Roman Empire'.

489. *Cloacae*: Latin, 'sewers', exactly as stated.

507. *Entrez, mes enfants!*: French, 'Enter, my children!'

557. *Domine!*: Latin, 'Lord!'

559. KYRIE ELEISON!: Greek, 'Lord Have Mercy!' The Kyrie is part of the Tridentine Mass.

562. *Kyrios*: Greek, 'a lord'.

567. *imperium*: Latin, 'empire, dominion'.

717–19. *. . . la tua pace . . . si tace*: Italian; taken from lines 92, 94 and 96 in Canto 5 of Dante's *Inferno*. Francesca da Rimini, one of the carnal sinners, is speaking to Dante (the words Stephen actually recalls are italicised): 'If the King of the Universe were our friend, we would pray him for *thy peace,* seeing that thou hast pity of our perverse evil. Of that which *it pleases thee* to hear and *to speak* we will hear and speak with you, *while* *the wind, as now, is silent for us.'* Stephen's interest however is less in the content of the passage than in the contrast between the light, tripping Italian rhymes *'pace, tace'* and his own dark, heavy ones ('mouth, south').

721.   *per l'aer perso*: Italian, 'through the black air' (*Inferno*, 5:89).

721-2.   *quella pacifica oriafiamma*: Italian, 'that peaceful oriflamme [gold flame]', (*Paradiso*, 31:127).

722.   *di rimirar fè più ardenti*: Italian '[he] made [my] eyes more ardent to gaze again' (*Paradiso*, 31:142).

754.   ITALIA, MAGISTRA ARTIUM: Latin, 'Italy, Mistress of the Arts'.

756.   *lex talionis*: Latin, 'the law of proportionate punishment', essentially the Roman version of 'an eye for an eye and a tooth for a tooth'.

910.   *Fuit Ilium!*: Latin, 'Troy has been' or 'Troy is no more' (Virgil, *Aeneid*, 2:235).

996.   *Nulla bona*: Latin, 'no goods' or 'no possessions'. Here it may simply mean 'no good'.

1056.   *Deus nobis haec otia fecit*: Latin, 'God has made this peace [or leisure] for us.' From Virgil, *Eclogues*, 1:6.

1057.   *Pisgah*: the mountain from which Moses was granted sight of the Promised Land (Exodus), though he was not allowed to enter it (Deuteronomy 34).

II

[8 · Lestrygonians]

Time: 1 p.m.
Locations: from Sackville Street, Westmoreland Street, College Green, Grafton Street left into Duke Street; thence across Dawson Street to Molesworth Street, Kildare Street and the National Museum

SUMMARY

Bloom, standing on the western side of Sackville Street, near O'Connell Bridge, is handed a throwaway leaflet announcing the imminent arrival of a revivalist preacher, the Revd John Alexander Dowie. He takes it, but soon in fact throws it away, into the Liffey at O'Connell Bridge. Before this he notices Simon Dedalus's daughter, her 'dress is in flitters', waiting outside Dillon's auction rooms on Bachelor's Walk. At the river, and after disposing of the throwaway, he buys two Banbury cakes in order to feed the hungry-looking gulls. After they quickly consume what he gives them, he reflects: 'I'm not going to throw any more. Penny quite enough. Lot of thanks I get. Not even a caw.'

Moving into Westmoreland Street, he sees coming towards him a 'procession of [five] whitesmocked sandwichmen' each bearing a board spelling out a letter of the name of the printing firm HELY'S (apostrophe S is carried on one board). These rather sad figures perambulate the city daily and we will encounter them again.

In Westmoreland Street he meets Mrs Josie Breen, an old friend of his and Molly's, who knew her under her own name of Josie Powell. Having fielded an inquiry as to why he is dressed in black ('Going to crop up all day, I foresee.') he asks Mrs Breen about her 'lord and master', Denis Breen, a noted Dublin eccentric. She informs Bloom about her husband's latest exacerbation: someone has sent him a postcard with the words 'U.p: up' on it. This obscure insult has driven Breen to consult various lawyers around Dublin and his wife is trailing in his wake. Bloom, having expressed his commiserations, then asks about a mutual friend, Mrs Purefoy, to be told that she is now three days in labour in Holles Street hospital, with 'a houseful of kids' at home.

At this point, Bloom pulls Mrs Breen aside to allow an even more noted—and genuine—Dublin eccentric pass by: this is Cashel Boyle O'Connor Fitzmaurice Tisdall Farrell, better known as Endymion, who allegedly fell into a vat at Guinness's brewery and has been 'Off his chump' ever since. He, too, is a figure who will recur in the book.

Mrs Breen then rushes off to join her husband, who is on his way to John Henry Menton's office, and Bloom proceeds towards Trinity

College. He passes *The Irish Times*, where he placed the ad that attracted Martha, and then the college, where he remembers his unusually imprudent involvement in the riots that attended the conferring of an honorary degree on the British imperialist Joseph Chamberlain in 1899.

His thoughts move to Parnell and his charisma and almost immediately after ('Now that's a coincidence') he sees Parnell's brother, John Howard, now Dublin city marshal. Bloom is struck by his ghostly resemblance to his brother. After this semi-mystical experience, Bloom encounters a real mystic, George Russell (AE), discoursing on his bike to a female companion about the esoteric meaning of 'the twoheaded octopus'. Bloom has little sympathy with these 'Dreamy, cloudy, symbolistic' people, although he does realise you 'Must be in a certain mood' to write poetry. In Grafton Street he sees another acquaintance, Bob Doran, out on 'his annual bend'.

Bloom's wanderings may have appeared purposeless, but in fact he has had a destination in mind: the Burton restaurant at 18 Duke Street, where he plans to have lunch. On arriving there, however, he is revolted by what he finds: a powerfully rendered passage describes the room crowded with guzzling, swilling men, all devouring what is put before them in an animal-like frenzy. Bloom beats a hasty retreat to the relative tranquility of Davy Byrne's pub, just three doors down, where he contents himself with a cheese sandwich and a glass of wine for the present. In the 'moral pub' he encounters another acquaintance, Nosey Flynn. Flynn inquires after Molly and Bloom takes the opportunity to tell about the concert tour. Once again, however, Bloom has to endure the painful mention of the name of Blazes Boylan; Flynn has heard something about the tour, and asks about Boylan's involvement. Having negotiated that hazard, the conversation moves safely on to horses, and Bloom is left free to commune with his wine. Under its influence, and while watching two stuck flies buzz on the windowpane, he has a vividly intense recollection of himself and Molly lying together on the Hill of Howth early on in their courtship: 'Me. And me now.'

Under the wine's influence also, he feels the need to go and urinate. While he is out of the bar, Nosey Flynn tells the proprietor, Davy Byrne, that Bloom is 'in the craft', in other words a freemason. This allegation is correct (Bloom at least has been a mason), though little is made of it by Bloom himself. Three more people enter the pub while Bloom is absent: Paddy Leonard, Tom Rochford and Bantam Lyons, whom we have already met briefly in 'Lotus-Eaters'. It emerges that Lyons has a special tip for the Ascot Gold Cup that he is reluctant to disclose to his friends. When asked who gave it to him he indicates the person who is just leaving the pub: Leopold Bloom. The reader may well be puzzled by this, not recollecting any occasion on which Bloom gave a tip for a horse (not to mention that such an activity seems highly uncharacteristic of him). It will be quite some time before this little mystery is cleared up.

Bloom departs Davy Byrne's, heading for the National Library, where he wants to obtain a copy of the Keyes ad that has already appeared in the *Kilkenny People* which he hopes to place. Musing on the different kinds of food eaten by gods and mortals, it has struck him that goddesses, consuming as they do only ethereal substances such as nectar and electricity, have no need of anuses. He hopes to verify this hunch by inspecting the statues of goddesses in the National Museum (Bloom apparently believes that late nineteenth-century sculptors would be authorities in such matters).

At Dawson Street he comes upon a 'blind stripling' trying to cross over to Molesworth Street. Bloom helps him across and is duly thanked. Bloom has reached Kildare Street and plans first to go left to the National Library when he suddenly spots 'Straw hat in sunlight. Tan shoes. Turnedup trousers.' He has no need or wish to look at the face – he knows it is Blazes Boylan coming along. Desperate to avoid him, Bloom instantly swerves right towards the refuge of the goddesses in the National Museum. In a flurry of brilliantly descriptive prose, Bloom reaches the museum gate and safety.

CORRESPONDENCES

In Book 10 of *The Odyssey*, Odysseus narrates how after leaving Aeolia for the second time, he and his ships come to the land of the Lestrygonians. A scouting party explores inland and is lured by a 'stalwart young girl' to the house of her father, Antiphates, king of the Lestrygonians. These turn out to be cannibalistic giants, who devour one of the search party and chase the others back to the ships, which are trapped in a confined bay. The ships are destroyed and the crews are slaughtered – all except for Odysseus's vessel, which he has taken the precaution of anchoring in a less vulnerable position. Odysseus and his men, by rowing with all speed, manage to escape.

In the Gilbert schema, Antiphates, the king of the Lestrygonians, is hunger; the decoy (Antiphates's daughter) is food; the Lestrygonians are teeth.

STYLE

After the extravagances of the preceding episode, this one reverts to the 'initial style' to which we have been accustomed. It is, though, more internally Bloom's episode than any that has gone before: as he meanders along, his meditations become more extended, more elaborate, harder to follow. He also displays some of Stephen's more literary ability to conjure up a scene at will: the young nationalist and the maidservant is a fine example, as is the imagined scene of the young lovers embracing.

Outside Bloom's musings, some of the pungent Dublin dialogue that had marked 'Hades' is again evident in this episode: the conversation between Nosey Flynn and Davy Byrne ('And here's himself and pepper on him.' 'Bad luck to big Ben Dollard and his John O'Gaunt.') has an authenticity and a hard edge that will later be emulated by Flann O'Brien and other Dublin writers. Paddy Leonard's remarks, when he discovers that the two people whom he has offered to buy a drink, Tom Rochford and Bantam Lyons, want only water and ginger ale, have a marvellous air of intermixed wonder and scorn that seems the very essence of lived speech.

Perhaps the most powerful passage, stylistically, is the description of the men eating in the Burton. The reader's own gorge starts to rise, along with Bloom's, as this catalogue of gluttony proceeds: the description is partly narrative, partly interspersed with Bloom's horrified reaction. It leads to a vision of nature red in tooth and claw: 'Eat or be eaten. Kill! Kill!' Brilliant as many of Joyce's rewritings of Homer are, this rendition of the world of the Lestrygonians is one of the strongest.

Great tenderness is evident in the rendering of Bloom's recollection of his trip to Howth with Molly, a passage I will return to later. Much of the effect is produced through very short phrases, with simple repetition: 'Joy: I ate it: joy.' Or: 'Pebbles fell. She lay still. A goat. No-one.'

Also most impressive, stylistically, is the way the confusion and haste of Bloom's thoughts after spotting Boylan in Kildare Street are conveyed: 'Sir Thomas Deane was the Greek architecture.' Sentences are rushed together in the way that Bloom is himself rushing to reach the museum. By now the style's ability to echo and mimic any activity the characters may engage in seems limitless.

COMMENTARY

As is evident from the summary, nothing much happens in this episode: Bloom meanders along through Dublin's centre, has the odd encounter, reflects on this and that, has a bite of lunch, makes his way to the museum. Something *almost* happens: he nearly runs into Blazes Boylan, but this encounter, which would have been dramatic enough, does not occur, and, in fact, never occurs in the course of the book.

So the significance of the episode lies not on the level of incident, but rather on the level of internal processes, both psychic and physical. Digestion is its dominant metaphor, and the emphasis is on the mechanical digestive process. The 'technic' in the Gilbert schema is 'peristaltic', referring to the mechanical process of contraction and expansion whereby food is digested and passed down the body. (Not surprisingly, the 'organ' of the episode is the esophagus.) Similarly, Bloom is himself transmitted, with occasional halts and delays, through the city's central artery, the O'Connell Street–Grafton Street route, to be evacuated finally into the National Museum. He himself reflects, at one low moment: 'Feel as if I had been eaten and spewed.' The emphasis throughout is on mechanical process, change and succession not as purpose-driven or humanly controlled, but rather as the work of inhuman forces: 'Cityful passing away, other cityful coming, passing away too: other coming on, passing on.' Movement itself is automatic, not linked to any controlling will within a person: Bloom's 'slow feet walked him riverward', as if the feet are working automatically and Bloom is sleepwalking.

In this vision of a Dublin without stable foundations, subject constantly to change and destruction, the citizens themselves appear as ghosts; the most striking instance is the appearance of John Howard Parnell, in every sense the shadow of his brother, a walking echo. Bloom's mental comment on him, 'Poached eyes on ghost', perfectly sums up his status, as well as launching a marvellous punning phrase, based of course on 'poached eggs on toast', into eternity. Just before that, we had encountered AE, whose generally ethereal philosophy is appropriate for such a world. Those who are not ghosts tend to be crazy, like Denis Breen and Cashel Boyle, etc., etc., or devouring fiends, like the eaters in the Burton.

In *The Odyssey*, Antiphates is the king of the cannibals; here, the note of cannibalism and blood sacrifice is struck from the beginning. Bloom's initial image of the king 'Sitting on his throne sucking red jujubes white' instantly parallels the devouring monarch of *The Odyssey*. Almost immediately after, Bloom reads in the leaflet thrust into his hand: 'All are washed in the blood of the Lamb. God wants blood victim.' Religion is linked to this devouring element: when Bloom first sees the Hely's sandwich-board men, he thinks of the priest he had earlier seen in St Andrew's Church with the letters I.H.S. on his vestments. The Hely's men are one of the book's principal symbols for the repetitiveness and routine of a daily round; following, as the sound echo between the name Hely's and the Greek word for the sun, *helios*, suggests, the sun around in its tracks, they epitomise the effects of the tyranny of the sun god that dominates the diurnal world of Dublin. The well-fed constables are the keepers of this ghostly communal order. The 'art' of the episode is architecture, but architecture is here an impersonal force, building and destroying almost in the same breath: 'Kerwan's mushroom houses built of breeze. Shelter, for the night.'

In this generally bleak prospect, there are one or two oases. These correspond, I think, to moments of pause in the peristaltic process, before the contraction and expansion rhythm resumes: two of them correspond to actual pauses in Bloom's wanderings. One is the recollection, early on in the episode, of his earlier life with Molly in the 1890s, when Milly was a baby. Another is the encounter with Mrs Breen; although tied to one of the more benighted figures in the book, she radiates stoicism and good sense, and Bloom's exchange with her is one of his most open of the day. More important, though, is Bloom's sojourn in Davy Byrne's. Here, in the calm and peace of the 'moral pub', prompted a little by the effect of a glass of wine, Bloom is able to relax from the incessant and almost frenetic mental activity that makes up most of his inner world, and which is itself a means of avoiding painful realities that he does not wish to confront, and allow some of the more difficult memories in. This succeeds a long passage in which Bloom in some sense gets inside the world of food, its uses and varieties, instead of just letting food get inside him. His reward, aided by the wine, comes in his heightened sense of personal memory: 'Touched his sense moistened remembered.' The scene then evoked, and which will recur in the book, especially at the end, is one of the most crucial and evocative in the novel. It is in a sense its foundational moment: Molly and Bloom lying together on Howth Head, exchanging lovers' vows and tokens. Particularly important, in this context, is Bloom's recollection of the seedcake which passes from one's mouth to the other's. No particular schema or correspondences are needed to underline the vast significance of this moment; it contains within itself all it needs to make its own importance. Especially striking is the dignity of Bloom, much put upon as he is, as he confronts this moment. And, lest there be any excessive sentimentality, we are kept in mind of present conditions by the references to the two flies, stuck on the windowpane, buzzing as Bloom reflects. Moreover, Bloom's final 'Me. And me now.' makes clear the chasm that separates him from that foundational moment.

The last oasis in the episode is the National Museum, whence Bloom escapes to avoid Blazes Boylan; he has been 'sent' there, as it were, by the thought of the divine goddesses and their heavenly beverages of nectar and ambrosia. So Bloom has moved, in terms of food, to a higher plane than the cannibalistic scenes and world displayed in the earlier part of the episode, helped on his way, I suspect, by memories of a crucial moment in his own past. Once again the hero of *Ulysses* has come through; in this sense 'Lestrygonians' is an epitome of the entire book—and yes, it's funny as well.

One instance of its wit comes when Bloom wonders 'Did I pull the chain. Yes.' This refers back to Bloom's toilet visit at the end of 'Calypso'. The pulling of the chain is not mentioned in the otherwise very detailed account of Bloom's defecation and the reader might well wonder whether it happened; the fact that we now, so many pages later, discover that it did indeed take place indicates the care and precise planning, along with the overall perspective, that make this novel so special. It is appropriate that the chain should be pulled in Lestrygonians, the food episode.

BIOGRAPHICAL/HISTORICAL

Line 13. *John Alexander Dowie*: (1847–1907) an American revivalist preacher who believed he was the third manifestation of Elijah. He was not in Dublin in 1904.

17.   *Torry and Alexander*: two American revivalists.

27.   *Butler's*: George Butler, manufacturer of musical instruments, 34 Bachelor's Walk.

28.   *Dillon's auctionrooms*: Joseph Dillon, auctioneer, 25 Bachelor's Walk.

90.   *Kino's*: J. C. Kino, a London clothier, had an outlet in Dublin, the West End Clothiers Co., 12 College Green.

98.   *Maginni*: Denis J. Maginni (born Maginnis), professor of dancing, 32 North Great Georges Street.

110.   *sir Robert Ball*: (1840–1913), astronomer royal and directory of the observatory at Cambridge. Born in Dublin.

126.   *Wisdom Hely's*: Hely's Ltd, stationers, printers, bookbinders, 27–30 Dame Street.

130.   *M'Glade's*: M'Glade's advertising firm, 43 Abbey Street.

159.   *Val Dillon*: lord mayor of Dublin, 1894–5; prominent
         Parnellite.

160.   *The Glencree Dinner*: an annual fundraising dinner in
         St Kevin's Reformatory, Glencree, Co. Wicklow (now
         the Glencree Reconciliation Centre).

160.   *Alderman Robert O'Reilly*: merchant tailor and
         politician.

171.   *Dockrell's*: Thomas Dockrell and Sons, wallpaper,
         decorators, 47–49 Stephen Street.

181.   *Bartell d'Arcy*: a character in 'The Dead', in *Dubliners*.

187.   *High school*: The Erasmus Smith High School, 40
         Harcourt Street. Founded in 1870.

203.   *Mrs Breen*: a friend of Molly's and Bloom's. Formerly
         Josie Powell, part of a family that Joyce knew well.

233.   *Harrison's*: Harrison Co., confectioners, 29
         Westmoreland Street.

282.   *Dr Horne*: Andrew J. Horne, one of the two masters
         of Holles Street lying-in hospital.

302.   *Cashel Boyle O'Connor Fitzmaurice Tisdall Farrell*: a
         well-known eccentric whose nickname was Endymion.
         Believed to have fallen into a vat at Guinness's
         brewery.

330–1.   *Lizzie Twigg*: a real person, a minor Celtic Revival
         poet.

337.   *James Carlisle*: manager and director of *The Irish
         Times*.

369–70. *the Burton*: the Burton Hotel, 18 Duke Street.

396.   *Tom Wall's*: Thomas Wall K.C., chief divisional
         magistrate of the City of Dublin Police District.

404.   *Owen Goldberg*: listed in *Thom's Directory* at 31
         Harcourt Street.

423–4.   *the day Joe Chamberlain was given his degree in
         Trinity*: Joseph Chamberlain (1836–1914) was an
         English politician who was doubly unpopular in
         Ireland because of his hostility to the Boers and his
         opposition to Home Rule. The conferral on him of an

honorary degree by Trinity College on 18 December
1899 did result in a considerable degree of disturbance
in the city, as Bloom recalls.

435.   *De Wet*: Christian R. De Wet (1854–1922), a Boer
         commander.

441–2.   *Harvey Duff*: a spy in Dion Boucicault's play *The
         Shaughraun*.

457.   *James Stephens' idea*: James Stephens, head centre of
         the Fenians. Stephens organised the IRB in circles,
         making it theoretically hard to inform on anyone
         beyond the immediate circle. The account of Stephens's
         escape given by Bloom is substantially accurate.

491–2.   *Kerwan's mushroom houses*: Michael Kirwan,
         building contractor, built low-cost houses for the
         Dublin Artisans' Dwellings Co.

496.   *The reverend . . . tinned salmon*: the Revd George
         Salmon (1819–1904), provost of Trinity from 1888 to
         1902.

500.   *Walter Sexton's*: goldsmith, jeweller, 118 Grafton
         Street.

500.   *John Howard Parnell*: (1843–1923), brother of
         Charles Stewart Parnell and in 1904 Dublin city
         marshal.

513.   *Mad Fanny*: Parnell's sister, Frances Isabel (1848–82).
         Leader of the Ladies' Land League, she moved to the
         US and wrote patriotic verses.

513.   *Mrs Dickinson*: Emily Parnell (1841–1918). Married
         to a Captain Arthur Dickinson and wrote a biography
         of her brother called *A Patriot's Mistake*.

515.   *David Sheehy*: Nationalist MP for Meath, 1903–18.
         Father of Hannah Sheehy Skeffington.

523–4.   *Beard and bicycle*: George William Russell (AE;
         1867–1935), leading mystic, poet, journalist,
         economist and land reformer.

552.   *old Harris's*: Morris Harris, dealer in objets d'art, etc.,
         30 Nassau Street.

553.   *young Sinclair*: William Sinclair, Morris Harris's grandson and uncle by marriage of Samuel Beckett.

573–4.   *professor Joly*: Charles Jasper Joly (1864–1906), astronomer royal of Ireland, director of Dunsink Observatory.

600.   *Pat Kinsella*: in the 1890s, owner of the Harp Musical Hall, 1–3 Adam Court.

600.   *Whitbred*: James W. Whitbread, manager of the Queen's Royal Theatre, Great Brunswick (now Pearse) Street.

697.   *Davy Byrne's*: David Byrne, wine and spirit merchant, 21 Duke Street.

737.   *Nosey Flynn*: a character in 'Counterparts', in *Dubliners*.

801.   *Myler Keogh*: a boxer named M. L. Keogh took part in a tournament against a British soldier named Garry on 29 April 1904. Keogh won, as he does here.

889.   *miss Dubedat*: the Misses Du Bedat, Wilmount House, Killiney.

891.   *Micky Hanlon*: M. and P. Hanlon, fishmongers and ice merchants, 20 Moore Street, Dublin.

950.   *John Wyse Nolan*: based on journalist John Wyse Power; his wife, Jenny, did run an 'Irish farm dairy … in Henry street'.

989.   *Tom Rochford*: 2 Howth View, Sandymount. On 6 May 1905, was involved in the attempted rescue of a sanitation worker overcome by sewer gas at the corner of Burgh Quay and Hawkins Street. The incident is anachronistically mentioned later in *Ulysses*.

1146–7. *All those women … in New York*: some 1,030 people died in a fire aboard the steamer *General Slocum* in New York harbour on 15 June 1904.

1174.   *Sir Thomas Deane*: Sir Thomas Newenham Deane (1830–99) and his son Sir Thomas Manly Deane (1851–1933) jointly designed the National Library and National Museum.

SELECT GLOSSARY

Line 36. Yom Kippur: the Jewish Day of Atonement, a day of fasting. It occurs in September or October, five days before the Feast of Tabernacles.

110. Parallax: the difference in apparent direction of an object when seen from two different points of view; in astronomy, the difference in apparent direction of a celestial body as seen from a point on the earth's surface and from some other point, such as the sun.

596–7. *Cherchez la femme*: French, literally 'look for the woman'; figuratively 'expect a woman to be the hidden cause'.

623. '*Lacaus esant* . . . : Italian, from Meyerbeer's opera *Les Huguenots* (1836). Bloom runs together and condenses the words '*La causa è santa*,' 'The cause is holy.'

890. *Du de la*: French, 'Of the', masculine and feminine forms.

1040–41. *Don Giovanni, a cenar teco/M'invitasti*: Italian, 'Don Giovanni, you invited me to sup with you.' From Mozart's opera *Don Giovanni*; spoken by the statue of Don Giovanni's dead enemy, the Commendatore, whom Don Giovanni had in mockery invited to supper. *Teco* means 'with you'.

II
[9 · Scylla and Charybdis]

Time: 2 p.m.
Location: the National Library of Ireland, Kildare Street, Dublin

SUMMARY

Again, the beginning is ultra-abrupt: 'Urbane, to comfort them [who? why do they need comfort?], the quaker librarian purred: . . .'. Just as we have established that what he purrs may have something to do with Goethe, the 'quaker librarian' (Thomas William Lyster) leaves, summoned by an attendant. A rude comment by Stephen (at least we know he is there, and who he is) follows his departure.

Also present in this room in the National Library are John Eglinton (W. K. Magee), at this time assistant librarian, and George Russell (AE), whom we last saw wheeling his bicycle in Grafton Street. They are soon joined by Richard Best, presented as an aesthetic young man who dabbles in French and Irish literature and who is also on the library staff. Best has just left Haines, last seen in 'Telemachus', who has rushed off to buy Douglas Hyde's *Lovesongs of Connacht* as part of his Irish immersion course. (The book, of course, has a certain ironic appropriateness, since, as has been mentioned in Episode 7, 'Aeolus', it is from it that Stephen has cadged his own poem.)

The conversation, especially at first, proceeds by indirections, allusions, hints. It is preceded by a couple of warnings from Russell, one about the irrelevance of discussing the mere authors of works – only what they have actually produced matters – and the other about the power of simple love songs to change the world. There is also much internal musing from Stephen, some of it very hard to relate to what is going on around him.

It becomes gradually clear, however, that some sort of debate or discussion is about to take place ('Unsheathe your dagger definitions') and that the subject of it is Shakespeare's relation to Hamlet (both character and play). The discussion proper, in which Stephen and Eglinton are the principal participants, begins with Stephen's question: 'Who is King Hamlet?' The conventional late-nineteenth-century wisdom would have it that in this play, regarded as the most personal of all Shakespeare's works, Shakespeare is the prince. It is this conventional wisdom that Stephen sets out to challenge, arguing instead that

Shakespeare is the ghost of Hamlet's father, the murdered king of Denmark whom Prince Hamlet is pledged to avenge.

It follows, in Stephen's view, that if Shakespeare is the dead king, then Prince Hamlet must be Shakespeare's only son, Hamnet Shakespeare, who died aged eleven in 1596. (The resemblance of the names is certainly striking.) It also follows, even more importantly from Stephen's perspective, that the guilty queen in the play, Gertrude, must be Ann Hathaway, Shakespeare's wife and Hamnet's mother. In the play, young Hamlet's disgust at the behaviour of his mother in marrying the king's brother, Claudius, is even more pronounced than his hatred of Claudius, the killer of his father, himself. Stephen is determined to drive home these parallels.

Russell once more protests against 'this prying into the family life of a great man' but Stephen forges on regardless. He adduces the facts that Ann Hathaway was considerably older than Shakespeare and that she was pregnant at the time of their marriage to suggest (in a curious reversal of the normal paradigm) that she virtually raped him ('tumbles in a cornfield a lover younger than herself', as Stephen puts it).

At this point, Russell has had enough. He rises, explaining he is due at the *Homestead*, the co-operative movement paper that he was involved in. Prior to his departure, there is much animated discussion between him, Eglinton, Best and Lyster (who has rejoined the group shortly before) about people and plans to do with the Literary Revival, and Stephen feels acutely his (largely self-imposed) isolation and detachment from the intellectual ferment around him.

Following Russell's departure, Lyster, particularly, asks to hear more. He has followed the logic of Stephen's argument: if Ann Hathaway is the queen, Shakespeare the deposed king, then Ann must have been unfaithful. Stephen confirms that this is indeed his view. The plays themselves are adduced in evidence: against the 'spirit of reconciliation' breathed by the late plays, Stephen insists that there can be no reconciliation if there has not first been a sundering and he also insists that some deep personal wound lies behind 'the hell of time' that produced *King Lear* and the other tragedies. He believes that what causes the later reconciliation is the birth of a granddaughter, a female child sufficiently removed from her grandmother to touch some secret spring in the poet's feelings.

Stephen also adduces the sonnets in evidence: he argues that Shakespeare's use of an intermediary to do his wooing for him with the dark lady of the sonnets indicates that his sexual self-confidence has been destroyed by Ann's vigorous 'wooing' in a cornfield, a violation from which he has never recovered.

At this point there is what the text itself calls an *entr'acte*, an intermission. The company is joined by a person we have not encountered since the first episode: Buck Mulligan. The atmosphere instantly lightens, from Mulligan's initial quip about Shakespeare being the 'chap that writes like Synge'. Mulligan has some cause for grievance: he and Haines had been waiting in the Ship pub, in lower Abbey Street, for Stephen to join them, as had been arranged in the first episode, with funds for further drinking. Instead, they receive a telegram from him: '*The sentimentalist is he who would enjoy without incurring the immense debtorship for a thing done.*' To add insult to injury, Stephen at the relevant time was drinking only a few doors away, at Mooney's in Abbey Street, although Mulligan does not know this. Mulligan also conveys the unwelcome news that John Millington Synge is out to 'murder' Stephen, having heard that the precocious poet pissed on his hall door in Glasthule. This leads Stephen to memories of his fraught meetings with Synge in Paris, where they were both in exile.

Lyster is once more called away, this time by a gentleman who wishes to consult the files of the *Kilkenny People*. We recognise the 'patient silhouette' waiting at the doorway. But in any case, Mulligan has already spotted Bloom in the National Museum engaging in the anatomical inspection of the goddesses' posteriors that we have seen him planning. This interest in the goddesses' rear ends makes him 'Greeker than the Greeks', in Mulligan's opinion. Bloom has left his card, and Mulligan seizes on it to identify him. Oddly enough, Mulligan is aware that Bloom knows both Stephen and his father, and he mentions this to Stephen in a manner that is in some sense a warning.

Following these diversions, the discussion resumes. Amid much Elizabethan fiddle-faddle, the next, startling step of Stephen's argument unfolds: Ann Hathaway has not just been unfaithful to her husband (who, of course, has been spending most of his time in London for many years while she remains in Stratford), she has been unfaithful with the poet's brother, Richard, and possibly also with another brother, Edmund. (The chief evidence for this surprising claim is that Richard and Edmund are the names of two of Shakespeare's more notable villains. And needless to remark, the testimony of the famous 'secondbest bed' in Shakespeare's will is also adduced.) While this exposition has been going on, Lyster again has to leave, this time summoned for a consultation with Father Dineen, presumably about the latter's great Irish–English dictionary.

This more or less concludes the argument, if argument is the right word. Challenged, Stephen instantly declares that he does not believe his own theory. Eglinton rather reasonably responds that in that case, he should not expect to be paid for it, as apparently Stephen does. He and Mulligan leave together, Stephen responding only very occasionally and reluctantly to Mulligan's continual badinage. As they go through the library's wide entrance hall, a dark figure passes between them. Stephen stands aside to let the figure pass and Mulligan greets him. Bloom (for it is he) walks out between them. Comically, Mulligan warns Stephen that the 'wandering jew', Bloom, 'looked upon you to lust after you' and advises him to 'Get thee a breechpad'. Mulligan, at least, is aware of Bloom's interest in Stephen, even if he interprets it in a very characteristic way. The two young men leave the library and the sight of two plumes of smoke ascending from the housetops in Kildare Street allows Stephen one last Shakespearean allusion, this time from *Cymbeline*.

CORRESPONDENCES

In Book 12 of *The Odyssey*, Odysseus narrates how having returned to Circe's isle after the visit to Hades, she gives him advice as to his best possible course for Ithaca. One route will take him between two points of land. One of the points is an impregnable, rocky island, the home of the six-headed monster Scylla, who always devours one man for each of her gullets. The other point is the abode of the monster

Charybdis, who sucks voyagers down into a vast whirlpool. Odysseus decides to take this route despite its perils. He manages to avoid Charybdis, despite the horrific sight of the vast whirlpool, but Scylla claims her due, seizing and devouring six of his men while they are gazing transfixed at the whirlpool, and doing her level best to include Odysseus among their number. However, he and the rest of his mariners escape her.

In the Gilbert schema, the Rock, where Scylla dwells, is Aristotle, dogma, Stratford; the Whirlpool (Charybdis) is Plato, mysticism, London; Ulysses is Socrates, Jesus, Shakespeare.

STYLE

This episode's style is ostensibly continuous with that of most of the preceding ones: there are no obvious stylistic flourishes like the newspaper headlines in 'Aeolus' to set it off. But in fact, a radical shift is underway: it is becoming less and less possible to talk of a 'narrative voice' that can be distinguished from what it narrates, that stands outside the subject matter of the episode. This was always something of a fiction anyway: even in the very first episode, the narrative voice was already deeply implicated in what it narrated, taking on the hue and the cast of the person or even thing it was describing. Gradually, over the previous eight episodes, the distinction between narrator/narrated has been fading, has been compromised. This is the 'Uncle Charles' principle, so called by Hugh Kenner because a classic instance of it is the account of Uncle Charles in the second chapter of *A Portrait*. The account of him, ostensibly objective and detached, is actually phrased in the words he himself would use: every morning 'he *repaired* to his outhouse but not before he had creased and brushed *scrupulously* his black hair' (italics added for emphasis). Much magnified in *Ulysses*, this means that each episode determines the way it will be narrated; there is no objective narrator out there to tell it. More and more, the episodes are beginning to narrate themselves. In this sense, ultimately, Joyce has no style of his own; there is only a set of styles, no one of which is carried any further than the particular occasion that gives rise to it.

In the current instance, the style is so thoroughly Stephen's that he might as well be the narrator of the episode as well as an actor in it. A quick instance will suffice: this is John Eglinton exchanging a glance with George Russell: 'Glittereyed his rufous skull close to his green-capped desklamp sought the face bearded amid darkgreener shadow, an ollav, holyeyed.' So much of this is filtered through Stephen's perception that it is useless to try to distinguish his contribution from that of any overt 'narrator'.

This is not just a matter, moreover, of Stephen's consciousness. His is, of course, the dominant one but there is a larger, Shakespearean/Elizabethan ambience that seems to transcend Stephen's own perception and powers. Thus at one point the text itself becomes a play, with speeches by the principal participants; at another, it turns into a form of Miltonic blank verse. These little flourishes seem engendered by the text itself—they are part of the decorum of an episode which has the Elizabethan world for its subject, just as headlines were part of the decorum of an episode that had newspapers for its subject. We as readers will get used to this. 'Scylla and Charybdis', if we survive it, as Ulysses did, is part of our induction into a new practice of reading.

COMMENTARY

This is one of the most puzzling of the episodes of *Ulysses*. Later episodes are more difficult to read in terms of style, but none seems as oblique in terms of content. What is the point of this hour in which Bloom hardly appears, in which we learn scarcely anything new about Stephen, and in which he and others discourse about a subject that seems to have only a very remote bearing, at best, on the issues that have so far arisen?

Stephen's theory of Shakespeare is wildly preposterous, if seen purely as a theory of Shakespeare. The evidence is notoriously scanty and can be read in any number of ways. It begins to make sense only when it is read allegorically, as a concealed statement of his own (and, unbeknownst to him) Bloom's condition. Seen this way, a few parallels become evident (and it is, of course, the case that links between the Sandycove tower and Elsinore had already been made in the first episode).

Stephen's theory is really a meditation upon paternity. It is animated by an intense misogyny: the hapless Ann Hathaway is seen as the author of all Shakespeare's woes. The underlying wish is to remove the process of paternity from all natural contingencies: 'What links them [father/son] in nature? An instant of blind rut.' This means that the role of begetting, and even more the role of the mother, are being set at naught – father/son relations are a mystical state, an apostolic succession that has nothing to do with the mere natural relationship so denominated. In fact the natural relationship is being violently rejected – by the end of Stephen's exposition, if I read it correctly, the very minimal role assigned to the actual Hamnet Shakespeare as Prince Hamlet has itself been usurped by Shakespeare himself, who, we learn, is in any case all in all. He plays ultimately all the parts, including those of his usurping brothers – all the parts, that is, except the inconveniently recalcitrant one of Ann herself, who continues to be the object of Shakespeare's bitter resentment, but who at least remains a separate person.

The point to retain from all the above allegory is Stephen's bitter rejection of his own natural begetting and situation. His own mother has let him down; she has abandoned him for another lover – death. (The fact that she hadn't much choice in the matter is neither here nor there – it's still a betrayal.) His actual father is, to say the least, unsatisfactory. Stephen wants to cast off the shackles of natural engendering. The tricky part in this transition is the role of the mother – libidinal attachment alone makes it hard to shake her off. Hence the need to cast all the blame on Ann Hathaway – 'By cock, she was to blame' – and to make Shakespeare the innocent if unlikely victim first of a near-rape and then of multiple betrayals. The hysterical aspect of Stephen's obsession emerges in these ranting passages.

The issue of the father is less problematical: Stephen's quest for a father (the 'theme' that some critics see as animating the book) ends in a satisfactory substitute for the real one: himself. Just as poor dead Hamnet Shakespeare disappears as the exposition proceeds, so Stephen ends up begetting himself, having effectively wiped the messy natural process of engendering and relationships off the agenda. Even the unfortunate fact of gender difference can be overcome, if not here on earth, at least in the economy of heaven: 'glorified man, an androgynous angel, being a wife unto himself.'

In theory, then, Stephen should be happy: he has worked his intense personal problems out in this allegorical mode, he is playing all the parts, as he wishes – but he does not sound happy. In reality, his guilt, remorse and self-laceration over his mother's death are as active as ever, as we shall see later. Imaginary solutions – even highly imaginative ones, as this is – do not always resolve real problems.

What of Bloom's role, if any, in all of this? Despite being absent in name, Bloom is in fact omnipresent in this exposition. A crucial way in which he 'gets in' is via Stephen's theory of ghosts. Shakespeare, for Stephen, is 'a ghost by absence', absence from Stratford. Bloom similarly is a ghost by absence, voluntary absence from 7 Eccles Street, where he has left a clear field for Blazes Boylan. One way of reading Stephen's theory is to say that Bloom is Shakespeare and therefore the usurped King Hamlet, while Stephen is Hamnet Shakespeare and therefore the avenging Prince Hamlet. This makes Molly an unlikely Ann Hathaway/Queen Gertrude, with Blazes Boylan as an even less likely Richard and Edmund cum Claudius. The correspondences have made it clear that Shakespeare is Ulysses; but Bloom is also Ulysses; therefore Bloom is Shakespeare. The logical consequence of this scenario is that Stephen, as the living son, should in some way revenge Bloom's usurpation and cuckolding by Boylan and Molly. This is not what happens, but it remains a vestigial possibility, faintly haunting the text as it proceeds.

Much of Bloom's actual situation corresponds with that of Shakespeare as outlined by Stephen. Indeed, it corresponds rather better than Stephen's own situation does: Bloom has in fact been usurped by Blazes Boylan, as Shakespeare allegedly was by his brothers and Bloom had a son who died young, as Shakespeare's did. As has been mentioned, Bloom and Shakespeare resemble each other as 'ghosts by absence'. However, the 'fitting' of other parts of the theory on to Bloom is problematical: the whole motif of revenge, the hatred of Ann Hathaway, all seem most un-Bloom-like. If Stephen's Shakespeare is indeed his portrait of an ideal father, then Bloom does not really fill the bill. Perhaps this is the lesson – a lesson in the adjustment of expectations – that Stephen learns as the day goes on.

Crucial to the episode is the dialectical structure that underpins it. Lyster, Best and especially Eglinton are not mere foils for Stephen's wit; they are engaged in a vibrant dialogue (the Platonic dialogues, especially the *Phaedrus,* certainly hover in the background) that sharpens and advances Stephen's thought. The Platonic context fits the occasional slight allusions to homosexuality that are dropped in the episode: 'douce youngling', 'ephebe', 'Phedo's toyable fair hair', etc. By the end, as we have seen, Stephen significantly revises his theory, making it far more solipsistic and far more artist-centred. This revision, as Joley Wood has argued, may well owe a debt to the dialogic structure of the episode, with ideas being challenged, explored and revised as it moves on.

The point of the Scylla and Charybdis passage in *The Odyssey* is that Odysseus makes his way through these two perils, though he is more at risk from the rock of Scylla. Steering between two extremes is often an aspect of this episode. Stephen steers a course in his exposition between the rock of Aristotelian dogmatism and the whirlpool of Platonic mysticism, though he veers much closer to the former. Often in the episode Shakespeare is shown poised between two poles, sometimes unable to choose between them. Stratford is one pole, the Warwickshire town that was the scene of his first undoing and which he is unable ever to really leave, and London, where he attempts to forget his psychic wound in 'scortatory love and its foul pleasures', is another. These correspond to Dublin and Paris in Stephen's personal odyssey.

At the end of the episode, there is a final passage between two poles. Stephen is standing on one side of the National Library's entrance hall, Mulligan on the other. This is not just a physical distance. Stephen reflects: 'My will: his will that fronts me. Seas between.' However, a man passes out between them, steering a careful course between these two warring entities. Prudence has once more brought Leopold Bloom/Ulysses out of danger.

BIOGRAPHICAL/HISTORICAL

Note: great care needs to be exercised in relating the personages who are portrayed in this episode to their historical originals. As the recent researches of Harald Beck and Clare Hutton have shown, a very distorted perception of them could be gained from their presentation in 'Scylla and Charybdis'. Of course a writer may well be entitled to do this; problems may arise, however, when the portrayal becomes so powerful, as here, as to virtually eradicate the subject. Some of these differences are noted below.

Line 1. *The quaker librarian*: Thomas William Lyster (1855–
         1922), director of the National Library of Ireland
         (1895–1920). It appears that, contrary to all the
         evidence of the text, he was not a Quaker. As his
         reference to Goethe would imply, he was a
         considerable German scholar, having translated a very
         substantial life of Goethe. A rather different portrait of
         him is presented in Oliver St John Gogarty's *As I Was
         Going Down Sackville Street*.

16.   *Monsieur de la Palice ... before his death*: an example
         of a ridiculously obvious statement, apparently uttered
         by the soldiers of the French Maréchal de la Palisse, to
         defend his activities (or lack of them) during the battle
         of Pavia in 1525.

18.   *John Eglinton*: the pseudonym of William Kirkpatrick
         Magee (1868–1961). A very influential essayist, he was
         assistant librarian of the National Library at this time
         and remained so until 1922, when he left Ireland at
         the founding of the Irish Free State. He is in many
         ways the prototype of revisionist intellectuals such as
         F. S. L. Lyons and Conor Cruise O'Brien. Joyce
         remained on friendly terms with him despite the rather
         scathing portrait presented here.

46.   *Russell*: George William Russell (AE), leading mystic and social reformer, first mentioned in Episode 2, 'Nestor', line 257, and several times thereafter, and glimpsed briefly in the previous episode, 'Lestrygonians'.

65.   *Dunlop*: Daniel Nicol Dunlop, Irish theosophist.

65.   *Judge*: William Q. Judge, Irish-American theosophist.

70–71.   *Mrs Cooper Oakley*: leading British theosophist.

71.   *H.P.B.*: Helena Petrovna Blavatsky (1831–91), Russian-born, the most important theosophist of the time. Already mentioned in Episode 7, 'Aeolus', line 783.

74.   *Mr Best*: Richard Irvine Best (1872–1959): the most travestied character in the episode. He was assistant director (1904–23) and director (1924–40) of the National Library and became a very considerable Celtic scholar in his own right, whatever his early aesthetic affiliations. He had already translated Joubainville's work on Celtic mythology by 1903.

113.   *Stephen MacKenna*: (1872–1954), Irish journalist, linguist and scholar of philosophy; translator of Plotinus.

130.   *Robert Greene*: (*c.* 1558–92), Elizabethan novelist, playwright and pamphleteer.

274.   *Moore's*: George Moore (1852–1933): Irish novelist who briefly but memorably became enamoured of the Revivalist cause in Ireland. A highly controversial figure in the Irish Literary Renaissance. He abandoned Ireland for good in 1911.

274.   *Piper*: William J. Stanton Pyper, a minor Literary Revival figure.

283.   *Louis H. Victory; T. Caulfield Irwin*: two minor Irish Revival poets.

301.   *Colum*: Padraic Colum (1881–1972): Irish poet and dramatist. A friend of Joyce.

301.   *Starkey*: James O'Sullivan Starkey (1879–1958), poet and editor. Changed his name to Seumas O'Sullivan.

301. *Roberts*: George Roberts, litterateur, actor, publisher: most notorious for his failure to print *Dubliners*.

302. *Longworth*: Ernest Longworth, editor of the Dublin *Daily Express*. Published reviews by Joyce.

306–7. *Miss Mitchell*: Susan Mitchell (1866–1926), wit, parodist and poet.

307. *Martyn*: Edward Martyn (1859–1923), playwright. An important figure in the Irish Revival, noted for his religious scruples.

309. *Dr Sigerson*: George Sigerson (1838–1925), physician, translator, poet.

311. *O'Neill Russell*: Thomas O'Neill Russell (1828–1908), Celtic revivalist and linguist.

312. *James Stephens*: (1882–1950), poet, novelist, folklorist; later a friend of Joyce, who was intrigued by his name and his date of birth.

317. *Mr Norman*: Harry Felix Norman, editor of the *Irish Homestead*.

322. *Synge*: John Millington Synge (1871–1909), leading dramatist of the day. Met Joyce in Paris in 1903, as recalled here by Stephen.

374–5. *Messer Brunetto*: Brunetto Latini (*c.* 1210–95), Florentine poet, unusually admired by Dante.

386. *Drummond of Hawthornden*: William Drummond (1585–1644), Scottish poet.

394. *Renan*: Ernest Renan, French critic and scholar.

418. *Mr Brandes*: George Brandes (1842–1927), highly influential Danish critic and writer.

419. *Mr Sidney Lee*: (1859–1926), leading English literary figure and Shakespeare theorist. His original name was Solomon Lazarus Lee.

439–40. *Mr George Bernard Shaw*: (1856–1950), the Dublin-born critic and playwright.

440. *Mr Frank Harris*: (1856–1931), critic, litterateur.

492. *Johann Most*: (1846–1906), German-American anarchist and secular prophet.

518.   *Vining*: Edward Vining (1847–1920), did indeed hold
         that Hamlet was a woman.

520.   *Judge Barton*: Dunbar Plunket Barton (1853–1937),
         judge of the High Court in Ireland, published *Links
         between Ireland and Shakespeare* in 1919.

561.   *Connery's*: owners of the Ship Hotel, 5 Abbey Street
         Lower.

582.   *Mr Justice Madden*: Dodgson Hamilton Madden
         (1840–1928), judge of the High Court of Ireland,
         published *The Diary of Master William Silence: A
         Study of Shakespeare and Elizabethan Sport* in 1897.

729.   *Dowden*: Edward Dowden (1843–1913), professor of
         English at Trinity College Dublin; well-known critic.

994.   *George Meredith*: (1828–1909), English novelist and
         poet.

1073.   *Herr Bleibtreu*: Karl Bleibtreu (1859–1928), German
         dramatist and critic. He did hold the theory attributed
         to him here.

1134.   *lousy Lucy*: according to local tradition, a landowner
         near Stratford called Sir Thomas Lucy whipped the
         young Shakespeare for stealing deer.

1141.   *M'Curdy Atkinson*: F. M'Curdy Atkinson, minor
         Dublin litterateur.

1159.   *Gregory*: Lady Gregory, who helped Joyce, and whose
         book *Poets and Dreamers* he did review in the *Daily
         Express* in forthright terms.

1221.   *Cymbeline*: Shakespeare's play *Cymbeline* does end
         with a 'druid peace'.

SELECT GLOSSARY

Line 2.   *Wilhelm Meister*: a novel by Goethe, in part of which
           the hero does discuss and even revise *Hamlet*.

5.   sinkapace: an Elizabethan dance (after the French
           cinque pas).

12.   corantoed: based on another Elizabethan dance, the coranto.

30.   *ollav*: standard anglicisation of Irish ollamh, a scholar.

34.   *Ed egli avea del cul fatto trompetta*: Italian, 'And of his arse he made a trumpet' (*Inferno*, 21:139).

62.   Hiesos Kristos: Greek, 'Jesus Christ'.

65.   Arval: mystical name for the ruling council of the theosophical movement, after the name of a Roman priesthood.

69.   sophia: Greek, 'wisdom', thought of as a person in theosophy.

69.   plane of buddhi: fourth plane of enlightenment in theosophy.

70.   karma: the law of moral balance in theosophy; somewhat akin to judgment in Christian religions.

72.   *Pfuiteufel!*: German, *pfui*: 'for shame'; *teufel*: devil.

114.   *il se promène ... de lui-même*: French, 'He walks along, reading the book of himself.' From the prose-poem, *Hamlet et Fortinbras*, by Mallarmé.

118–21.   *Hamlet/ou/Le Distrait/Pièce de Shakespeare*: French, 'Hamlet; or, the absent-minded one. A play by Shakespeare'.

222–3.   *Liliata rutilantium*: see glossary, Episode 1, 'Telemachus', lines 276–7.

236.   (*absit nomen!*): Latin, 'let the name be absent!' The phrase involves a play on the stock Latin expression *absit omen*, 'let there be no ill omen'.

237.   Socratididion: the diminutive of Socrates, frequently translated 'sweet Socrates'.

237.   Epipsychidion: an invented Greek word (invented by Shelley) meaning something like 'soul out of my soul'.

238.   caudlelectures: word derived from nightly harangues delivered to her husband by Margaret Caudle in Douglas Jerrold's *Curtain Lectures*.

239.   archons: Greek, the ruling magistrates.

281. mahamahatma: Sanskrit, maha: 'great'; mahatma: 'wise one'.

282. chelaship: 'chela' in Buddhism is a novice in the mysteries.

298. Argal: a corruption of the Latin *Ergo*, 'therefore'.

314. *Cordoglio*: an invented Italianised version of 'Cordelia', but also a word meaning 'sorrow of heart'.

315. Nookshotten: an archaic word meaning 'pushed into a corner', hence 'neglected'.

321. ild: Elizabethan English, reward.

330. chopine: Elizabethan English, woman's shoe with a thick sole.

366–7. *Ta an bad ... Taim in mo shagart*: Irish, 'The boat is on the land. I am a priest.'

367. beurla: bastardised Irish, 'English'.

374. *E quando ... l'attosca*: Italian, 'And when it [the basilisk] looks upon the man, it poisons him'; from an Italian version of Brunetto Latini's *Li livres dou tresor*.

413. *Tir na n-og*: Irish, 'the land of youth'.

425–6. *L'art d'être grandp ...* : French, an almost complete rendering of the phrase, 'The art of being a grandf[ather]'.

430–31. *Amor ... concupiscimus*: Latin, two conjoined phrases from Aquinas's *Summa contra Gentiles*: something like: 'Love indeed wills something good to something; hence when we desire a thing ...'

452. buonaroba: Italian, 'a commonplace thing'; also in Elizabethan slang 'a good thing', 'an easy mark'.

455. coistrel: Elizabethan, 'ruffian, knave'.

484. *Entr'acte*: French, 'intermission'.

491. *Was Du verlachst ...* : German proverb, 'What you mock you will nevertheless serve'.

500. *Gloria ...* : Latin, 'Glory to God in the Highest'.

564. mavrone: Anglicised Irish for *mo bhrón*, 'my sorrow'.

570. pampooties: moccasins worn by Aran Islanders.

579.   *C'est vendredi saint!*: French, 'It's Good Friday!'

616.   Kallipyge: Greek, 'beautiful-buttocked'.

636.   capon's: tasty food transferred as an epithet to the woman.

638.   lakin: Elizabethan contraction of 'ladykin', a term of endearment.

641.   Cours la Reine: a street in Paris.

642.   *Encore . . . veux?*: French, 'Twenty sous more. We will do nice little nasty things. Darling? You want to?'

666.   giglot: Elizabethan term for 'lascivious, wanton'.

716.   *Separatio . . . thalamo*: Latin, 'Separation from board and bedchamber', Mulligan's variant on the standard phrase, *Separatio a mensa et thoro*, 'Separation from board and bed'.

762.   *Mingo . . . mingere*: Latin, the principal parts of the verb 'to make water, to urinate'.

765.   *Sufflaminandus sum*: Latin, 'I ought to be repressed [in speaking]', alluding to a comment by Ben Jonson that Shakespeare's natural fluency should sometimes have been curbed.

770–71.   *Amplius . . . multos*: Latin, 'Further. In human society it is of greatest importance that there be friendship among the many.'

773.   *Ora pro nobis*: Latin, 'Pray for us'.

775.   *Pogue mahone! Acushla machree*: Irish, 'Kiss my arse! Pulse of my heart!'

797.   *Requiescat!*: Latin, 'May she rest!'

811.   *inquit Eglintonus Chronolologos*: Latin cum Greek, 'Quoth Eglinton the chronicler'.

817.   the unco guid: Scottish dialect, 'the exceptionally righteous'; the title of a poem by Robert Burns.

831.   *nel . . . vita*: Italian, 'in the middle of the journey of our life', the opening line of Dante's *Divine Comedy*.

842–3.   *Amor matris*: Latin, 'a mother's love', or 'love of a mother'.

848.   *Amplius ... Postea*: Latin, 'Further. Heretofore. Once again. Afterwards.' Terms used in Scholastic argument, e.g. Aquinas.

907.   (*piano, diminuendo*): Italian, 'softly, with diminishing volume'.

919.   (*a tempo*): Italian, 'keeping time'.

921.   (*stringendo*): Italian, 'forcefully'.

926.   honorificabilitudinitatibus: Latin, 'in the condition of being loaded with honours'. Believed to be the longest Latin word and hence a stock joke.

938.   meacock: Elizabethan, a spiritless or weak man.

939.   *Autontimorumenos ... Stephanoumenos*: Greek, 'Self-tormentor. Ox-soul of Stephen.' The latter phrase is used by Stephen's classmates as he passes on his way to the beach in the climactic scene of *A Portrait of the Artist as a Young Man*.

940–41.   S.D ... *S.D.*: Italian, 'S.D: his woman. Oh yes – his. Gelindo resolves not to love S.D.'

947.   *Stephanos*: Greek, 'crown', or 'garland'.

954.   *Pater, ait*: Latin, 'Father, he cries'. Icarus's cry to Daedelus in Ovid's *Metamorphoses*.

995.   *Que voulez-vous*: French, 'What do you expect?'

1003–4.   Protasis ... catastrophe: the four principal divisions of ancient drama: protasis: the introductory material; epitasis: developing the main action; catastasis: the climax of the action; catastrophe: the final event, such as death in tragedy or marriage in comedy.

1070.   Eclecticon: combines 'eclectic' with 'Eglinton'.

1079.   *Egomen*: Greek: 'I on the one hand'.

1089–90.   *Summa contra Gentiles*: Latin, 'treatise against unbelievers', the title of one of Aquinas's major works.

1109.   I gall his kibe: from *Hamlet*, '[I walk so close to him] I rub a blister on his heel'.

1179.   *marcato*: Italian, 'in an emphatic manner'.

II
[10 · Wandering Rocks]

ST XAVIERS. R.C.C. DUBLIN. 1193 W.L.

Time: 3 p.m.
Location: the streets of Dublin

SUMMARY

Note: 'Wandering Rocks' consists of nineteen 'mini-episodes', into all but four of which is interpolated a fragment of another action that is occurring simultaneously, but at a different place in Dublin. The following summary will indicate each interpolation at the end of each section, with line numbers. Some, but not all, of the interpolations refer to the principal action of another section, and where appropriate this is indicated.

Section 1

Father John Conmee S.J., superior of the Jesuit community in Gardiner Street, is setting out from Gardiner Street to the O'Brien Institute for Destitute Children, Artane, run by the Christian Brothers, to see about placing Patrick Dignam, eldest son of Paddy·Dignam, in the institute. He has been requested to do so by Martin Cunningham, and Father Conmee is anxious to oblige that 'good practical catholic'. In Mountjoy Square he meets the wife of Mr David Sheehy MP and stops for some genteel conversation with her. He then gives three young Belvedere boys whom he encounters a letter 'for father provincial' to post. He next greets the 'stately, silverhaired' Mrs McGuinness, a pawnbroker. Saluting various citizens, he walks down Great Charles Street to the North Circular Road, then along Portland Row. He turns left into the North Strand Road, and reaches Newcomen Bridge, where he takes a tram in order not to traverse 'the dingy way past Mud Island' (now Fairview Park). He descends from the tram at the Malahide Road and walks the rest of the way. Father Conmee, who is very aware of history, thinks first of the Lords Talbot de Malahide, and then, by way of a book he is planning on the history of Jesuit houses, of Mary Rochfort, countess of Belvedere, sequestered away by her jealous husband at Gaulston, Rochfortbridge, near Mullingar, in the eighteenth century, on suspicion of having been unfaithful with his brother. Father Conmee can easily see himself as a priest of those times. As he reaches more rural parts on the Malahide Road, he remembers his time as rector of Clongowes in Co. Kildare. He begins to read his office, but is slightly distracted by the sudden emergence of a young man and woman from a nearby field. He blesses them both gravely and continues reading.

Interpolation

56–60.   'Mr Denis J. Maginni . . . Dignam's Court'. Dignam's Court is off Great Britain (now Parnell) Street, about a half-mile away from Father Conmee's current location.

Section 2

Corny Kelleher, who works for the undertaker H. J. O'Neill, is standing at the door of the premises in the North Strand Road. (Father Conmee has already greeted him as he passed by.) Constable 57C passes by, and he and Corny have a very cryptic conversation, culminating in the constable announcing that 'I seen that particular party last evening'.

Interpolations

213–14.   'Father Conmee . . . Newcomen Bridge'. Newcomen Bridge is a short distance away from O'Neill's premises at 164 North Strand Road.

222–3.   'a generous white arm . . . Eccles Street'. Eccles Street is slightly north-west of the North Strand Road. The 'generous white arm' belongs, of course, to Molly Bloom (see Section 3).

Section 3

A one-legged sailor makes his way up Eccles Street, uttering his begging refrain: '*For England, home and beauty*'. He passes Number 7, where 'gay sweet chirping whistling' is interrupted by his plea. A coin is flung to him over the area railings by a woman's arm. An honest urchin who is passing by drops it into the sailor's cap.

Interpolation

236–7.   'J. J. O'Molloy's white careworn face . . .'. Occurs in St Mary's Abbey, just off Capel Street, in Section 8.

Section 4

Katey and Boody Dedalus, sisters of Stephen Dedalus, return to their home in St Peter's Terrace, Cabra, having failed to obtain any money for the books they had attempted to pawn from Mrs McGuinness, the pawnbroker. Their elder sister, Maggy, tells them that another sister, Dilly, has gone to meet their father, Simon, in an attempt to get money from him and Boody comments: 'Our father who art not in heaven'.

Interpolations

264–5. 'Father Conmee . . . Clongowes fields . . .'. Actually a recall of Father Conmee reminiscing about his time in Clongowes as he walks along the Malahide Road in Section 1.

281–2. 'The lacquey . . . Barang!' The scene at Dillon's auction rooms on Bachelors Walk, where Simon Dedalus does in fact meet Dilly in Section 11, lines 649–50.

294–7. 'A skiff . . . George's quay'. The throwaway about Alexander J. Dowie that Bloom had thrown away into the river back in Episode 8, 'Lestrygonians', line 57, is making its way down the Liffey.

Section 5

Blazes Boylan is in Thornton's fruit and flowers shop at 63 Grafton Street, getting a basket of fruit made up. He includes in the basket a 'bottle' and a 'small jar' that he has already purchased and he asks the 'blond girl' who is serving to have them delivered to an address which he writes down. He notices the Hely's sandwich-board men whom Bloom had already seen pass by. The girl tickles his fancy but he goes no further with her than to ask to use her telephone.

Interpolation

315–16. 'A darkbacked figure . . . Merchant's Arch . . .'. Bloom, some distance away, is scanning books on a hawker's cart. See Section 10.

Section 6

Stephen Dedalus is talking in College Green to Almidano Artifoni, an Italian music teacher of his acquaintance. Artifoni urges him, in Italian, not to let his fine voice go to waste, saying he should not sacrifice himself in this way. Stephen gives no promises, however, and Artifoni trots off to catch the Dalkey tram.

Section 7

Blazes Boylan's secretary, Miss Dunne, receives a telephone call from her employer, checking up on messages and giving her some instructions. She has just begun to type something when the call comes through, and has got as far as the date, '16 June 1904' (the only time it is formally announced). She tells Boylan that 'Mr Lenehan' has rung to say he will be in the Ormond Hotel at four.

Interpolations

373–4.   'The disk shot down . . .'. Tom Rochford's 'invention' to indicate the different music hall turns is being demonstrated to Lenehan, McCoy and Nosey Flynn. See Section 9.

377–9.   'Five tallhatted . . .'. The Hely's sandwich-board men that Boylan spotted from Thornton's in Section 5 pass along at the top of Grafton Street.

Section 8

Ned Lambert, a seed merchant, is in St Mary's Abbey, one of Dublin's most historic sites, just off Capel Street, with a Church of Ireland clergyman who is interested in history, the Revd Hugh C. Love, of Rathcoffey, Co. Kildare. Ned Lambert explains to the visitor that this is the place where Silken Thomas, the rebellious earl of Kildare, renounced his allegiance to King Henry VIII. They are joined by J. J. O'Molloy, last seen in the 'Aeolus' episode. The clergyman departs, intending to return and take a photograph on a subsequent occasion. Before J. J. O'Molloy can tell Ned Lambert the purpose of his visit, Lambert develops a violent sneezing fit, partly due, he says, to the draught at Paddy Dignam's funeral.

Interpolations

425. 'From a long face ... chess board': John Howard Parnell. See Section 16.

440–41. 'The young woman ... twig'. The woman in the couple Father Conmee encounters on the Malahide Road. The words used to describe her action are identical. See Section 1, lines 201–2.

Section 9

In his premises in Crampton Court, just off Dame Street, Tom Rochford is showing Lenehan, McCoy and Nosey Flynn his invention to indicate which music hall 'turn' is now 'on'. Lenehan promises to mention it to Blazes Boylan, who is, of course, a concert promoter, down in the Ormond Hotel, and he and McCoy leave. As they go along Sycamore Street, Lenehan tells McCoy about Tom Rochford's heroic act in rescuing a man overcome by sewer gas down a manhole. The two discuss the upcoming Gold Cup race: Lenehan, who is backing Sceptre, tells of meeting Bantam Lyons going in 'to back a bloody horse someone gave him that hasn't an earthly'. He then identifies the 'someone' as Leopold Bloom, whom they spy scanning books on the hawker's cart under Merchants's Arch. Lenehan, as they go along Wellington Quay, proceeds to tell McCoy 'a damn good one' about Bloom. He claims that when he and the Blooms were at the Glencree Reformatory dinner, he and Molly were seated together in the jaunting car on the way home. Lenehan took advantage of this proximity to enjoy what he could of Molly's charms, while Bloom (who is keenly interested in astronomy) was pointing out the stars of the Milky Way to the other occupants of the car, Chris Callinan and the jarvey. Finally Molly asked Bloom to identify a tiny star 'miles away' (a slight understatement). Bloom, for once, is stumped, but is rescued by Chris Callinan, who declares that the star is *only what you might call a pinprick*. Lenehan is most amused by the unintended reflection on

Bloom's sexual prowess but seeing that McCoy, whose own wife is also a concert singer, does not share his feelings, he adds defensively that Bloom is 'a cultured allroundman . . . There's a touch of the artist about old Bloom'.

Interpolations

470–75. 'Lawyers of the past . . .'. Occurs again in Section 10, lines 625–31.

515–16. 'The gates of the drive . . . viceregal cavalcade'. See Section 19.

534–5. 'Master Patrick . . . porksteaks'. See Section 18.

542–3. 'A card . . . Eccles street'. See Section 3, lines 250–51.

Section 10

Leopold Bloom is scanning the books on the hawker's cart under Merchant's Arch, looking for works that might appeal to Molly's taste for erotic titillation (and his own). One or two are suggested by the salesman and rejected, but he alights on a volume called '*Sweets of Sin*', and finds its plush prose very much to his taste. He tells the shopman that he will purchase it and is assured: 'That's a good one'.

Interpolations

599–600. 'On O'Connell bridge . . . dancing &c.' See Section 1, lines 56–60.

625–31. 'An elderly female . . . Corporation.' See Section 9, lines 472–5.

Section 11

Dilly Dedalus, spotted already by Leopold Bloom in 'Lestrygonians', meets her father outside Dillon's auction rooms on Bachelors Walk and asks him for money. A difficult scene ensues, with Mr Dedalus grudgingly giving her a shilling and then, under further pressure, producing two more pennies. Mr Dedalus strides off, making sarcastic comments about the 'little nuns!', whom he obviously suspects of undermining his position with his daughters.

Interpolations

651–3. 'Bang of the lastlap . . . College Library'. The Trinity
College Sports are also referred in Section 19, lines
1258–60.

673–4. 'Mr Kernan . . . James's street'. See Section 12, lines
718–20.

709–10. 'The viceregal cavalcade . . . out of Parkgate.' See
Section 19, lines 1180–81.

Section 12

Tom Kernan is walking along James's Street, pleased with the order
for tea he has booked for his company, Pulbrook Robertson. He
rehearses with pleasure his encounter with the publican, Mr Crim-
mins, and admires the skill with which he wheedled the order out of
him. Drawing near St Catherine's Church, he reflects on the execution
of Robert Emmet and also recalls the fate of another patriot, Edward
Fitzgerald, who escaped from his pursuers in the same area. He is
roused from these reflections on Ireland's patriotic past by the sight
of the vice-regal cavalcade going along the quays, and is most disappointed to have missed the chance of greeting his excellency.

Interpolations

740–41. 'Hello, Simon . . . stopping'. See Section 14, lines
881–2.

752–4. 'North Wall . . . coming.' Bloom's throwaway, already
observed in Section 4, lines 294–7.

778–80. 'Denis Breen . . . Collis and Ward'. Denis Breen, last
seen in Episode 8, 'Lestrygonians', lines 309–13 on his
legal quest.

Section 13

Stephen Dedalus is in Fleet Street, looking at jewels in a jeweller's
window, and reflecting on his own struggle, as an artist, to 'wrest old
images from the burial earth'. He goes down Bedford Row and stops
at a book-cart. Suddenly he is approached by his sister Dilly, who has

just bought a French primer at the cart with some of the money her father has so reluctantly given her. The exchange between the two is difficult: Stephen is internally overcome again with guilt and remorse at the plight of his family – but he is also fearful of 'drowning' with them. He makes no practical move to help his sister, preferring to wallow in his misery.

Interpolations

818–20.   'Two old women . . . cockles rolled'. The two women
           Stephen first spotted on Sandymount Strand in
           Episode 3, 'Proteus', lines 29–34.

842–3.   'Father Conmee . . . vespers'. A continuation of Father
           Conmee's journey from the point where we left him at
           the end of Section 1.

Section 14

Simon Dedalus meets a friend, Father Cowley, on Ormond Quay. Father Cowley is under pressure from the moneylender, Reuben J. Dodd, who is attempting to recover a debt by seizing some of Cowley's property. They are joined by another acquaintance, Ben Dollard, something of an expert in these tangled legal matters, who assures Father Cowley that since his landlord, the Revd Hugh C. Love, has the prior claim on any goods and chattels, Dodd's writ 'is not worth the paper it's printed on'.

Interpolations

919–20.   'Cashel Boyle . . . Kildare Street club'. Cashel Boyle
           O'Connor Fitzmaurice Tisdall Farrell, the wandering
           eccentric last sighted in 'Lestrygonians', lines 295–303.

928–31.   'The reverend Hugh . . . the Ford of Hurdles.' Mr Love's
           progress after his visit to St Mary's Abbey in Section 8.

Section 15

Emerging from Dublin Castle, Martin Cunningham, Mr Power and another friend, John Wyse Nolan, discuss the collection they are trying to raise for young Patrick Dignam. It is noted, with some surprise, that Bloom has contributed five shillings. Martin Cunningham accosts Jimmy Henry, the assistant town clerk, hoping to enlist him in the cause. They enter Kavanagh's wine rooms at 27 Parliament Street, where they find the city sub-sheriff, Long John Fanning, waiting for them. Fanning cannot remember Paddy Dignam, but before the conversation can advance any further, they are distracted by unusual noise and colour outside: the vice-regal cavalcade passing by.

Interpolations

962–3.   'Bronze by gold'. From the start of the next episode, 'Sirens'.

970–71.   'On the steps of . . . descending'. Happens very close to the scene of this section, but is, in fact, an interpolation.

984–5.   'Outside la maison Claire . . . liberties'. Jack Mooney's brother-in-law is, in fact, Bob Doran, 'hero' of the story 'The Boarding House' in *Dubliners*. McCoy has already mentioned to Bloom that Doran was 'on one of his periodical bends' in Episode 5, 'Lotus-Eaters', lines 107–8.

Section 16

Buck Mulligan and Haines are in the Dublin Bakery Company's tearooms at 33 Dame Street. Mulligan tells Haines that Stephen Dedalus's wits have been 'driven astray' by 'visions of hell'. They agree that he is paralysed by the idea of eternal retribution and 'can never be a poet'. However, Mulligan says that Stephen plans to write something 'in ten years'. Haines meanwhile is anxious to ensure that he is being served 'real Irish cream'. He does not wish to be 'imposed on'.

Interpolations

1063–4.   'The onelegged sailor . . . England expects . . .'. See Section 3.

1096–9.   'Elijah . . . bricks.' Bloom's throwaway again. See Episode 8, 'Lestrygonians' and Sections 4 and 12.

Section 17

Almidano Artifoni walks past Holles Street to Mount Street. He is followed by Cashel Boyle, etc., himself followed at some distance by the blind stripling whom Bloom has helped cross the road in 'Lestrygonians'. Having reached the corner of Merrion Square and Holles Street, Cashel Boyle turns around and on his way back brushes against and buffets the blind stripling. The stripling snarls insults after him.

Section 18

Young Patrick Dignam, son of the late Paddy, is walking along Wicklow Street, bringing pork-steaks home to his mother. He finds the house of mourning dull, and is distracted by the sight of a poster in a shop window advertising a boxing match. However, the match is well over. In Nassau Street he remembers he is mourning and wonders if others notice. This leads him to memories of his father's death, and he attempts to come to terms with the reality of that fact and with the notion of an afterlife.

Section 19

The lord lieutenant and his entourage sally forth from the vice-regal lodge in the Phoenix Park to inaugurate the Mirus bazaar in Ballsbridge in aid of funds for Mercer's Hospital. This section then describes the viceroy's progress through the city from the Phoenix Park gates to Northumberland Road. He is greeted by many of the people already mentioned in this episode (some of them have appeared in earlier episodes), but there are some rather unexpected obeisances, not least the River Poddle's 'tongue of liquid sewage'. He passes Trinity College, where the college races are under way: the runners are enumerated. The last to salute him is Almidano Artifoni's 'sturdy trousers swallowed by a closing door' on Northumberland Road.

CORRESPONDENCES

In Book 12 of *The Odyssey*, Circe outlines two possible routes to Odysseus that he may take to get home. One is via Scylla and Charybdis, the other is through the Wandering Rocks. These latter, rocks that drift around the ocean, are virtually impassable for ships; only one vessel, Jason's *Argo*, has ever managed to get through them. Odysseus, as we know, chooses Scylla and Charybdis, so the encounter with the Wandering Rocks does not actually occur in *The Odyssey*. The Wandering Rocks are sometimes identified as the Symplegades, two rocks at each side of the Bosphorus, the entrance to the Black Sea, which sometimes clashed together. The Bosphorus is the narrow sea strait dividing Europe and Asia.

In the Gilbert schema, the Bosphorus is the Liffey, the European bank of the Bosphorus is represented by the Viceroy, the Asian bank by Father Conmee and the Symplegades by the Groups of Citizens.

STYLE

After the extravagances of 'Scylla and Charybdis', this episode returns, virtually for the last time, to the style we have become accustomed to from prior episodes: ostensibly objective description, fairly clearly defined internal monologue. By now, however, the complications with this apparently clear distinction, in reality present from the beginning, are much more manifest. Certain sections of this episode *do* operate in this way: Section 8, the one involving Lenehan and McCoy, features a detached narrative voice that does not appear to pick up any inflections from the persons being narrated. Other sections, however, the more bravura and showpiece ones, blur the distinction very thoroughly.

In the opening one, for example, that featuring Father Conmee, the narrative voice is neat, tidy, categorical; very like the cast of Father Conmee's mind: 'At the Howth road stop Father Conmee alighted, was saluted by the conductor and saluted in his turn.' As Beckett would say, 'There at least is something that admits of no controversy' (*Malone Dies*). So once again the narration is in no sense neutral, it is thoroughly compromised by what it is telling. The lessons of 'Scylla and Charybdis' have been thoroughly learned.

Perhaps the most striking aspect, stylistically, of this episode is that the 'stream of consciousness' technique is extended beyond Bloom and Stephen. We gain direct access to the minds of some other characters. This has not happened before, and rarely happens again. Father Conmee himself is the first such instance. Here he is on Father Bernard Vaughan: 'A zealous man however. Really he was. And really did great good in his way.' His neat and tidy, judgmental mind is being reflected directly in the appropriate prose.

Similar instances occur with Mr Kernan, with Miss Dunne, even a little with Blazes Boylan in Thornton's shop: 'Blazes Boylan looked into the cut of her blouse. A young pullet.' The second 'sentence' is a direct rendering of Blazes Boylan's perception, the only such rendering in the book. The most striking and moving application of the technique, however, is in Section 18, that dealing with young Patrick Dignam. The young boy's feelings and perceptions are expressed with total immediacy: 'And they eating crumbs of the cottage fruitcake, jawing the whole blooming time and sighing.' Later, he attempts to engage with the truth of his father's death, trying to express what he cannot really understand: 'Death, that is. Pa is dead. My father is dead.' Short though the section is, *Ulysses* contains few more touching passages.

COMMENTARY

This is the episode where a good map of Dublin is indispensable. The city is spread out before us and it is possible to plot the spatial co-ordinates of virtually all the characters in it at any given time. In 1982, the centenary of Joyce's birth, the entire episode was played out on the streets of Dublin. It is here that the 'spatial form' of *Ulysses* finds maximum expression: Dublin is a stage or a space where multiple destinies are unfolding simultaneously. This insistence on simultaneity abolishes the historical dimension in favour of a continuous present, a frozen instant of time where someone will forever be just about to step on to the Howth tram. It is another way of expressing the paralysis which Joyce initially diagnosed in Dublin, and which, far from repudiating, he explored all the more deeply and thoroughly in his later works. The 'technique' of the episode is called 'Labyrinth', and Dublin here is a labyrinth, with no clue or thread to lead one out of it.

Appropriately, therefore, the kind of obliquity which we have already encountered in the conversations at the funeral and in the newspaper office – the sense of being excluded from something through some basic unfamiliarity with the Dublin world – is even more pronounced here. When Martin Cunningham and Mr Power are discussing people they could approach to subscribe money to support Paddy Dignam's son, Mr Power suggests: 'You could try our friend' (a sufficiently cryptic remark in itself). 'Boyd?', Martin Cunningham replies: 'Touch me not'. And that is it – the reader has no way of understanding it any further without the external knowledge that 'Boyd' is William A. Boyd, general secretary of the Young Men's Christian Association, a Protestant organisation and therefore suspect in the eyes of Dignam's friends. You can either feel that this makes meaning a matter of knowledge that in its way is just as esoteric as the higher reaches of theosophy or you can feel, more correctly I believe, that perhaps here meaning is not the whole point, that the sense of being immersed in a world and its discourse counts for more than understanding everything that it is being said. So the obliquity is integral to the experience.

In 'Wandering Rocks', no character is more or less important than any other: even Bloom and Stephen take their place among the others. In that sense this is a very democratic episode: the plight of Master Patrick Aloysius Dignam receives as much attention as that of Stephen Dedalus. One effect of the interpolations is to destabilise each section's ostensible narrative, to draw our attention away from it, to frustrate narrative flow and insist on the equal primacy of something happening somewhere else. Where then is a centre? In this episode there is none; there are instead two clear frames, church and state, and between these the citizens wander and drift like the rocks which

Odysseus would have had to dodge. Bloom and Stephen are as embedded in this frozen world as anybody else. The frames are, of course, provided by Father Conmee and the viceroy, the first section and the last, and between these immutable poles the citizens' lives unfold themselves.

Some of the sections seem very inconsequential; what is the point, for instance, of the brief passage involving Miss Dunne, Boylan's secretary? It very marginally advances the action, in so far as we learn that Lenehan wants to meet Boylan in the Ormond at four. But there must be more to it than that – or must there? Given critical ingenuity (and a massive amount of it has been lavished on *Ulysses*) more significance could no doubt be extracted from it – and probably has been. But perhaps it is more to the point to say that there actually isn't much point, that the little section is there to thicken the texture of this Dublin world, a world of which bored secretaries most certainly form part. And it does, after all, supply us with the date – no trivial piece of information. The section involving Corny Kelleher may seem even more irrelevant, but that is not quite the case – this is one of these Dublin instances where much is going on beneath the surface, Corny Kelleher being a police tout and having a special understanding with Constable 57C.

Nonetheless, some of the sections do have an important bearing on what went before and what is to come after – even if sometimes only obliquely. It is striking, for instance, after hearing a good deal about false and usurping brothers in the previous episode, that Father Conmee's meditations include one about an allegedly cuckolded brother who exacts a harsh revenge on his wife. The pictures of the plight of Stephen's family in Sections 4, 11 and 13 certainly heighten our sense of his dilemma and anguish. We may also be inclined to judge him more harshly because of it; his anguish is not matched by any action to alleviate the misery he feels so intensely.

One element that is emphasised quite strongly is Dublin's history, thus running somewhat counter to the frozen spatial form that seems to dominate the episode. The Revd Hugh C. Love is keenly aware of it in St Mary's Abbey; so is Mr Kernan, who thinks about rebel figures such as Emmet and Lord Edward Fitzgerald in Section 12. However, this preoccupation is sharply undercut when the same Mr Kernan rushes to greet the vice-regal cavalcade as it passes by. History is firmly in the past, as it is for Mr Love; it has no bearing on the static present.

In the previous episode we have heard much about sons that have lost their fathers and fathers who have lost their sons. In this one we encounter an actual son who has lost his father: in the experience of young Patrick Dignam we find something that transcends the schemas and structures that underlie *Ulysses* and we come close again, after the wonderful Davy Byrne's scene in 'Lestrygonians', to the real sources of Joyce's genius. Static the world of 'Wandering Rocks' may be; emotionless it certainly is not.

HISTORICAL/BIOGRAPHICAL

Line 1.　　*The superior, the very reverend John Conmee S.J.*:
　　　　　John Conmee (1847–1910) was rector of Clongowes
　　　　　Wood College during Joyce's time there and prefect of
　　　　　studies (headmaster) in Belvedere in the early 1890s.
　　　　　He was instrumental in having Joyce admitted as a
　　　　　pupil there despite his father's inability to pay. He was
　　　　　superior of the Jesuit church of St Francis Xavier in
　　　　　Gardiner Street from 1898 until 1904. He is buried in
　　　　　the Jesuit plot in Glasnevin Cemetery.

17.　　　　*'The wife of Mr David Sheehy M.P.'*: Bessie Sheehy.
　　　　　Her husband David (mentioned in 'Lestrygonians')
　　　　　was MP for South Galway and then for South Meath
　　　　　up to 1918. They were the parents of Hanna Sheehy-
　　　　　Skeffington and of Mary Sheehy. Joyce knew the
　　　　　family well. They lived at 2 Belvedere Place, just off
　　　　　Mountjoy Square.

43–4.　　　*Jack Sohan, Ger. Gallaher, Brunny Lynam*: the names
　　　　　apparently conceal a Joycean joke, since Jack Sohan
　　　　　was the name of a well-known pawnbroker, Ger
　　　　　Gallaher a brother of the notorious journalist Ignatius

Gallaher, and Brunny Lynam's name is linked to a bookie's that Lenehan visits in Section 10.

56.   *Mr Dennis J Maginni*: professor of dancing, 32 North Great George's Street. His real name was Maginnis, but of course 'Maginni' sounded much more impressive.

59.   *lady Maxwell*: lived at 36 North Great George's Street.

61.   *Mrs M'Guinness*: Mrs Ellen McGuinness, pawnbroker, 38–39 Gardiner Street Upper.

83.   *Aldborough house*: Lord Aldborough (died 1801) bankrupted himself by building the house at a cost of £40,000 between 1792 and 1798.

86.   *Mr William Gallagher*: grocer, 4 North Strand Road.

110–11. *the reverend Nicholas Dudley C.C.*: *Thom's Directory* for 1904 lists a Revd J. D. Dudley as curate of St Agatha's Roman Catholic Church, North William Street, near the North Strand Road.

156.   *Lord Talbot de Malahide*: the story Father Conmee recalls concerns, not Lord Talbot de Malahide, but the son of Lord Galtrim and his fiancée, Maud, daughter of Lord Plunkett. The groom was called away just after his wedding to fight a marauding party and was killed. Maud later married Lord Talbot de Malahide (died 1329).

163.   *Mary Rochfort*: (1720–90) was married to the first earl of Belvedere. He suspected her of committing adultery with his brother and imprisoned her for many years on the Rochfort estate at Gaulston near Mullingar.

233.   *Katey and Boody Dedalus*: clearly based on two of Joyce's sisters, though it is difficult to be sure which two. Given the spirit that Boody shows later on, it is possible she is May Joyce. It is hard to imagine the very conventional Eva or Florence Joyce saying: 'Our father who art not in heaven'. Another possibility is Mabel Joyce, who died in 1911.

261.   *Maggy*: clearly based on Margaret (Poppy) Joyce, the eldest of Joyce's sisters.

338.   *Almidano Artifoni*: named after the owner of the Berlitz school of languages in Trieste, where Joyce taught. An Italian called Benedetto Palmieri did teach music in Dublin at this time, and it is possible the character is based on him.

378.   *where Wolfe Tone's statue was not*: in 1898 a foundation stone for a statue of Wolfe Tone was laid at the corner of St Stephen's Green facing Grafton Street; the statue was never erected there.

408.   *silken Thomas*: Ned Lambert's account of Silken Thomas's rebellion is mostly accurate.

437.   *The reverend Hugh C. Love*: Joyce has transposed to a fictional Church of Ireland clergyman the name of the son of the Joyce family's landlady at 29 Windsor Avenue, Fairview. In the book, as soon emerges (Section 14), Mr Love is the landlord of the very same property.

444.   *the earl of Kildare*: Ned Lambert's story about the Great Earl of Kildare, Gerald FitzGerald and the burning of Cashel Cathedral, including his remark about the archbishop, is historically attested.

464.   *Tom Rochford*: Rochford's part in the attempted rescue of a man overcome by sewer gas (in which others were also involved) did happen, but in 1905; Joyce has moved it back somewhat. It took place at the junction of Burgh Quay and Hawkins Street; a memorial is still there to mark it.

644.   *Dilly Dedalus*: clearly based on another of Joyce's sisters, the one described in most detail. Eileen Joyce seems the most likely, although May cannot be ruled out.

652.   *J. A. Jackson, W. E. Wylie, A. Munro, H. T. Gahan*: these cyclists are named as having taken part in the Trinity College bicycle sports in the report of the *Evening Telegraph* on 16 June 1904.

740.   *Father Cowley*: a spoiled priest, one who retains the title 'Father' but has no other link with the church. He is probably to be identified with the 'Father Keon' of 'Ivy Day in the Committee Room' in *Dubliners*.

785.   *lord Edward Fitzgerald*: a leader of the 1798 rebellion, he did escape from Major Sirr, his pursuer, in the Watling Street area, in the way Kernan describes, though he was arrested through the treachery of the 'sham squire', Francis Higgins, shortly afterwards.

812.   *Old Russell*: Thomas Russell, lapidary and gem cutter, 57 Fleet Street.

930.   *Tholsel*: literally, 'toll-collector's booth', a medieval building in Skinner's Row, now Christchurch Place, which served as a guild hall, courthouse and council chamber. It was demolished in 1806.

967.   *Boyd*: William A. Boyd, secretary of the (Protestant) Dublin Young Men's Christian Association.

968.   *John Wyse Nolan*: based on the Dublin journalist John Wyse Power.

971.   *Abraham Lyon*: councillor for Clontarf West ward.

982:    *Jimmy Henry*: assistant town clerk.

984–5. *Jack Mooney's brother-in-law*: Bob Doran, the central character of the story 'The Boarding House' in *Dubliners*. McCoy has already mentioned to Bloom in 'Lotus-Eaters' that Doran is on 'one of his periodical benders'.

995.   *long John Fanning*: based on Long John Clancy, sub-sheriff of Dublin.

1175.   *William Humble, earl of Dudley*: (1866–1932), lord lieutenant of Ireland 1902–6.

1175.   *Lady Dudley*: real name Rachel Gurney.

1176.   *lieutenantcolonel Heseltine*: Lieut Col C. Heseltine was an aide-de-camp in the viceroy's establishment.

1258–60. 'M. C. Green ... W. C. Huggard': the names of these runners are taken from the *Irish Independent*, 17 June 1904. The *Independent's* list gets one of the names

(J. B. Jeffs for J. B. Jones) wrong through dirty type,
and Joyce reproduces this error.

1262.   *Mr M. E. Solomons*: optician and Austro-Hungarian
consul, 19 Nassau Street.

SELECT GLOSSARY

Line 4.   *Vere dignum et iustum est*: Latin, 'It is indeed right
and fitting': the opening phrase of the preface which
begins the Eucharist of the Mass. There is, of course,
an implied pun on the name 'Dignam'.

147–8.   *Le Nombre des Élus*: French, 'The Number of the
Elect'.

168.   *eiaculatio seminis . . .* : Latin, 'ejaculation of semen
within the natural female organ'. The Catholic
Church's formula for full sexual intercourse.

182.   *Moutonner*: French, 'to present a frothy or fleecy
appearance'.

193.   *Pater* and *Ave*: Latin, literally 'Father' and 'Hail'. The
opening words of the Lord's Prayer and the Hail Mary.

194.   *Deus in adiutorium*: Latin, 'God, [come] to [our] aid'.
The opening words of Psalm 70 and the beginning of
the office of nones (read at 3 p.m.).

196–8.   *Res in Beati . . . iustitiae tuae*: Latin, '*Res* in Blessed
are the undefiled' (*Res* is the Hebrew letter that begins
the twentieth section of Psalm 119, called 'Blessed are
the undefiled'). 'Thy word is true from the beginning:
and all your righteous judgments [endure] forever.'

204–5.   *Sin . . . cor meum*: *Sin* is the Hebrew letter that begins
the twenty-first section of Psalm 119: Latin, 'Princes
have persecuted me without reason; and my heart is in
awe of thy words.'

338–62.   *Ma! . . . Tante belle cose!*: Italian, 'But! . . . I too had
these ideas when I was young like you. At that time I
was convinced that the world was a beast. It is a pity.

Because your voice ... would be a source of income,
you see. But instead, you are sacrificing yourself.
—A bloodless sacrifice.
—Let us hope. But, listen to me. Think about it.
—I'll think about it.
—But seriously, though?
—Look, here it is! [my tram]. Come and see me and
think about it. Goodbye, dear fellow.
—Goodbye, maestro. And thank you.
—For what? Excuse me, eh? All the best!'

840–41.   *Stephano Dedalo ... palmam ferenti ...* : Latin, 'For
          Stephen Dedalus, best pupil, bearing the palm.' The
          standard formula for Jesuit school prizes.

849.   *Se el yilo ... Amen.*: garbled Spanish-Arabic which
          could be interpreted to mean 'Little heaven of blessed
          femininity! Love me alone! Holy! Amen.'

918.   *basso profondo*: Italian, 'a deep bass voice'.

1011.   *locum tenens*: Latin, literally 'holding the place'; acting
          as a substitute.

1054.   *mélange*: French, 'mixture'. Here, a mix of fruit in
          thick cream.

1068.   *idée fixe*: French, 'fixed idea', referring to an
          obsessional neurosis.

1113.   *Coactus volui*: Latin, 'having been forced, I was
          willing.'

1216.   *dernier cri*: French, 'the last word', 'the latest fashion
          trend'.

II
[11 · Sirens]

Time: 4 p.m.
Location: the Ormond Hotel, Ormond Quay, Dublin

SUMMARY

Miss Lydia Douce and Miss Mina Kennedy, the barmaids in the bar of the Ormond Hotel, have seen the viceregal cavalcade go by. After the excitement, they settle down for their afternoon cup of tea, brought to them by a rather unmannerly server. They take their tea sitting down behind their counter, and while doing so discuss the state of Miss Douce's skin after her recent holiday in Rostrevor. This leads on to memories of an 'old fogey' in the chemists, Boyd's, whom Miss Douce approached for advice on her skin problem; mention of his mannerisms prompts peals of laughter from the two young ladies.

Meanwhile Bloom is walking west along Wellington Quay, on the other side of the river. He is keenly aware that the time is nearing four o'clock, the hour of Boylan's assignation with Molly. He now needs to eat, having forgone his lunch, and is turning over various venues (the Clarence, the Dolphin) in his mind. Bloom also wants to pen a reply to Martha's letter, which he had received that morning.

Mr Dedalus, last seen walking along the quays, enters the bar. He orders a glass of whisky and inquires about Miss Douce's holiday. Lenehan also arrives, and tells Simon Dedalus of his drinking session with Stephen in Mooney's in Abbey Street. Mr Dedalus wanders over to the piano in the saloon, and Miss Douce mentions that the blind piano tuner had been in that morning. Mr Dedalus plays, but does not sing, some of *Goodbye, Sweetheart, Goodbye*.

Bloom meanwhile is buying some stationery in Daly's tobacconist's at Number 1 Ormond Quay. He spies a jaunting car on Essex Bridge, near the Ormond, with a familiar figure mounted on it: Blazes Boylan. Lured by a morbid compulsion, he resolves to follow it and quickly leaves the shop.

Boylan arrives at the Ormond and is hailed by Lenehan, whose manner to him is remarkably similar to his manner towards Corley in the story 'Two Gallants' in *Dubliners*: 'See the conquering hero comes.' Bloom has followed Boylan with due prudence and, virtually at the door of the Ormond, encounters Richie Goulding. Both are hungry and both decide to eat in the Ormond. Bloom feels that he will be safe in the dining room: 'See, not be seen.'

Boylan has been observed with special favour by Miss Douce, who serves him with grace a sloe gin. The clock strikes four and at Lenehan's prompting Miss Douce performs for them both the trick known as *sonner la cloche* (sound the bell). This consists of snapping a garter against the thigh (while keeping one's leg decently covered, of course), thereby producing a distinctive smacking sound. Miss Douce daintily describes Lenehan's gloating reaction as 'the essence of vulgarity' but it certainly has an effect on Boylan, who immediately drains his glass, leaves the premises and jumps into his waiting hackney car accompanied by a breathless Lenehan. A disappointed Miss Douce (her performance was really for Boylan) languishes behind. Bloom, now ensconced in the hotel dining room with Richie, hears him depart and knows where he is going: 'He's off. Light sob of breath.'

As Boylan departs, Ben Dollard and Father Cowley enter, Dollard still reassuring Cowley that all will be well in his problem with Reuben Dodd. Meeting Mr Dedalus, they discuss a concert where Dollard was at a loss for a dress suit and Bloom came to the rescue. This leads on to some chat about Molly, while Bloom in the dining room consumes liver and bacon and Richie steak and kidney pie. They are served by 'bald', 'bothered' (deaf) Pat, waiter of the Ormond.

Boylan sets off on his way to Eccles Street, and the text keeps track of his progress (Lenehan has been disposed of somewhere *en route*). Bloom meanwhile himself remembers the night Ben Dollard was stuck for a dress suit and the rather ill-fitting garment with which he and Molly supplied him. Dollard has begun to sing the bass part of *Love and War*, a duet about the conflicting claims of the two grand passions.

Two gentlemen have entered and are served by Miss Kennedy. They are followed by the solicitor George Lidwell. Dollard has finished and Father Cowley takes over the piano. He begins to sing *M'appari* from Flotow's opera *Martha,* but this is just to encourage Simon Dedalus to take up the song. In the opera, the aria is sung by the hero, Lionel, at a stage when he believes that he has irretrievably lost his beloved Martha. It contrasts former happiness with current

woe and ends on a note of deep longing for Martha to return. It therefore has intense relevance both for the bereaved Mr Dedalus and the
cuckolded Bloom.

Mr Dedalus yields to his friends' entreaties and, accompanied by
Cowley, embarks on the aria. He sings an English version of it, which
is probably familiar to everyone in the premises. Certainly Bloom and
Goulding, listening in the dining room, recognise it. As he sings,
Bloom reflects on the power of music: 'Love that is singing: love's old
sweet song.' He winds the elastic band of his packet of envelopes
tightly around his fingers. 'Words? Music? No, it's what's behind',
Bloom reflects as Simon's voice gains in power. Bloom is struck by the
coincidence that the aria is from *Martha,* while he is just about to
write a letter to a woman ostensibly of that name. The song mounts
to a climax and at that intensely charged climax, Bloom, Simon and
Lionel (the character who sings the aria in the opera) merge in some
consummation of loss and longing.

All present are intensely moved by the singing, Richie Goulding,
Mr Dedalus's brother-in-law, from whom he is totally estranged, not
least. Tom Kernan, meanwhile, has 'strutted in'. The elastic band that
Bloom has been winding about his fingers snaps as Boylan's cab
jingles into Dorset Street. Bloom, having consumed his liver and bacon,
then decides to embark on his letter to Martha. To conceal this operation from Richie's prying eyes, he pretends he is replying to a job
advertisement. His composition pushes the implicitly erotic tone of
the correspondence a little further (each letter is clearly designed to do
this) with phrases such as 'You naughty too?' and urging her to call
him 'that other word' (in fact she wrote 'world') which she refrained
from using in her previous epistle. He ends the letter on a melancholy
note, reflecting 'they like sad tail at the end': 'I feel so sad today . . . So
lonely.' He is painfully aware that Boylan's car would by now have
reached Eccles Street.

As Lydia Douce listens to a shell that Lidwell holds up to her ear,
another song is requested, this time from Ben Dollard. Dollard obliges
with the patriotic Irish ballad 'The Croppy Boy', the saga of a 1798
would-be rebel youth who is duped by a British trick into revealing
his subversive intentions to an army officer in the confessional and

subsequently executed. Caught up in the singing, Bloom, who had intended to leave, stays listening and remembering other times with Molly. As Lydia Douce listens, her hand passes up and down the 'smooth jutting beerpull'. At the same time the words 'With a cock with a carra' indicate that Boylan has reached his destination.

Bloom decides to leave just before the end of the ballad, as a new sound has begun to make itself heard: 'Tap. Tap. Tap.' These are the taps of the blind piano tuner's cane, as he makes his way back to the Ormond to retrieve his tuning fork, which he had left there. The melancholy ballad ends to great acclaim just before the piano tuner arrives.

Bloom, having left the premises, feels an internal pressure obliging him to release wind. He attributes this to the glass of cider he has consumed (Bloom is careful to trace the cause of every symptom). Avoiding a woman he identifies as 'the whore of the lane', he stands in front of a window displaying the closing words of Robert Emmet's speech from the dock, and, taking advantage of the noise of a passing tram, farts loudly as he reads Emmet's concluding *I have done*.

CORRESPONDENCES

In Book 12 of *The Odyssey*, Odysseus tells how the enchantress Circe warned him about the danger of the two Sirens who would attempt to trap him on his voyage home. Their song would make him and his men forget their journey, and lure them to their deaths on the Sirens' rocky island. If he wants to hear their song without endangering himself, he must stop the ears of his men with wax, tie himself to the mast of his vessel, and order his men not to release him no matter how much he protests. Odysseus follows this advice. He hears the Sirens' song, which promises both pleasure and wisdom, without disaster because his deafened men refuse to untie him and he and his crew pass safely by their island.

In the Gilbert schema, the Sirens are the barmaids, and their island is the Ormond bar. The Linati schema also mentions Orpheus: the relevance of this musical maestro, who charmed the king of the underworld with his lyre, and who also beat the Sirens at their own game by playing music more beautiful than theirs, is clear in this musical episode.

STYLE

With this episode, we embark on the novel's real 'odyssey of style'. The style of 'Sirens' is startlingly innovative. From the initial list of disjointed phrases to the concluding 'Pprrpffrrppffff' of Bloom's fart, language is teased, twisted, inverted, perverted in order to create an acoustic surround. Although we can still make out the reasonably familiar mode of Bloom's interior monologue, it is caught up in a nexus of linguistic devices that constantly threaten to overwhelm it. Each episode aspires to be a total environment; as the book goes on, they become more and more successful in that task. 'Sirens' creates a complete sound world, a surrounding ambiance through which the characters move and which is prior to anything they might think, say, feel or even sing. Style is beginning to be foregrounded.

Multiple musical puns ('Listen sharp', 'Tenors get women by the score'), multiple onomatopoeiac effects ('Tschink. Tschunk.' – glasses being clinked together; 'Diddleiddle addleaddle ooddleooddle' – urine descending into a chamber pot; 'Imperthnthn thnthnthn' – the boots' version of Miss Douce's 'impertinent insolence') reinforce the dominance of sound. However, these are so glaring that they scarcely need noting, let alone commentary. More subtle and more startling effects are also involved.

The first surprising experience for the reader is the list of sixty 'items' or elements that precede the actual opening of the episode's 'narration'. These (apart from the final 'Begin!') are all phrases that will occur sequentially in a defined context in the text. Seen in isolation here, the phrases are like motifs or snatches of tunes in an overture that will take on meaning only when the full opera is staged. They will stay in the listener's memory so that when they appear in 'full dress', as it were, they will be recognised as such. The ultimate effect is to abolish sequential narrative in favour of words, mere words; we are being obliquely warned as to the nature of the text that awaits us.

The 'technique' of the episode is described in the Gilbert schema as a *fuga per canonem* ('a fugue according to rule'). Joyce told Harriet Weaver in a letter that the episode was structured as the 'eight parts' of such a fugue. The relatively recent (2002) discovery of Joyce's listing in Italian of these eight parts and of their source (2007) in an article on the fugue form in the *Grove Encyclopaedia of Music* by the English composer Ralph Vaughan Williams shows that Joyce was not hoaxing in this claim. (The discovery was made by Susan Brown and is reported in an article in the online journal *Genetic Joyce Studies*.)

Identifying how each part corresponds to an aspect of 'Sirens' remains a matter of considerable debate. But some aspects are clear and actually have been since Stuart Gilbert's first guide to *Ulysses*: the fugue's 'subject' is Music, the barmaids, the Sirens themselves. The 'reply' to this subject is Bloom. The 'counter-subject' is, appropriately, Boylan. The songs that are sung in the barroom, principally 'The Croppy Boy' and 'M'appari', or 'When First I Saw', are the 'divertimenti' or 'episodes' that form extrapolations from the fugal structure. The notable passage towards the end: 'Near bronze from anear near gold from afar they chinked their clinking glasses all, brighteyed and gallant, before bronze Lydia's tempting last rose of summer, rose of Castile. First Lid, De, Cow, Ker, Doll, a fifth: Lidwell, Si Dedalus, Bob Cowley, Kernan and big Ben Dollard' (lines 1269–72) is the *stretto* (roughly, 'climax') of 'Sirens'.

The fugal structure does at least help to unite an episode in which many diverse actions or motifs are at play. At least five can be enumerated, with some side activities as well. These are: i) the barroom and saloon scene itself, with the barmaids and the singing; ii) the Bloom motif, also in the Ormond Hotel but in a different part of it, also involving Richie and Pat; iii) the Blazes Boylan motif, involving Boylan on his car, stopping off at the Ormond and then *en route* to Eccles Street, marked by the words 'jingling' and 'cock'; iv) the 'tap' motif of the blind stripling who comes to the Ormond to retrieve his tuning fork; and v) Bloom's fart, the coda, in every sense, of the episode. The purpose of the fugal form seems to have been to enable Joyce to develop these different scenarios, while holding them together in a unified composition.

COMMENTARY

So far, in a sense, *Ulysses* has only been taxiing down the runway; now, it really begins to take off. So much is going on in the 'Sirens' episode that it is difficult indeed to obtain a clue that might begin to make some sense of it, rather as it is difficult, in listening to a complex fugue, to hear the subject that actually is there holding the different voices together. One such clue in this instance is the Homeric parallels, which actually are helpful, more helpful than they were in the previous episode, where they were very sketchy.

We know, for instance, that the Sirens are the barmaids, Miss Douce and Miss Kennedy. Armed with this information, we can interpret a phrase such as 'they cowered under their reef of counter' more literally than might otherwise seem warranted; these are, after all, sea nymphs of a sort. The shell, which is mentioned just in passing as an ornament of the bar, something Miss Douce brought back from her holiday in Rostrevor, also takes on a new significance. Similarly, when Miss Douce draws down the blind of the Ormond bar, the phrase 'slow cool dim seagreen sliding depth of shadow' is brilliantly suggestive of a submarine ambience.

These sirens do sing a little: Miss Douce trills a line from the light opera *Floradora*, but their seductive quality has more to do with their gender than with their voices. There are phrases such as 'tempting poor simple males' that indicate their siren-like qualities in this connection. In fact, though, when one of them engages in the most overtly seductive action (Miss Douce's performance for Boylan and Lenehan) it backfires, from her point of view: Boylan has other fish to fry and is sharply reminded of that fact by what he has heard, leaving Miss Douce to muse on his behaviour.

The actual seductions of song are the province of the men: Ben Dollard, Simon Dedalus, Father Cowley. Unlike their Homeric counterparts, these singers are *themselves* seduced by what they sing; this is a crucial difference. The songs they sing express but also numb the pain that gives them birth: Mr Dedalus sings 'of a heart bowed down', but his singing is also a means of relieving that grief, one of the very few available (the other obvious one is drink). This is in no sense to belittle the wonderful musical culture that is being expressed in this bar: Joyce of all people is fully aware of it. But in the economy of the 'Sirens' episode, music is assigned a certain function: it is a means of entrapment and is represented as such. It is in this sense that Bloom is a 'counter-subject' to the episode's fugal 'subject', music itself. Bloom does not fall under the sway of sound as do the other denizens of the bar. He hears and is deeply moved by Simon Dedalus's singing of 'M'appari', he feels the fate of the croppy boy, but he retains a certain crucial distance. This despite the fact that both songs have a special resonance for Bloom: 'M'appari' as a song of lost love, 'The Croppy Boy' as dealing with the death of a young boy who 'alone is left of my name and race' (Bloom draws an explicit parallel with his dead son, Rudy). As the episode goes on, Bloom becomes more and more sceptical of music's power: 'Music. Gets on your nerves,' he goes so far as to muse on his way out of the Ormond, and he reflects: 'Cowley, he stuns himself with it: kind of drunkenness.' Nor has he much time for 'enthusiasts', who, he ponders are 'Always talking shop. Fiddlefaddle about notes.'

Similarly, he reflects, apropos of the croppy boy, after the song is over: 'All the same he must have been a bit of a natural not to see it was a yeoman cap.' These opinions may seem surprising from one who is in fact a lover of music, but Bloom is also Ulysses, the hero who survives the Sirens' singing. Once again his vital detachment has brought him through another peril.

The episode poses many problems for a reader. Negotiating the style – its many transitions, its play, its obliquities – is difficult enough. There is also a disconcerting sense that games are being played with the reader, who is being teased and even taunted at times: 'Upholding the lid he (who?) gazed in the coffin (coffin?) at the oblique triple (piano!) wires. He pressed (the same who pressed indulgently her hand), soft pedalling, a triple of keys . . .'. The process of understanding, the questions a reader will ask, are being echoed but also parodied here; yes, it is helpful to know that the 'He' of the passage is Simon Dedalus and that what's being referred to is a piano, but the information is imparted in an almost sneering manner that is more undermining than enhancing of the reader's confidence.

Similarly, when Bloom is eating his liver and bacon, the text goes: 'As said before he ate with relish the inner organs . . .'. In one way it's nice to be reminded of Bloom's predilection for such nourishment; in another way, though, there's a touch of 'remember?' about it that can be quite off-putting. At the very least the process of narration is being foregrounded, attention is being drawn to it; instead of the seamless 'service' the reader expects in this regard, the reader is being forced to attend to the process, even to treat it as prior to the thing being told. To do this requires a considerable adjustment of conventional expectations, and one can feel that it's being insisted on rather forcefully.

Games are not only being played with the reader; they are also being played with the characters. All of them (Bloom included) are subjected to this treatment to a greater or lesser degree; they suffer such indignities as having their names foreshortened in the interests of musicality: 'Lid, De, Cow, Ker, Doll . . .'. Bloom at one point becomes 'Bloowho' (also an instance of playing with the reader). It can be seen also in the treatment of the deaf waiter, Pat, who is largely a figure of fun: 'Pat is a waiter hard of his hearing. Pat is a waiter who waits while you wait. Hee hee hee hee.' Without being over-moralistic about it, Pat's humanity tends to disappear in this heightened stylistic mix.

As the above passage illustrates, there is, I feel, in the episode, an atmosphere of repressed hysteria, a 'will to power', that affects its entire presentation. There is a clear reason for this: this is the hour, in the course of the day, when Boylan's fateful assignation with Molly takes place. The text as a whole, and not just Bloom, is striving to cope with this painful fact; it is being narrated, because it has to be, but elaborate textual games are being staged to divert attention from its import, if not from its actuality.

However, if a certain dehumanisation is the cost of some of these procedures, that, too, has its limits. Bloom, as we have seen, does not succumb to music as both expression/anaesthetic of psychic pain; he keeps his distance and his dignity, despite the verbal exuberance that surrounds him. Listening to the words of 'The Croppy Boy': 'He bore no hate.' Bloom reflects: 'Hate. Love. Those are names. Rudy. Soon I am old.' A passage like this, which actually has nothing to do with Molly and Boylan, preserves the essential integrity of Bloom, 'unconquered hero', through the many trials and tribulations that the text itself subjects him to.

BIOGRAPHICAL

Line 64.   *miss Douce . . . miss Kennedy*: fictional, although miss Kennedy's address, 4 Lismore Terrace, Drumcondra, is a real one.

343.   *Richie Goulding*: Stephen's uncle; evoked in 'Proteus' and appears in 'Wandering Rocks', line 471.

562–3.   *George Lidwell*: J. George Lidwell, solicitor, 4 Capel Street. A friend of Joyce's father, who frequently used his office as a covering address, he advised Joyce, not very helpfully, during his protracted negotiations with George Roberts over the printing of *Dubliners* in Dublin. He died in 1919.

878–9.   '*Barton James*': James Barton is attested in *Thom's Directory* for 1904 as living in Harmony Avenue, Donnybrook.

SELECT GLOSSARY

Line 2.   Imperthnthn thnthnthn: the rude echo by the Ormond's 'boots' of Miss Douce's 'impertinent insolence'.

17–18.   *Sonnez . . . La cloche!*: French, literally, 'Sound the bell'; here referring to the smack of Miss Douce's garter against her thigh.

43.   *Naminedamine*: Latin, correctly '*Nomine domine*', 'In the name of the Lord'.

67. *eau de Nil*: French, literally 'water of the Nile', a pale greenish-blue cloth.

264. *en ville*: French, 'in town'.

264. *sur mer*: French, 'by the sea'.

541. *Amoroso ma non troppo*: Italian (in music), 'Soft and tender, but not too much so'.

594–5. *M'appari ... l'incontr ...*: Italian, 'The whole of love appeared to me; that encounter [filled] my sight ...'. The Italian version of Lionel's aria in Flotow's *Martha*; Simon Dedalus sings it in an English-language version.

610. *Sonnambula*: Italian, *The Sleepwalker*, an opera by Vincenzo Bellini. Richie whistles an aria, 'Tutto è sciolto', 'All is lost now', from the opera. Also the title of a poem by Joyce.

805–6. *Corpus paradisum*: Latin, literally 'the body of paradise'. Combining two fragments of the funeral service that Bloom has heard at Paddy Dignam's obsequies earlier in the day.

844. *Blumenlied*: German, 'Flower song'.

975. *quis est homo*: Latin, 'Who is the man?', from Rossini's (not Mercadante's) *Stabat Mater*.

990. *Qui sdegno*: Italian, 'Here indignation', the opening words of the aria 'In diesen heil'gen Hallen', from Mozart's *The Magic Flute*.

1033. *mea culpa*: Latin, 'through my fault', part of the Act of Contrition.

1036. *corpusnomine*: Latin, literally 'body in name': Bloom is again misremembering parts of the funeral service he heard that morning.

1245. *da capo*: Italian, 'from the start'; in music, a direction to repeat a passage.

II

[12 · Cyclops]

Time: 5 p.m.
Location: Barney Kiernan's public house, 8–10 Little Britain Street,
off Capel Street, and intersected by Green Street

SUMMARY

Note 1: the 'Cyclops' episode is narrated by an unidentified narrator whose voice dominates the action. The Gilbert schema refers to him as 'Noman' and this is the term I have adopted.

Note 2: the episode is punctuated by a number of passages which are vast expansions of the material already narrated (or occasionally anticipating this material), written in the form of parodies of various styles of public discourse. Each of these is described as it comes up under the rubric 'Parody'.

Noman is standing at the corner of Arbour Hill and Stony Batter when he is met by Joe Hynes, the journalist whom we have already encountered at the funeral and in the newspaper office. Noman explains that he is now working as a debt collector and is trying to recover a debt from a plumber named Geraghty for goods he purchased from a merchant, Moses Herzog.

Parody (lines 32–51): style of legal documents, obviously pertaining to the Geraghty-Herzog imbroglio.

Joe Hynes suggests that they call into Barney Kiernan's in Little Britain Street; he wants to tell 'the citizen', who is already there, about the meeting of cattle traders in the City Arms Hotel.

Parody (lines 68–99 and 102–17): nineteenth-century and Anglo-Irish revival 'versions', such as Lady Gregory's and Standish O'Grady's, of Irish sagas and legends. The passage actually describes the area around Little Britain Street and St Michan's Churches, particularly the fine fruit, vegetable and fish market between St Michan's Street and Arran Street. After a brief interjection bringing us back to Geraghty, the parody goes on in the same vein to describe the many animals that throng the area due to the presence of the cattle market nearby on the North Circular Road.

The pair enter Barney Kiernan's and find 'the citizen' ensconced inside. This character, who is never given any other name, is presented as an Irish nationalist of the deepest hue. He is accompanied by his dog, a 'mangy mongrel' called Garryowen, of whom and from whom much more will be heard. Three pints are ordered, at Hynes's expense.

Parody (lines 151–205): again in the style of revivalist and earlier nineteenth century versions of Irish myths and legends. The passage is a mock-heroic description of the citizen, his garments and his dog.

Noman evinces surprise that Joe Hynes has the money to pay for the drink, and Joe explains that 'the prudent member' (this is apparently enough to identify Bloom) gave him 'the wheeze' (we may or may not remember that Bloom had mentioned to Hynes back in the newspaper episode that the cashier's office was open). Noman mentions that he had spotted Bloom in the area a short time previously. (In the previous episode Bloom had reflected that he had an appointment to meet the people involved in the efforts to provide for Paddy Dignam's offspring at Barney Kiernan's, whence they are to go to Sandymount to see the widow.)

Parody (lines 215–17): Bloom's arrival in the area rendered in the same style of versions of Irish heroic legend.

Mention of the newspaper leads the citizen to comment bitterly on the English (and therefore anti-national) origins of the death notices in that day's *Irish Independent*.

Parody (lines 244–8): the arrival of Alf Bergan, preceding Denis Breen and his wife, is prefigured in the style of the more flowery nineteenth-century translations of Homeric and other heroic epic.

Bergan enters the pub in fits of laughter. His laughter awakens Bob Doran, last seen in 'Wandering Rocks', who has been sleeping unobserved in a corner of the pub. Bergan points out Denis Breen, the recipient of the 'U.P.: up' card, as he passes by the door, still in quest of a lawyer, with his wife, Josie, behind him, and he tells the other pub occupants about the joke played on Breen. Breen has been to the city sub-sheriff, Long John Fanning, with his complaint, and mention of the sub-sheriff prompts Joe Hynes to ask about the next hanging scheduled for Mountjoy. (Looking after executions was part of the sub-sheriff's duties.) Bergan orders a drink.

Parody (lines 287–99): the serving and paying for the drink are described in a style that again evokes Victorian versions of Greek legends.

The citizen has noticed Bloom walking up and down outside the pub door. The reference to hanging leads Bergan to produce letters from hangmen that he has obtained in the course of his employment as assistant to the sub-sheriff. The awakened Bob Doran has been growing ever more truculent, so to create a diversion Noman asks Bergan about the health of a mutual friend, Willy Murray. Bergan replies that he has just seen Murray with Paddy Dignam, a reply that produces general consternation. Bergan is informed that he could not have seen Dignam, since the latter is dead, and Bergan is duly 'flabbergasted'.

Parody (lines 338–73): theosophical-type account of a spiritualist's séance, describing Paddy Dignam's state in the afterlife.

Parody (lines 374–6): lamentation for Dignam, in the style of stilted versions of Irish legend.

Bob Doran becomes at first angry with Christ and then emotional at the news of Dignam's death.

Parody (lines 405–6): further lamentation for Dignam, in the style of the previous parody.

Bloom, meanwhile, who has been hanging around the door of the pub, is finally persuaded to come in by the citizen. He declines a drink, but is prevailed upon to take a cigar. A hangman's letter, offering his services in an upcoming execution, is read out. Bergan describes how the job is done.

Parody (lines 446–9): the hangmen described in the style of popular versions of medieval romances, with a distinct Biblical resonance added.

The discussion of the techniques of hanging leads on to a sort of discussion of the morality of the practice, in which, interestingly enough, Bloom seems to espouse its utility as a deterrent. This is soon diverted, however, by the fascinating revelation, proferred by Alf Bergan, the expert in these matters, that the hanged man dies complete with an erection. Bloom explains that there is a scientific reason for this, and that it is not, as someone suggests, because the 'ruling passion is strong in death'.

Parody (lines 468–78): pseudo-scientific report for a medical journal, possibly of evidence tendered in a court, concerning Bloom's explanation of the physiological effects of hanging.

Hanging, naturally, leads the citizen on to a roll-call of patriots executed by the British. Bloom's attempts to put up a counter-argument are fiercely rebuffed.

Parody (lines 525–678): a newspaper's feature-type account of a public execution of a patriot. The various accounts of the execution of Robert Emmet may well supply a template.

The dog, Garryowen, having rebuffed the drunken Bob Doran's efforts to cosset him, turns his attentions to Noman and Joe Hynes. Neither is particularly keen to engage with him, so the citizen calls him over and he and the dog engage in a species of dialogue, the citizen talking to him in Irish and the dog growling in response.

Parody (lines 711–47): another newspaper item, this time a 'puff' or promotional article for a public meeting featuring a verse recitation by Garryowen, proof of his near-human abilities.

More drinks are ordered, and Bloom is again pressed to partake. He explains that he is in the pub just to meet Martin Cunningham over the matter of the bestowal of Paddy Dignam's estate.

Throughout, Noman has been steadily putting Bloom down in the course of his narration; he does this to everyone, in fact, but there is a special venom in his dismissals of Bloom. On this occasion he claims that Bloom was nearly prosecuted for selling foreign lottery tickets. In fact, this appears to have happened, (it is mentioned in 'Lestrygonians', lines 184-5, and will be mentioned again by Molly), but Noman is keen to milk it for all it is worth.

Bob Doran, in maudlin mode, asks Bloom to convey his condolences to Mrs Dignam and Bloom promises to do so.

Parody (lines 786–99): Doran's exchange with Bloom rendered in the style of genteel nineteenth-century fiction.

Doran then leaves, accompanied by some appropriately sarcastic internal comments from Noman, harking back to the manner in which Doran was trapped into marrying Polly Mooney in the story 'The Boarding House' in *Dubliners*.

The drinks arrive, and the conversation turns to the likely next lord mayor. Nannetti, last seen in the newspaper episode, is mentioned, and Joe Hynes reports that Nannetti was at the cattle traders' meeting in the City Arms Hotel earlier that day. This leads on to a discussion of foot-and-mouth and other animal diseases and Bloom, who had once worked in a cattle trader's yard, intervenes to advocate humane methods.

Parody (lines 846–9): Bloom as advocate of kindness to animals in the style of a child's first reader.

Hynes then mentions that Nannetti is going to London that night to ask questions about foot-and-mouth disease in the parliament the next day. Bloom becomes quite concerned when he hears this, as he wanted to see Nannetti about the ad he is hoping to place in the paper. But Nannetti is in fact departing.

Parody (lines 860–79): the style of a newspaper report of proceedings in the House of Commons about foot-and-mouth disease, with interjections by Irish members.

Joe Hynes starts to laud the citizen's sporting prowess, and this leads on to a discussion of the benefits of Gaelic sports as against 'shoneen' games such as lawn tennis.

Parody (lines 897–938): a newspaper report of a public debate (heavily biased in favour of the patriotic side) as to the merits of reviving the ancient Gaelic sports; Bloom, as the only dissenter, gets short shrift.

Mention of sport brings up the Keogh-Bennett boxing match (mentioned in 'Wandering Rocks'), a bout in which Blazes Boylan trained the victor, Keogh. This immediately arouses Bloom's anxieties, and he attempts to divert the conversation to tennis. To no avail, however; the others remain focused on Boylan's success.

Parody (lines 960–87): the Keogh-Bennett contest described in the flowery sports journalism style of the time.

Alf Bergan then mentions that Boylan is now organising a concert tour in the north, and Bloom is finally forced to acknowledge that his cuckolder is the current topic of conversation. He confirms the concert tour plan, confirms that his wife is part of it and, no doubt reluctantly, declares that Boylan is 'an excellent man to organise'. Noman instantly picks up the implications of this for Molly's relations with Boylan (the only person in the book, outside the fantasy 'Circe' sequences, to do so) and comments in characteristic style: 'Hoho begob says I to myself says I.' Characteristically also, though, his comments on Boylan, and on Boylan's father, are almost equally scathing.

Parody (lines 1003–7): Molly described in the style of nineteenth-century versions of medieval romance.

Parody (lines 1008–10): the entrance of J. J. O'Molloy and Ned Lambert described in pompous mock-heroic terms.

O'Molloy and Lambert are greeted by the others. Noman once again instantly deduces that O'Molloy has got Lambert off the grand jury list in return for money (we saw this operation begin back in 'Wandering Rocks') and foresees that O'Molloy's career will end in tears. References are made to the Denis Breen postcard and O'Molloy, as a barrister, warns that a libel action against whoever sent the card (strongly believed to be Bergan) could easily lie. The citizen makes abusive comments about Breen (and by extension Bloom) as a 'half and half' (with a strong sexual implication) and a 'pishogue' (one who is under an unlucky spell).

Trouble is temporarily averted, and the conversation moves on to various recent court cases, including one in which Reuben J. Dodd was involved and which was dismissed with contempt by the judge.

Parody (lines 1111–40): a combination of legal terminology and high romantic inflated diction, descriptive of court proceedings.

Mention of Reuben J. Dodd, seen as Jewish, gives the citizen a chance to indulge in some anti-Semitism, with Bloom as his real target. Bloom, however, ignores it, and attempts to get Joe Hynes, who owes him money, to take up the matter of Keyes's ad with Myles Crawford, the *Evening Telegraph* editor. However, the atmosphere has soured considerably. Reference to 'the adultress and her paramour' (Dervogilla and Dermot MacMurrough) chimes uncomfortably for Bloom with his own situation, as do the predictable leerings over a picture of a misbehaving 'society belle' in a magazine that Alf Bergan produces.

A diversion of sorts is provided by the entrance of Lenehan and John Wyse Nolan. The citizen asks Nolan about the city council meeting to discuss the revival of the Irish language, mentioned already in 'Wandering Rocks'.

Parody (lines 1183–9): a brief report of the corporation meeting, done in the style of nineteenth-century versions of medieval romance and legends of chivalry.

This topic again provides the citizen with an opportunity to launch into an anti-British tirade; he encounters some opposition from J. J. O'Molloy, and from Bloom, which he roughly overrides.

Parody (lines 1210–14): the citizen's defiance in the style of 'medieval-type' stories that we have previously encountered.

Lenehan, meanwhile, is in the dumps. We soon discover why: the horse which he has backed in the Gold Cup, Sceptre, and which he has also tipped to Boylan, has been well beaten by a rank outsider, Throwaway. It is at this point that it becomes clear that Bloom had inadvertently tipped the winning horse to Bantam Lyons way back in the 'Lotus-Eaters' episode; Lyons had taken Bloom's remark, that he was just about to 'throw away' the paper, as a concealed hint or tip. So Bloom is a victor (and over Boylan!) without knowing it.

The argument about British imperialism and Ireland has become more heated: the citizen has now launched forth on an exposition of the many Irish natural resources that the British have taken; prominent among these are the trees of the country.

Parody (lines 1266–95): a newspaper account of a fashionable society wedding; in this case, of course, all present are named after trees and the whole account has a suitably sylvan tone.

The citizen continues his exposition of the wrongs of Ireland, his tone rising in vituperation and hurling incidental abuse at the French *en passant*. He is strongly backed by most others in the pub, with only J. J. O'Molloy and Bloom offering some opposition. Among the many barbarous practices attributed to the British are corporal punishment in the navy, graphically described.

Parody (lines 1354–9): corporal punishment in the British navy delineated in the form of the Apostles' Creed.

As the tirade goes on, Bloom becomes more and more excited and resentful. He feels that much of it is directed against him, even if not explicitly. He denounces 'national hatred among nations', only to be confused and flustered over the question of what a nation is. He asserts unequivocally that Ireland is his nation, an assertion met by a deeply sceptical spit from the citizen. This requires the use of his face-cloth 'to swab himself dry.'

Parody (lines 1438–64): the citizen's handkerchief described in the style of a newspaper feature-type article on an ancient illuminated manuscript, such as the Book of Kells.

As the argument gets more heated, Bloom begins to assert his Jewish identity, alluding to the persecutions then going on in North Africa. Challenged to 'stand up' to the injustice 'with force like men', Bloom changes tack: rather than seeing 'Force, hatred, history, all that' as 'life for men and women', he asserts that the 'very opposite of that' constitutes life: love, the opposite of hatred. With this parting comment he prudently and temporarily leaves, to go around to the courthouse to see if Martin Cunningham is there.

Parody (lines 1493–501): universal love expressed in namby-pamby adult baby-talk.

In Bloom's absence, the vituperation against him continues. A skit from the *United Irishman* mocking the imperialist trappings accompanying the visit of a Zulu chief to England is read out. (This is virtually an expansionary parody in itself.) Animosity against Bloom is heightened when Lenehan declares that his visit to the courthouse is merely a blind; he has gone to collect his winnings on Throwaway. Lenehan knows about Bloom's alleged involvement with Throwaway because Bantam Lyons had told him that it was Bloom who gave him the tip. Ironically enough, Lenehan has put Lyons off backing the horse.

Noman leaves to 'pumpship' (urinate) and when he returns stories about Bloom's doings are being swapped around: it is even claimed by John Wyse Nolan that it was Bloom who gave the original idea for Sinn Féin to Arthur Griffith. Martin Cunningham then arrives, accompanied by Jack Power and an Orangeman called Crofter, Crofton or Crawford.

Parody (lines 1593–620): the arrival of the trio at Barney Kiernan's done in the style of a nineteenth-century historical novel.

Martin Cunningham is looking for Bloom to accompany them to Mrs Dignam's. In Bloom's absence, however, he confirms that Bloom did indeed draw up the plans for Sinn Féin 'according to the Hungarian system'. Abuse of Bloom moves from racial to sexual matters. Doubts are cast on the paternity of his two children and deep scepticism is voiced as to his sexual competence: 'I wonder did he ever put it out of sight.'

Martin Cunningham agrees to have a drink prior to going and says as a toast: 'God bless all here.'

Parody (lines 1676–750): a mock solemn account of a sacred procession leading to a blessing of Barney Kiernan's and all within it.

Bloom re-enters and this time the citizen's anger, especially over the alleged 'bet', gets full vent. Martin Cunningham hurries Bloom out of the premises and on to the coach which is waiting outside. He urges the driver to hasten on his way.

Parody (lines 1772–82): the departure of the coach rendered as a mythological vessel setting forth on the waves, accompanied by 'a many nymphs' to speed it on its way. The style is again that of a nineteenth-century version of a mythological story.

Bloom has departed, but the citizen takes off after him, with Garryowen at his heels. An appreciative crowd has gathered outside the pub to witness this scene. Bloom is on the car, but is now highly excited and shouts out large claims for the Jews, including one that really angers the citizen: that Christ was a Jew. The citizen vows 'by Jesus' to brain Bloom for using the Holy Name in vain. He runs back into the pub and grabs a Jacob's biscuit box that has already featured in the episode.

Parody (lines 1814–42): Bloom's departure rendered as a newspaper account of the farewell of an important foreign dignitary, such as royalty, after a state visit.

The citizen flings the box at Bloom just as the car is heading off. Garryowen, not to be outdone, takes off after the car 'like bloody hell'.

Parody (lines 1858–96): the throwing of the box rendered as a newspaper account of a natural disaster, such as a major earthquake.

The car gets around the corner of Little Britain Street with the dog after it and Bloom standing up in it still shouting and gesticulating.

Parody (lines 1910–18): Bloom's final departure rendered in Biblical prose as the ascension of the prophet Elijah into heaven. The final phrase, 'like a shot off a shovel', brings matters back to earth.

CORRESPONDENCES

In Book 9 of *The Odyssey*, Odysseus tells how he and his men arrived in the land of the one-eyed giants, the Cyclopes, cruel and inhospitable 'louts'. He and his men go to the cave of the giant Polyphemus. The giant instantly devours two of the men and then falls asleep. Odysseus and his followers are imprisoned in the cave and the next evening two more of the men are devoured. Odysseus, however, having prepared a sharp stake, plies Polyphemus with wine. The giant asks Odysseus his name and is told his name is *outis*, 'Noman'. Polyphemus falls into a drunken stupor and Odysseus puts out his single eye with the burning stake. The giant's neighbours, having heard his cries, gather round and ask Polyphemus who has made him cry so loudly. He replies 'Noman' and his neighbours respond that in that case he does not need any help. Odysseus and his men are able to flee from the cave by hiding among the blinded giant's sheep. As they board their ship, Odysseus flings a last taunt back to the Cyclops; in response the giant hurls rocks after their vessel. Luckily, they miss. As a parting shot, however, the giant calls on his father, Poseidon, the god of the sea, to thwart Odysseus in his journey homeward and to ensure he loses all his companions and his ships and has a bitter homecoming. This prayer is granted.

In the Gilbert schema, the anonymous narrator is the 'Noman' figure, the (non-)identity Odysseus temporarily assumes; Bloom's cigar is the stake, and the challenge that the departing Odysseus hurls at the giant is represented by the apotheosis of Bloom (his ascension into heaven) at the end of the episode. The identifications of the citizen with Polyphemus and of Bloom with Odysseus are obvious.

STYLE

The technique of this episode is called in the Gilbert schema 'gigantism': this is clearly meant to reflect the giant qualities of the Cyclops. Stylistically, it is expressed most obviously in the parodies that punctuate the narration. However, gigantism is not confined to those passages; the voice of Noman is itself massively given to exaggeration, to inflated claims, to gigantic vituperation. For the citizen, similarly, exaggeration is second nature; everything he says is overstated, the animosity driving him leads him always to hyperbole. So the parodies are just one mode of highly exaggerated discourse, a literary or journalistic mode; the discourse of the pub customers is equally exaggerated in its own way.

At the same time, the contrast between the two modes allows plenty of opportunity for bathos, from the 'Begob he was what you might call flabbergasted' which leads on to the pompous description of the séance, to the '—And so say all of us, says Jack' that follows the elaborate staging of the blessing of Barney Kiernan's. As Swift showed long ago, gigantism works only if there is something to contrast it with: and there is plenty in this episode to counterpoise against the lofty tone of the official parodies. Vituperation is one mode of exaggeration, but it is a very different mode from the would-be nobility of the interpolated passages here.

The parodies themselves are somewhat unusual exercises in the genre; the term 'parody' usually refers to a subversive or mocking imitation of a particular passage or author; here, though, they are rather parodies of a certain style of discourse or narration. Very few specific 'originals' have been found for these parodies (the account of the Keogh-Bennett boxing match, for instance, is rather close to a newspaper report of a similar match that took place in Dublin at this time). And these *are* parodies, not pastiches: a pastiche is a straight imitation of another text, while a parody contains a more or less overtly absurd or exaggerated element to undercut the original. And in this episode, of course, exaggeration is the keynote.

The style of discourse or narration being parodied is hard to define exactly. It is, in general, though, a nineteenth-century 'high-falutin'' literary-journalistic style, in particular the mode of bad translations of heroic sagas. Words such as 'lo', 'comely', 'peerless' abound. All revolutionary literary movements—and *Ulysses* is part of one such revolutionary movement called Modernism—need something against which to define themselves, a preceding literary mode or language that can be seen as outmoded and *passé*. Romanticism was able to use eighteenth-century poetic diction for this purpose. Similarly, Modernism could feed on the inflated diction of later nineteenth-century literary language in order to point up its own ironic self-awareness. Part of what is happening in these 'Cyclops' parodies is linked to that effort.

As the parodies go on, however, as they become longer and more elaborate, they begin to go beyond their apparent goal. One particular parodic effect, the enormous lists and catalogues, begins to take on a life of its own. The more absurd these are, the better; ridiculous juxtapositions (the Queen of Sheba next to a Dublin publican called Acky Nagle of 25 North Earl Street) are of the essence. It becomes doubtful whether the word 'parody' really describes what is happening any more. Whatever was being parodied—the target text, vague anyway, as we have seen—is forgotten as the parody begins to take off, to become self-delighting in a way that transcends parody's normal satiric purpose.

The parodies are just one of the main stylistic innovations of this episode. The other is the voice of Noman. The entrusting of the episode's narration to this 'character' results in the second most pulsating, vibrant linguistic performance of the whole book (Molly Bloom's being, of course, the first). Noman's language is the Dublin argot in all its intensity, comedy and awfulness. No greater demonstration could be given of the oft-claimed thesis that Dublin's energies were primarily linguistic. His voice, and the voices of the other characters, except for Bloom, of course, make this the most entertaining episode for many readers, so much so, indeed, that its power can sometimes unbalance the work. Molly Bloom's monologue aside, it is Joyce's finest exercise in a living, rather than in a literary or journalistic language (these are supplied in heightened form for contrast): hence its wide appeal.

COMMENTARY

'Cyclops' is such a hugely enjoyable episode that it is difficult to detect any underlying seriousness. Its predominant mode is comic; readers are not wrong to take it in that sense. But there is a serious sub-text: it emerges, for instance, in the recurrent focus on executions, punishments and non-judicial killings (not just in Ireland). To an extent the episode reprises the themes of 'Aeolus', the newspaper episode: as in the newspaper office, the citizen posits against the hated British empire a notional Irish empire that sounds very like the one it is to supplant; the long parody execution scene exploits to the full the cult of death and blood sacrifice that seems to accompany all visions of empire, of whatever racial origin (the battle of the Somme was happening as Joyce was writing this episode). The seriousness emerges also, of course, in the way in which Bloom is viewed by the others present: his Jewishness, far from evoking their sympathy for him as a member of another oppressed minority, rather leads to his total ostracism; whatever about the New Jerusalem, the New Ireland will not have any room for Jews by all appearances. All these are very serious matters, but they are contained within an essentially comic frame.

Much critical debate in recent times has focused on the way in which this episode is to be read, on the values to be perhaps inferred from it. A traditional reading, following the lines suggested by the Homeric parallel, sees Bloom as the moral victor, the router of the citizen and the dark, primitive, pre-Enlightenment values he is supposed to represent. Bloom, then, is the apostle of universal love, whose enlightened virtues he embodies. As against this, it has been argued firstly, that some of the citizen's comments on such things as Ireland's natural resources sound very like some of Joyce's own comments in his lectures and journalism in Trieste, and secondly, that the nationalism the citizen represents proved historically to be the agent of Irish modernisation and the music of the future. To accept this view is to understand the Homeric parallels as being intended entirely ironically, which is actually an old-fashioned approach. It is also, more seriously, to attach too much weight to the arguments being advanced on either side of this pub brawl, as if this was a debate at an academic conference: the episode *is* serious, but not at the ideological or discursive level where these readings operate. Bloom is not really proposing a model of universalist Enlightenment rationalism for Ireland: he is defending himself against attack.

If the world of Noman and the citizen *does* triumph in this episode, it does so not through ideological correctness or through having history on its side, but rather through sheer linguistic exuberance. The episode's *effect* on readers works counter to its official programme. Long experience of reactions to 'Cyclops', and the fascinating experience of hearing it read by a fine company of Dublin amateur actors, have convinced me that readers and listeners respond with delight to Noman's and the citizen's rantings, even, or especially, when they know them to be slanderous and vituperative. In that sense, Noman has the last word.

A more serious issue for readers, perhaps, concerns the tone of this episode and the tone the entire book is taking. A good instance is provided by the parody passage concerning the Paddy Dignam séance and the subsequent parody lamentation. Can this be the same person whose son we observed just two episodes ago quietly mourning his father and whose death and funeral provided the pretext for Bloom's descent to Hades? What has happened to this book when an aspect of it that seemed one of its most serious elements has now become an object of mockery and mirth?

The question is one of the most fundamental that can be raised about *Ulysses*; properly to answer it requires a total reading of the novel in all its aspects. Around the stage of the 'Sirens' episode, the book undergoes a paradigm shift whereby nearly everything in it becomes overtly comic: Bloom's plight, Stephen's plight are submerged under torrents of sheer style. Their basic situations do not alter and the book continues to deal with and explore them, but these characters have lost their privileged positions; they no longer feel like the main sources of the book's concerns. These concerns have shifted on to language itself, its internal workings and its own developmental logic. Through it all, Bloom and Stephen struggle on, and part of the book's pathos is to watch them preserve what dignity they can under the relentless pressure of the verbal and stylistic edifices that surround them. Each episode, as mentioned already, is a total environment; Bloom, Stephen and their problems have to take their places within this stylistic economy. In 'Cyclops', Bloom is himself the object of some of the parodies; he is no more privileged in that regard than anybody else. But he forges on, a 'darkness shining in the brightness' of nationalism's glad new day.

BIOGRAPHICAL/HISTORICAL

Line 17.　*Moses Herzog*: *Thom's Directory* for 1904 lists an M. Herzog at 13 St Kevin's Parade, Portobello. According to Louis Hyman, in *The Jews of Ireland*, he was an itinerant grocer.

20.　*Geraghty*: *Thom's* lists an M. E. Geraghty at 29 Arbour Hill. Occupation unknown.

58.　*The citizen*: based on Michael Cusack (1847–1907), founder of the Gaelic Athletic Association. In appearance and manner the portrayal of the citizen is not too far removed from the actual Cusack; he did apparently refer to himself at times as 'Citizen Cusack'. He also appears briefly in *Stephen Hero*.

189.　Michelangelo Hayes: an Irish painter (1820–77), who adopted the name of his rather more illustrious Italian predecessor.

190.　*Peter the Packer*: Lord Peter O'Brien of Kilfenora (1842–1914), notorious for his attempts to 'pack' juries with pro-British citizens.

194.　*Waddler Healy*: Archbishop John Healy of Tuam (1841–1918), noted for a waddling gait.

195.　*Valentine Greatrakes*: an Irish healer (1629–83)

198.　*Acky Nagle, Joe Nagle*: two Dublin publicans who had a public house at 25 North Earl Street.

249.　*Alf Bergan*: a friend of Joyce's father, he was a clerk in the offices of David Charles, solicitor, Clare Street, Dublin. He lived in Clonliffe Road, and died in about 1951. In 1904 he was assistant to the sub-sheriff of Dublin. Joyce corresponded with him in the 1930s, especially around the time of John Stanislaus Joyce's death. The kind of practical joke of which he is here suspected seems to have been very characteristic of him.

430. *H. Rumbold*: the name of the British minister to Bern, in Switzerland, Sir Horace Rumbold, at the time of Joyce's quarrel with the British Consulate in Zurich. He was marked down as an enemy.

1589. *Crofton*: an Orangeman who had been a colleague of John Joyce in the office of the collector general of rates. He is a character in the story 'Ivy Day in the Committee Room', in *Dubliners*.

SELECT GLOSSARY

Line 148. *a chara*: Irish, 'my friend'.

265. *Bi i dho husht*: phoneticised Irish, more properly *Bí i do thost*: 'Be quiet'.

339. tantras: in theosophy, prayers.

341. etheric double: the 'spiritual' aspect of a living person in theosophy.
jivic rays: the *jiva* is the life energy.

346. pralaya: period between death and rebirth.

350. atmic development: the plane of pure existence, the highest plane.

358. Maya: the physical, sensuous universe.

474. *corpora cavernosa*: Latin, 'the cavernous bodies'. In medicine, erectile tissue.

478. *in articulo . . . capitis*: medical Latin, 'at the moment of death through the breaking of the neck'.

523. *Sinn fein amhain*: Irish, 'ourselves alone'.

556. Bacibaci Beninobenone: Italian, 'Kisskiss prettywell'.

558. Petitépatant: French, 'Pittypat'.

560. Schwanzenbad-Hodenthaler: German, 'Penis in bath-Valley of testicles'.

560–61. Marha Virága Kisászony Putrápesthi: Hungarian: 'Cow Flower Mademoiselle Putrapesthi'.

561–2.   Athanatos Karamelopulos: Greek, 'Deathless Sweet-seller'.

562–4.   Hidalgo . . . Malaria: Spanish, 'Sir Noble Knight Mr Pecadillo and Words and Lord's Prayer of the Evil Hour of Malaria'.

565.   Goosepond: pun on Russian *gospodin*, 'Mister'.

567.   Chuechli-Steuerli: Swiss German, 'Little cake-little tax'.

569.   Kriegfried Ueberallgemein: German, 'Universal war-peace'.

593.   *Gladiolus Cruentus*: botanical Latin, 'Bloody gladiolus flower' (*Gladiolus* itself means 'sword').

600–601.   Hoch . . . *evviva*: national expressions for 'hooray' 'your health' and 'long life' in, respectively, German, Japanese, Hungarian, Serbo-Croatian, pidgin, modern Greek, English, French, Arabic and Italian.

708.   *pro bono publico*: Latin, 'for the public good', a stock pseudonym used by newspaper letter-writers.

735.   englyn: a metre in Welsh verse.

819.   *Slan leat*: Irish, 'your health'.

859.   *Sluagh na h-Eireann*: Irish, 'The Host of Ireland', a patriotic society.

884.   *Na bacleis*: Irish, 'don't mind it'.

897–8.   *Brian O'Ciarnain's*: Irish, 'Barney Kiernan's'.

898.   *Sraid . . . Bheag*: Irish, 'Little Britain Street'.

1058.   pishogue: a standard English form of an Irish word meaning a charm, or a superstitious practice. Here it is a variant of the Irish word *piteog*, defined by Dinneen as an effeminate person.

1205.   *cabinet d'aisance*: French, literally, 'cabinet of ease', water closet.

1209.   *Conspuez . . . Albion*: French, 'Scorn the English! Perfidious Albion!' medher: Irish, a cup.

1211–12.   *Lamh Dearg Abu*: Irish, 'The Red Hand Forever'.

1213.   *Raimeis*: Irish, 'Rubbish'.

1291–2.   *in horto*: Latin, 'in the garden'.

1653.   *En ventre sa mère*: French, 'in the belly of his mother'.

1721–2. *in Epiphania Domini . . . Surge, illuminare*: Latin, the entrance chant for the Mass on the Feast of the Epiphany. The lesson begins 'Surge, illuminare': 'Arise and shine'.

1722–3. *Omnes . . . venient*: the gradual of the Mass for the Epiphany: 'All [the people] are coming from Saba'.

1740–43. *Adiutorium . . . tuo*: Latin, 'Our help is in the name of the Lord./Who made Heaven and Earth./The Lord be with you./And with thy spirit.' A response prayer that precedes the formal blessing.

1746–50. *Deus . . . nostrum*: Latin, 'God, by whose word all are sanctified, pour your blessing upon these created things: and grant that whoever, giving thanks to you, uses them in accordance with your law and your will, may by calling on your holy name receive through your aid health of body and protection of soul, through Christ our Lord.' The standard 'Blessing for all things.'

1841.   *Visszontlatasra . . . Visszontlatasra!*: Hungarian, 'See you again, dear friend. See you again!'

1884.   *missa pro defunctis*: Latin, 'Mass for the Dead'.

1915.   *Abba! Adonai!*: *Abba*: Syriac-Greek 'Father'; *Adonai*: Hebrew, 'Lord'.

II
[13 · Nausicaa]

Time: 8 p.m.
Location: Sandymount Strand

SUMMARY

'Three girl friends', Cissy Caffrey, Edy Boardman and Gerty Mac-Dowell, are enjoying the evening sun on Sandymount Strand, beside the Star of the Sea Church. (In those days the strand extended much closer to the church wall than now.) With them are Cissy's two little twin brothers, Tommy and Jacky, and Edy's even younger brother, baby Boardman, aged eleven months. Tommy and Jacky have 'a slight altercation' over the design of a sand castle they had built, in the course of which the castle is itself destroyed, but Cissy settles matters between them. Tommy joins Cissy and Edy, and Edy makes a pointed remark about Gerty as Tommy's girlfriend. However, Tommy remains distressed and Cissy whispers to Edy Boardman to help him relieve himself behind the push-car, 'where the gentleman couldn't see'.

Gerty meanwhile is seated some distance from the others, lost in thought. She is brooding on her notional (very notional) 'beau', Reggy Wylie, who appears to have cooled in his attentions of late. She makes no reply to Edy's sharp remark. A 'gnawing sorrow' is haunting her. Twenty-one-year-old Gerty does not believe that Reggy Wylie will ever be worthy of her and she longs for 'a manly man' to take her in his arms and for the opportunity to make a home for him.

Tommy has finished his business behind the push-car, but he now wants the ball that has been given to baby Boardman. Cissy takes it off baby by a ruse and sends it flying along the strand with Tommy after it. Meanwhile the men's temperance retreat is being held in the Star of the Sea Church, with rosary, sermon and benediction. The girls can hear the sound of the organ from the church, the men recite the litany of Our Lady of Loreto, and Gerty reflects sadly on the damage that drink has done in her own home.

The twins have another altercation over the ball; Jacky kicks it so far that it heads towards the seaweedy rocks well down the strand. A gentleman who is seated on the rocks intercepts the ball, however, and at Cissy's request throws it to her. The ball, though, as if it has a will of its own, lands exactly at Gerty's feet. She succeeds in kicking it away and after doing so looks over at the gentleman seated on the rocks. The face that meets hers is 'the saddest she had ever seen'.

The litany of Loreto continues in the church, the twins play with their ball, and baby Boardman claps hands and tries to say 'Papa'. However, baby protests loudly when Cissy discovers that he is 'possing wet' and that his clothes have to be adjusted.

Gerty finds the twins and baby most annoying and wishes Cissy and Edy would take them away. She is conscious of the attention of the dark stranger seated opposite her; she is sure he is a foreigner, and she notices that he is in deep mourning. She knows on the instant that he is her 'dreamhusband'.

Listening to the litany of Loreto being recited from the church, Gerty remembers Father Conroy there and his kindness to her when she had something embarrassing to tell him in confession. She would like to get him a present such as a clock, but she has noticed that the priests already have a clock in their presbytery with a 'canarybird' that comes out to tell the time.

The inveterate twins are quarrelling again and Cissy is obliged to run down the strand after them past the strange gentleman. Gerty watches her long gawky run with scorn.

The litany continues and then the choir sing the 'Tantum Ergo Sacramentum'. Gerty sways her foot in time to the singing and takes off her hat. Both actions are duly noted by the gentleman sitting opposite. Edy Boardman has observed the interaction between them and says sharply to Gerty: 'A penny for your thoughts'. Gerty replies that she was wondering what the time was (a subtle hint that it is time for Edy to go) and Cissy Caffrey goes over to the strange gentleman to enquire. He takes his hands out of his pockets to check his watch. However, his timepiece is stopped but he guesses it is after eight.

The choir is still singing and as it does so, Gerty swings her leg 'more in and out in time'. The gentleman has put his hands back in his pockets and Gerty feels her passions being aroused under his gaze.

Edy and Cissy prepare to go, but Edy has a parting shot at Gerty, asking her if she is 'heartbroken about her best boy throwing her over' (a reference to Reggy Wylie). Gerty nobly replies that because it's a leap year, she can pick whoever she chooses.

As dusk descends and the bell rings out for the benediction and a startled bat flies out of the belfry and the atmosphere becomes ever more romantic, Gerty surrenders to the ambience, to the enraptured gaze of the stranger sitting opposite and vows to be 'wild, un-trammelled, free'.

At that moment a skyrocket from the Mirus bazaar fireworks in nearby Ballsbridge bursts overhead; the other two girls, complete with baby and twins, dash off down the strand to see more, leaving Gerty alone with the stranger. She notices that 'his hands and face were work-ing'; she leans far back as if to see the fireworks better, giving him a full view of her legs up to her drawers. She leans farther and farther back and at the moment of maximum exposure 'a long Roman candle' bursts in the sky above, scattering a stream of golden sparks against the sky.

Then 'all melted away'. Gerty gets up, casting Leopold Bloom '(for it is he)', a look in which reproach and forgiveness are commingled. Before going she takes out her handkerchief and wafts a little perfume from it in Bloom's direction.

Bloom watches her as she departs and notices that she goes very slowly and with care because Gerty is lame. (She had already adverted obliquely to that fact, mentioning 'that one shortcoming' caused by an accident on Dalkey Hill.) Bloom, left alone, reflects 'Poor girl!'.

Nonetheless, his satisfaction at what he has just witnessed is in no way diminished; he is glad he did not masturbate over Martha's letter in the bath that morning. He realises that his watch stopped at half past four, just when Boylan and Molly would have been together. The pain of that realisation, however, is blunted by what has just hap-pened (Bloom has in fact ejaculated just as the Roman candle burst and Gerty's exposure was at its height: this is made clear by his need to recompose his wet shirt). He goes on to reflect on the inevitability and ubiquity of sexual attraction and the apparently innate nature of female response: 'Something inside them goes pop.' Was Gerty aware of what he was doing, he wonders, and answers: 'Course.'

The encounter has left him weary, but has nonetheless done him good, after his experiences in Barney Kiernan's and in Dignam's house in Newbridge Avenue, Sandymount. (Bloom has come to the seashore after his visit to nearby Dignam's.) He reflects on women's involvement in the two most basic moments of life, birth and death: 'Washing child, washing corpse'. Thoughts of birth remind him of the plight of Mrs Purefoy, who, as we learned in 'Lestrygonians', has been in labour for three days in Holles Street Hospital, and he resolves to call in to ask after her.

Bloom is still arranging himself after his masturbatory activities (it is at this point we learn that he is not circumcised). Renewed musing on the 'coincidence' of his watch stopping at about the time of Boylan's and Molly's tryst leads to reflections on the power of magnetism, as manifested between him and Gerty.

He catches the scent of her perfume, leading to further musings on attraction at a distance and the different effects of male and female odours. Ever the scientist, Bloom attempts to smell himself to verify what a 'man smell' would be like. He is surprised to find that he emits an odour of lemons and then realises that he is detecting the smell of the soap he has been carrying around since morning. This reminds him that he has neglected to return to the chemist's to collect the lotion he ordered and to pay: 'Bad opinion of me he'll have'.

Bloom sees a man passing by on the beach, a man whom Gerty had already noticed and who regularly takes a constitutional along the strand. Bloom wonders who he might be and thinks idly of writing a prize-winning story (as he already did back in 'Calypso') called 'The Mystery Man on the Beach'.

The Bailey light flashes on Howth Head, and the romance of the scene begins to get through to Bloom: 'All that old hill has seen'. One of the things it has seen, of course, is him and Molly locked in their fateful embrace. Bloom remembers this and thinks: 'Take the train there tomorrow'. But he decides that there is no point: 'Returning not the same'. More memories of his early days with Molly assail him.

Fortunately, he is distracted by the flying of the bat, which makes him, characteristically, wonder 'what they're always flying for'. This leads him on to thoughts of birds migrating over seas and of the lives and perils of sailors.

A last Roman candle goes up from the Mirus bazaar. The nine o'clock postman goes around the houses of Sandymount, the lamplighter illuminates the lamps, the newsboy is hawking the final edition of the

Evening Telegraph, bearing the result of the Gold Cup race, and Howth settles down for the night's slumber.

Bloom remembers his daughter, Milly, and her fearlessness on a choppy excursion in Dublin Bay in a vessel called the *Erin's King*. Molly's memories of her childhood in Gibraltar also come into his mind; she always thought she'd marry a lord or a rich gentleman. Why Bloom? 'Because you were so foreign from the others.'

Bloom looks back on the day: the most depressing moment, he feels, has been the visit to Dignam's (the one extended incident involving Bloom in the book which we do not witness at firsthand). He reflects on the irony of the name of the Scottish Widows Insurance Company where Dignam had a policy: 'Takes it for granted we're [men] going to pop off first'.

He spies a piece of paper on the strand with something written on it but is unable to read it. He picks up a stick and begins to write on the sand with it: 'I . . . AM . . . A.' Weary, he throws the stick away and thinks vaguely about returning the next day to see Gerty again. But by now he is fairly indifferent to Gerty and even to Boylan's activities with Molly: 'Let him.' He drifts into a half-slumber in which various elements of his preceding musings return in very jumbled form.

The little bat is still flying about and in the priests' house the clock that Gerty MacDowell remembered seeing strikes the hour of nine. The 'canarybird' emerges nine times to proclaim the last word of Bloom's 'I . . . AM. A.': *Cuckoo*.

CORRESPONDENCES

In Book 5 of *The Odyssey*, Odysseus finally departs from Calypso's island. No sooner has he set forth in his craft than his vessel is wrecked through the enmity of Poseidon, the sea god. Odysseus is rescued by the nereid, Leucothea, and by Athena. He is washed up at the mouth of a river on the shore of the Phaeacians' land. He hides under some bushes and, exhausted, falls asleep. In Book 6, the Princess Nausicaa and her maids come to the river to wash the palace laundry. (Nausicaa has in fact been prompted by Athena to go to the river this day.) At the river, after doing the washing, Nausicaa and her maids play a ball game. At one point, Nausicaa throws the ball badly and it lands in a stream. The party gives such a shout of alarm – 'a lusty cry of tall young girls' – that Odysseus, who has lost all his clothes in the shipwreck, is awoken. He emerges from the bushes, having protected his modesty with an olive branch. The maid-servants are so frightened by his appearance that they flee, but Nausicaa stands her ground. Odysseus pleads with her for help and assures her he means no harm. Nausicaa takes pity on him; she reprimands her maids: 'Does the sight of a man scare you?' Nausicaa's first feeling is compassion but after Odysseus has discreetly bathed himself, been somewhat 'improved' by Athena and put on the new clothes Nausicaa has provided for him, the princess feels 'he looks like one of heaven's people. I wish my husband could be as fine as he …' Nausicaa then arranges for Odysseus to meet her father, King Alcinous, who entertains him royally and eventually helps Odysseus to pursue his voyage.

In the Gilbert schema, Phaecia is represented by the Star of the Sea Church and Nausicaa by Gerty MacDowell. Significantly, in the Linati schema the Sense (meaning) is given as 'The Projected Mirage'.

STYLE

The 'technic' of *Nausicaa* is given in the Gilbert schema as 'tumescence/detumesence'. This obviously enough refers to the swelling of Bloom's member in the first part of the episode, and its subsidence in the second part. Less literally, it also refers to Gerty's growing excitement as her (non-)engagement with Bloom proceeds. The episode works by contrast between the inflated, flowery, sentimental, quasiromantic language of Gerty's part, and the flat, deflated, disillusioned language of Bloom's part. Gerty's part is characterised by long, elaborate, confused sentences; Bloom's, as in his previous internal monologues, by short, clipped reflections, their very brevity mirroring a mind that is 'less deceived', to use Philip Larkin's term. The physical gap between them on the strand is mirrored by the stylistic gap between their different discourses.

Joyce, in a well-known letter to Frank Budgen, described the language of the first part of 'Nausicaa' as 'a namby-pamby jammy marmalady drawersy (alto là!) style with effects of incense, mariolatry, masturbation, stewed cockles, painter's palette, chitchat, circumlocutions, etc., etc.' (From the previous episode on, valuable comments that Joyce made in letters to and conversations with Budgen are available; Budgen was almost the only person with whom Joyce seriously discussed the novel as he was writing it. Unfortunately, he got to know Budgen only about midway through the writing, so these helpful materials are not available for the earlier episodes.)

Surprising as the sudden stylistic flourish of the first part of 'Nausicaa' may seem, it should not be totally unexpected for readers; in one way it is just another mode of social discourse being exploited for all it is worth, in the same way that certain literary and journalistic discourses were in the previous episode. Instead of being an interpolation, as in 'Cyclops', this form of discourse here takes over half an episode, and becomes the sole means through which we get to know a character. It is as if we knew Alf Bergan, say, only through the 'parody' passages that involve him in 'Cyclops'.

Another way in which this style resembles the interpolations in 'Cyclops' is that no precise source text for it can be found; the word 'parody' seems even less appropriate here than it does for the 'Cyclops' passages. There are obvious general sources in popular romantic fiction, in pietistic Catholic literature, especially to do with the Virgin Mary, in women's magazines, in advertisements, in the 'society' columns of newspapers, etc. But to see the style as solely a literary matter may be too limiting: there is in it a certain tone of voice, the voice of bourgeois Dublin femininity, that is rather more difficult to describe than it is to intuit. It is apparent in such phrases as 'Master Jacky who was really as bold as brass there was no getting behind that' or '(Edy Boardman prided herself that she was very *petite* but she never had a foot like Gerty MacDowell, a five, and never would ash, oak or elm)'. The source of these locutions is not literary, even taking literature at its most popular level; it is in some sense communal, and it is, for me, unmistakably female. So in addition to everything that Gerty, like a latter-day Madame Bovary, has absorbed from popular literature and which is shaping her sense of the world, there is also a cocoon of received female locutions which define that world and in which she is inescapably wrapped. The style enacts that entrapment.

Bloom's deflated and deflationary discourse, on the other hand, is something in the nature of a farewell. This is the last time we encounter the pattern, with which we are now reasonably familiar, of a third-person narration accompanying an internal monologue in a voice we have come to know as Bloom's. We do hear that voice again, in the Nighttown episode, but with a very different stylistic context surrounding it.

In this episode, on its last appearance, the 'initial style' undergoes some modification. For one thing, the role of the 'narrator' is drastically reduced: Bloom's inner world is given with a minimum of narrative interference. This is helped, of course, by the fact that Bloom is doing nothing other than sitting on a rock, at his most static; there is nothing much to narrate. Narration is confined to simple indicators such as 'Mr Bloom watched her as she limped away'; 'Mr Bloom inserted his nose'. Whenever the narration becomes more extended, as it does occasionally, it almost imperceptibly slips back into the Gerty MacDowell mode: 'From house to house, giving his ever welcome double knock, went the nine o'clock postman.' And at the very end the narration definitively goes back to the tone with which it began in order to proclaim Bloom a cuckoo; this is in a sense Gerty's revenge. So we are not really back to the tone of the opening episodes: Bloom's own inner world and the world of the book have moved too far apart for that. The narration is paying only minimal attention to its job of narrating Bloom; it is, even in this second part of 'Nausicaa', far more interested in the effects it can generate on its own.

COMMENTARY

The first part of 'Nausicaa' is one of Joyce's most astonishing achievements. What is wonderful is the way in which the different elements—Gerty's musings, Bloom's dark presence, the retreat going on in the Star of the Sea, the Mirus bazaar fireworks, even the bat – are gradually blended together to produce the climax of Bloom's masturbation and Gerty's maximum exposure. A good example is Gerty moving her foot in time to the *Tantum ergo*, bringing the two worlds together. The prose gains in power and intensity, the elements become more and more fused, as it goes on, moving inexorably to one great goal. It is no wonder the passage had such a powerful effect on a writer such as Vladimir Nabokov, who frequently expressed his admiration of it.

The first part of 'Nausicaa' also represents Joyce's most radical negation yet of any gap between narrator and narrated. There has never, in fact, been a clear distinction between the two, but here the narration and the person being narrated are seamlessly one in an unprecedented way. The 'Uncle Charles principle', mentioned in the discussion of 'Scylla and Charybdis', here receives its maximum expansion to date. The episode that is closest to it in this respect, if only by contrast, is 'Scylla and Charybdis' itself, where Stephen's consciousness, his verbal universe, did to some extent take over, almost hijack, the narration; it became infected by his sensibility, taking on an Elizabethan, Latinate, monkish and paradoxical hue in response to his pressure.

In the case of the first part of 'Nausicaa', the reverse occurs: Gerty's sensibility is flooded, overpowered, by the narrative discourse, the verbal universe, that surrounds her. So total is her submersion in this dominant discourse that it is possible to wonder if Gerty is real at all, if she has any existence outside this framework that seems to constitute her. 'Art Thou Real, My Ideal?', the maudlin poem that Gerty remembers, has a very literal meaning in this context.

The nature of this discourse that envelops Gerty has been sketched out already in the comments on style. It is romantic, tawdry, 'feminine', sedulously averted from whatever it finds disagreeable, endlessly self-deceiving. It is also very powerful, creating an alternative reality that in its own way is just as powerful a reality as any other. A case in point would be Gerty's 'reading' of Bloom's behaviour as he watches her; Bloom may well be right when he concludes that she is well aware of what he is doing, but this superficially distasteful fact is completely occluded from her discourse as she fantasises about the dark stranger sitting opposite her. Terms such as 'erred' and 'sinning' are the nearest she gets to a conscious recognition of Bloom's activities. So the discourse that constitutes Gerty is not just pathetic and silly: it is a particular way of interpreting the world to consciousness in a form that is at least bearable. Almost anything can be made acceptable if it is couched in a suitably saccharine formulation.

At the same time, while this discourse does have its own power, it also works to take over completely the person who adopts it. Gerty, as mentioned, seems to have no reality outside this world; it has so thoroughly entered her spirit that one gets no sense of her as a person apart from it. And while it obviously can serve certain purposes, to be so completely absorbed in a tissue of cliches and truisms, in a huge collection of unexamined assumptions, can hardly be said to be empowering. There is no sense that Gerty *ever* thinks differently from this, that this verbal construct, which might well have its uses in the particular situation in which she finds herself *vis-à-vis* Bloom (she would not be the first or the last person to tell herself a convenient story in a particular situation), is ever relinquished by her in favour of some more adequate means of addressing the world. And, we need to remember, Gerty is twenty-one, not seventeen.

So completely is Gerty absorbed into this verbal universe that her very reality is in question: is it possible that someone could be so completely a construct as this and retain any reality (or at least any credibility as a character in a novel, which in this case is the same thing?). There are a couple of possible answers to that question, one internal to *Ulysses*, the other external. One answer is that by the time Joyce came to write the 'Nausicaa' episode, he had lost interest in such matters as character, credibility, novelistic depth; the book's concerns have shifted to the linguistic level, to surface, to verbal constructs for their own sakes. In this sense, the first part of 'Nausicaa' is another great triumph of style (Hugh Kenner has commented, for instance, on the many syntactical distortions into which Gerty's mode of discourse leads her – distortions that are entirely intentional on the author's part). If this triumph of style has to be achieved at the cost of the weakening of the reality of a given character (the last major new character introduced into the book), the loss is held to be worth bearing.

Again, the first part of 'Nausicaa' aims to create the total environment which is the book's major concern at this stage. Gerty, Cissy, Edy are reduced to figures in this all-encompassing stylistic landscape: the mode of tumescence.

Another reason, though, why Gerty's reality as a character is questionable, at best, is that the particular discourse that surrounds her – the discourse of Edwardian bourgeois femininity – is singularly powerful and all-embracing. It is not impossible for an individual, a subject, to be swamped by it to the point that no other reality is perceptible or available. Gerty in her way embodies the plight of many who have been subjected to a cultural construct so powerful it can seem to be nature. Nor are we, living at a time when dominant discourses (different, but still dominant) have expanded enormously in power since Gerty's day, in any position to look on Gerty with amused pity: the whole point about these modes is that you don't know they are determining you.

'Tumescence' (swelling) is the mode of Gerty's part of the episode; 'detumescence' is the mode of Bloom's. There is, in fact, a flat, disillusioned, occasionally sour quality to Bloom's reflections that would tend to confirm a traditional view of the after-effects of masturbatory activity. He is pleased at what has happened, but at the same time he refers to Gerty as 'that little limping devil', 'little wretch' and 'that female'. Bloom's 'less deceived' mode comes as a welcome relief after the overblown fantasy of the first part, but it is, if anything, a little *too* lowering (the entire episode is a matter of extremes, with no real balance in between).

One of Bloom's major preoccupations during his apparently random musings on the strand is, naturally enough, attraction at a distance, the experience he has just gone through with Gerty. He is struck by the 'coincidence' that his watch stopped at half past four, the time when Boylan and Molly would have begun their tryst, and he wonders idly about a possible magnetic influence. He notices the perfume Gerty leaves behind and wonders whether there is a 'man smell' that women would correspondingly pick up. All these musings seem to push the episode into a virtual sphere; they are about substitutes for physical contact, about the language of implication and suggestion. Their delicate eroticism is counterpoised against the harsh reality of the encounter going on at the same time in Number 7 Eccles Street, and is another part of Bloom's attempt to avert his gaze from it.

Bloom also has some reflections which are appropriate to the mariner that Ulysses is. He meditates on the difficult life of sailors, on shipwrecks – suitably, since in the corresponding episode of *The Odyssey* Odysseus is shipwrecked. This is one of the few moments when the Homeric parallel makes itself unambiguously felt; otherwise its relevance is more problematic than in other episodes. Gerty does do Bloom a favour, as Nausicaa does to Odysseus, but its actual effects are much more ambiguous than in the case of *The Odyssey*. At best it produces a stunned indifference, not unlike the condition of the people back in 'Lotus-Eaters': 'Let him'. The problematic nature of Bloom's position, despite Gerty's good offices, is made clear at the end, when, in a brilliant stroke, the cuckoo clock in the presbytery proclaims Bloom's actual status – and Gerty, complete with appropriate style, is explicitly brought in to make this finding: 'she noticed at once that that foreign gentleman that was sitting on the rocks looking was

> Cuckoo
>
> Cuckoo
>
> Cuckoo.'

This is one adventure that Ulysses does not survive unscathed.

BIOGRAPHICAL

Cissy, Tommy and Jacky Caffrey, Edy and baby Boardman, Gerty MacDowell: The name MacDowell was quite common in the Sandymount/Ringsend area, but no Gerty has been uncovered among them. (A 'Mrs MacDowell', presumably Gerty's mother, has been mentioned by Master Patrick Dignam in 'Wandering Rocks'.) One amusing detail that might escape a reader's notice is that the citizen's dog, Garryowen, is, in fact, the property of Gerty's maternal grandfather Giltrap (this is referred to by the 'Cyclops' narrator). Gerty's feelings about the dog are far more tender than were Noman's.

The name Caffrey is too widespread to make it possible to pin down Cissy. A family named Boardman lived in North Richmond Street when the Joyces were there; Edy Boardman seems to combine the name of Eily and Eddie Boardman, two family members.

Line 196. *Reggy Wylie*: fictional brother of the real W. E. Wylie, who was one of the bicycle racers in the Trinity College sports. The family did not live off or on the London Bridge Road.

283. *the reverend John Hughes S.J.*: a priest in St Francis Xavier's Church, Upper Gardiner Street.

448. *Father Conroy*: Father Bernard Conroy, 5 Leahy's Terrace, curate at the Star of the Sea Church in 1904. Bloom later thinks that 'Gabriel Conroy's brother' is curate at the church. In 'The Dead', Gabriel's brother is called Constantine and is curate in Balbriggan, very far away. It seems that Joyce, on finding an actual Father Conroy *in situ* in Sandymount, transferred Gabriel's brother to this parish. His first name is never given in *Ulysses*. At this point the line between fact and fiction is very blurred.

448. *Canon O'Hanlon*: the Very Revd Canon John O'Hanlon, parish priest of the Star of the Sea parish, Sandymount. In reality, he was a very distinguished churchman, the author of a multi-volume collection of lives of the Irish saints. He died in 1905, and the national school at the Star of the Sea Church is named after him.

SELECT GLOSSARY

Line 442. *Ora pro nobis*: Latin, 'Pray for us'. The response in the litany of Our Lady of Loreto.

486. *Tableau!*: French, literally 'a picture' or 'a sight'; here more like 'What a show!' Bloom uses the same word,

in one of the subterranean correspondences between his reflections and Gerty's.

498.   *Tantum ergo*: Latin, a hymn, actually consisting of the last two verses of St Thomas Aquinas's *Pange Lingua*, in honour of the Blessed Sacrament. The words quoted mean 'so great therefore a sacrament'.

574.   *Panem de coelo praestitisti eis*: Latin, 'You have given them bread from heaven'. Part of the benediction ceremony.

675.   *Laudate Dominum omnes gentes*: Latin, 'Praise the Lord all ye peoples'. The opening line of a psalm sung at the conclusion of the benediction ceremony.

862.   *Lacaus esant taratara*: Bloom's previously garbled version of *La causa é santa* (Italian, 'the cause is holy') from Meyerbeer's opera *Les Huguenots*. See Episode 8, Lestrygonians, lines 623–4.

1149.   *Faugh a ballagh!*: Derived from Irish *Fág an bealach*: 'Clear the way!'

1157.   tephilim: Hebrew; tephilin (the usual spelling) are little boxes containing verses from the Torah, which are strapped on to the arm or forehead during morning prayers. The word Bloom wants is *mezuzah*, a scroll placed at the doorpost of a house.

1208–9. *Buenas . . . hermosa*: Spanish, 'Good evening, senorita. The man loves the beautiful young girl.'

II
[14 · Oxen of the Sun]

Time: 10 p.m.
Location: the National Maternity Hospital, 29–31 Holles Street

SUMMARY

Note: This summary will not enumerate the different styles employed in this episode; these will be listed in the section on style and discussed in the commentary. Instead, it will attempt to outline the course of the 'action', as if there were no stylistic screen between reader and events narrated.

The episode begins with a triple invocation (each item repeated three times). The first invocation means 'Let us go to the right at Holles Street', the second is a prayer for fertility to the sun, to the horn of plenty, and to Dr Andrew Horne, Master of Holles Street Hospital, and the third is the cry of a midwife announcing the birth of a boy.

This is followed by a statement that careful provision for the processes of childbirth is an index of the moral wellbeing of any society. Among the Celts, we are told, there has always been a particular awareness of the importance of such provision and therefore commodious and well-appointed premises have been constructed for that purpose.

At one such hospital, the National Maternity Hospital in Holles Street of which Dr Alexander Horne is master, Leopold Bloom arrives as night falls. He is greeted by Nurse Callan who brings him into the hospital just as lightning flashes in the sky outside. Bloom inquires first after a Dr O'Hare whom he used to know and is told, to his sorrow, that the doctor died three years ago in the Isle of Man. He then inquires after Mrs Purefoy and is told that she is still in labour and that she has been in that state for a full three days. The nurse says that the hour of delivery is nigh but that it has been the hardest birth she has ever encountered. Bloom feels much sympathy for Mrs Purefoy's plight.

As they are speaking a door opens and a loud noise of conversation emanates from a room off the hall. A Dr Dixon emerges: he knows Bloom, having treated him for a bee sting in the Mater Hospital some time previously. He invites Bloom to join the company inside and Bloom accepts, being weary of his wanderings.

On the table in the room are bottles of beer, glasses, bread and a can of sardines. Dr Dixon offers Bloom a drink, which he makes show of accepting, although he surreptitiously empties most of it into his neighbour's glass. Nurse Callan begs the company to lessen their noise, in view of the condition of Mrs Purefoy and other labouring women in the rooms above.

Bloom recognises Lenehan among the company present and expresses to him his pity for Mrs Purefoy's plight and his hope that her ordeal will soon be ended. Lenehan is too busy cadging drinks to care much for Mrs Purefoy's case.

The other persons present are medical students called Vincent Lynch, Madden, Francis 'Punch' Costello, a Scotsman called Crotthers, and Stephen Dedalus, whom we have not encountered since 'Wandering Rocks'. Malachi Mulligan, also last seen in 'Wandering Rocks', is expected to join them. When Bloom arrives the company is debating the vexed issue of whether a pregnant mother in a medical emergency should have to die when a medical intervention might result in the abortion of her unborn child. Madden says that such a case had arisen in Holles Street a year ago and that both mother and stillborn child died, the husband declining to authorise intervention to save her as contrary to his religious beliefs. Most of those present support the mother's prior right to live. However, Stephen, and to some extent Madden, refuse to accept this general view, Stephen claiming that both parties are now glorifying God, the mother in purgatory and the baby in limbo. What, he asks, of those who, through contraceptive devices, 'impossiblise' 'Godpossibled' souls? Stephen insists that the propagation of life, endowed with a soul, is the only appointed aim and goal of sexual activity, and that it is appropriate that the earthly mother, who is 'but a dam to bear beastly', should be the one to die if it comes to a choice.

Bloom's opinion is invited; being given to dissembling, and seeking an answer that will please all, he replies that risking the life of the mother in order to save the life of the child would be the best course, since thereby the church would obtain both birth money (for a baptism) and death money (for a funeral service). Despite this brutal response, however, he remains full of pity for the travail of women in childbirth. He remembers his own dead son and is grieved to see Stephen, whose father he knows well, drinking heavily and wasting his substance in this riotous company.

Stephen continues in the same vein in which he has commenced. Venturing into theology, he asserts that in woman's womb the word becomes flesh but in the womb of the imagination, the mind of the maker, flesh becomes word, a far more noble destiny. He then engages in a put-down of the Virgin Mary (Eve, of course, is dismissed out of hand, as having sold us all for 'a penny pippin'). He refuses to allow Mary to be more than another creature of God, despite her eminence and power.

At this point, probably to the relief of the reader, Punch Costello bawls out a bawdy song: this brings another nurse, Nurse Quigley, rushing in to enjoin him to restrain himself. The company all turn on Costello, and peace temporarily returns. Stephen continues to expostulate; his discourse becomes more personal in tone, covertly alluding to his difficult position in the tower, where he has been spurned 'for a merchant of jalaps'. Both Moses and Hamlet, parallels for himself that Stephen has often employed in the course of the day, are invoked, and it is evident that if anything his sense of himself as a prophet without honour has grown only more acute.

He begins to recite a parody of *The House that Jack Built* comparing God's creation to Jack's house, when a long roll of thunder in the street outside terrifies him. Bloom attempts to calm him, pointing out that it is just a 'natural phenomenon', but Stephen is not so easily reassured. He has neither the scientific rationalism of Bloom nor the (at least partial) piety of one of the other young men, Madden, to sustain him. He had once possessed such piety, but 'Carnal Concupiscence' (Bunyan is the author being parodied) had undone him. All of the company, we are told, are in thrall to this same carnal concupiscence; they fear neither venereal diseases nor the inadvertent begetting of children, since they are each possessed of 'a stout shield' (a condom) to preserve them from such misfortunes.

Out on Merrion Square, near Holles Street, meanwhile, the rain is pouring down in torrents. Mulligan, on his way to join the company, is caught in the downpour. He meets Alec Bannon, who has just come from Mullingar, and the two of them make their way to Holles Street in the rain, Bannon enthusiastically telling Mulligan of a 'skittish heifer' (Milly Bloom) he has met in Mullingar.

Back in Holles Street, Lenehan tells Stephen that Garret Deasy's letter has duly appeared in the *Evening Telegraph*. Stephen, however, has no desire to see it. Costello inquires what the letter is about and is told it concerns foot-and-mouth disease in Irish cattle. Bloom, who has been listening carefully, is shocked to hear that a foot-and-mouth epidemic is feared; he expresses doubts on the matter, and opines it may just be 'the hoose or the timber tongue.'

Stephen, however, by now well advanced in drink, hotly insists that it is indeed foot-and-mouth, having it on the best authority that Irish bulls are indeed in danger from the disease. This leads on to a brilliant extended fantasy, in which most of the company share, based on Irish bulls and the Papal bull *Laudabliter* that authorised King Henry II to invade Ireland.

Mulligan now arrives, accompanied by Bannon. He immediately discloses his scheme to set up a national fertilising centre, with himself as chief fertiliser, to counteract the decline in the population and the entrapment of Irish womanhood by nunneries and sterile clergy. Mulligan notices Bloom, and inquires if he is in need of any professional services. Bloom assures him that he is not, and that he is in the hospital merely to ask after the condition of Mrs Purefoy.

Crotthers, the Scottish student, is chatting with Bannon, who shows him a locket bearing Milly Bloom's image. Bannon reminisces warmly about his time with Milly, and expresses deep regret that he did not have a condom along with him to enable him to consummate their pleasures. However, he reflects, tomorrow is another day.

Nurse Callan enters and calls away Dr Dixon. Mrs Purefoy's labour is at an end; she has given birth to 'a bouncing boy'. After the nurse's departure, Punch Costello makes a grossly sexual comment on her, for which he is rebuked by Dixon and by the others. He retracts, swearing his allegiance to the church and honouring his father and his mother.

Bloom has been sitting among this gathering, feeling somewhat out of place. He greatly dislikes the comment of Costello and some of the other crude remarks, but he does make allowance for youth and inexperience. He also feels greatly relieved that Mrs Purefoy's ordeal is over. Listening as some of the group question the paternity of Mr

Purefoy while others express their admiration for his potency at his advanced years, Bloom reflects with some wonder that in a very short time the conferral of a degree will turn these young blasphemers into models of respectability. However, he further realises, he is himself in no position to pass judgment on these youths; his own behaviour is not free from reproach (the correspondence with Martha, the recent scene with Gerty and an apparent attempt to debauch a scullery maid being cases in point).

The news of Mrs Purefoy's delivery leads to an animated discussion of monstrous, difficult and abnormal births. Bloom attempts to moderate the tone, without success, as the drink continues to flow freely around. Mulligan mentions that he is to meet Haines at Westland Row station at ten past eleven, in order to take the train to the tower.

Bloom falls into a reverie, remembering the days of his own youth and his hopes on setting forth as a travelling salesman. He recalls also his first sexual encounter and speculates idly that he may have fathered a son without knowing it. However, he is aware that such speculations are vain. Bloom becomes caught up in a romantic vision of beasts marching to the Dead Sea; this resolves itself into a vision of a radiant female, a constellation amid the heavens, her emblem finally a ruby-coloured triangle.

Costello and Stephen have been at Clongowes together; Costello asks Stephen about various people they had known there; neither has any idea of their whereabouts, but in any case, says Stephen, they are but phantoms, whom he can conjure up and dismiss at will. Lynch declares that they are all awaiting the work that Stephen has within him to bring forth. Lenehan makes an unfortunate remark about Stephen's mother, at which he almost withdraws from the gathering. However, he is distracted by the conversation's sudden turn to the outcome of the Gold Cup race. Lynch meanwhile mentions that he has encountered Father Conmee that very day (an incident described in 'Wandering Rocks'). Lenehan seeks to console himself for the failure of 'Bass's mare' (the losing Sceptre was indeed owned by a member of the Bass brewing family) by helping himself to some of Bass's beer, but Mulligan enjoins him to refrain, pointing out that Bloom is gazing, apparently rapt in reverie, at the red triangle that then, and still, adorns the label on a bottle of Bass. This is the ruby triangle in which Bloom had been absorbed in mystic contemplation. Bloom, however, is not so lost to the world; he has merely been recollecting some private transactions of his own. Noticing Lenehan's intention, he swiftly helps him to the drink.

Another general discussion follows, on topics connected with birth and childhood. Bloom raises the question of how gender is determined. No particular progress is made on that matter, so Bloom instead addresses the issue of infant mortality – the death of a child of healthy parents. Various suggestions are thrown about to account for the phenomenon, none of them very edifying. By far the most bitter, however, is Stephen's: that an omnivorous Deity, having consumed mainly mature meat, might occasionally appreciate a dish of newly born veal.

The relief and joy of the Purefoys at the birth of their ninth child is evoked, but Bloom is preoccupied by the bitterness of Stephen's remarks. He remembers the first time he saw him, at a garden party in mutual friends' at Roundtown, when Stephen was just a child and he wonders at the prematurely disillusioned figure he now beholds.

At this point, however, Stephen utters the word that gives the signal for a general exodus: 'Burke's!', the nearest pub, at the corner of Holles Street and Denzille (now Fenian) Street. The company encounter Dixon descending from the labour ward with the news that mother and baby are well, but they are far too intent on their goal to pay attention. Bloom goes with them and Dixon also tags along. With a final commendation of Theodore Purefoy in his role of progenitor, we follow the group *en route* to Burke's.

They are observed as they proceed by the urchins of Denzille Lane, who call out, 'Jay, look at the drunken minister coming out of the maternity hospal!' (referring to Stephen in his black garb). On arriving at Burke's, an issue instantly arises concerning who's going to pay for 'this here do'. Stephen, however, is the one with the money (he has already displayed his wealth to his companions, falsely claiming he received it as payment for a literary work). There is some discussion about Bloom: Dixon mentions having treated him for the bee sting, and Lenehan tells of Molly's charms. The drinks go round; there seems to be some resentment (possibly on Mulligan's part) that Stephen is not sufficiently quick with 'the readies'. Some form of quarrel seems to be under way.

Lenehan spots Bantam Lyons (who nearly had the right horse in the Gold Cup, thanks to the unwitting Bloom, but who was put off it by Lenehan) in the snug. Understandably enough, he is anxious to avoid him. In the general confusion, it emerges that Lenehan obtained the hot tip Sceptre through an intercepted telegram from the owner to a friend in the police depot.

More drink is ordered, and Alec Bannon experiences a more unpleasant recognition than Lenehan's: he realises that Bloom is Milly's father. He is anxious to get away and Mulligan uses the opportunity to slip away with him, leaving Stephen in the lurch. The prayer at the end of Mass, some of which is given straight in Episode 5, 'Lotus-Eaters', is being parodied by an unidentified voice throughout.

Another recognition occurs in this episode of recognitions: the man in the macintosh, whose identity had so puzzled Bloom at the funeral earlier, turns up and is identified as Bartle the Bread, an inhabitant of the Richmond Asylum. Amid frenetic discussion of motor racing, the Russo-Japanese War, etc., etc., time is called by the curate and what is left of the party moves out into the night. The fire brigade is passing by, *en route* to a blaze.

A very drunken Stephen suggests to Lynch that they head for 'the kips' (the brothel quarter) across the river. Bloom seems to be in the vicinity, since Lynch asks Stephen about him. On the way to Nighttown, they see a poster on the Merrion Hall advertising the visit of the gospeller Alexander J. Dowie (mentioned in 'Wandering Rocks') and the episode closes with a stirring sample of his sermonising.

CORRESPONDENCES

In Book 12 of *The Odyssey*, Odysseus and his crew pass through Scylla and Charybdis and arrive in Trinacria (modern Sicily), the home of the sun god, Helios. Circe has warned him of the danger of hurting the sun god's oxen, and Odysseus is reluctant to land on the island. However, his men are weary, and demand to have a rest. Odysseus makes them swear they will not touch any of the animals on the island. Bad weather maroons them on Trinacria; Odysseus goes inland to pray for relief, but while doing so falls asleep. Eurylochus, the most rebellious of his crew, persuades the others to slaughter the cattle around and have a feast. Odysseus is horrified on his return. The weather turns fair, and they embark again, but in the meantime Helios has complained to Zeus, the father of the gods, about the killing of his cattle. As soon as the ship sets forth, Zeus destroys it with a bolt of lightning, and all the crew, except Odysseus, are drowned. The shipwrecked Odysseus is washed up on Circe's island.

In the Gilbert schema, Trinacria is the hospital, the daughters of Helios, Lampote and Phaethusa, who alert him to the slaughter of the herds, are Nurses Callan and Quigley; Helios is Dr Horne (joint master of Holles Street at the time), the crime which corresponds to the killing of the oxen is fraud.

STYLES

The episode is written as a succession of parodies of passages of English prose, tracing its development from Latin and Anglo-Saxon up to the late nineteenth century. It breaks down at the end into a babel of contending voices. Unlike in the previous episodes, the word 'parody' really is appropriate here: the style of individual authors, sometimes of recognisable passages, is being directly imitated.

This development of English prose corresponds to the growth of the foetus in the womb: the episode is in nine parts to parallel the nine months of pregnancy. In a letter to Frank Budgen, Joyce stated that the hospital is the womb, Bloom the spermatozoon that enters it, the nurses the ovum and Stephen the embryo. He even drew a chart, now in the British Library, with nine concentric circles, each expanding outwards, to mark the nine months of pregnancy and with the name of an author written on each circle to indicate the stage of prose development arrived at. These activities will be further discussed in the commentary; in this section I will list the various parodies and mark the nine parts of the episode. Not all the parodies have been definitively identified; there are a few grey areas, and they can be further refined, but this list is reasonably comprehensive. One element that recurs is what Joyce called the 'double-thudding Anglo-Saxon motive' ('Before born babe bliss had') to suggest the movement of the oxen's hoofs.

When writing this complex episode, Joyce derived much material from various anthologies of prose that he consulted. Research carried out in recent years has convincingly shown that, in writing the episode, Joyce did not just draw his material from passages in the anthologies devoted to the particular style he was parodying, but also from any and every era which the anthology represented. This has led to the radical suggestion that the various parodies throughout the episode do not in fact represent any particular era or authorial style, but are entirely random and arbitrary.

When we lift our eyes from the trees to the wood, however, we find that this is not so: the various paragraphs are, in each one's overall effect, generally representative of a particular author or, sometimes, era. Familiarity with the styles of these writers indicates that Joyce's passages are indeed generally in the style or ethos of a given writer. Certainly, the discovery does have implications for the textual stability of the episode, and I will consider these further in my new (2022) Epilogue, but it is still fully valid, I believe, to continue to indicate, as I have done here, the various authors and epochs being parodied.

Parody 1 (lines 7–32): 'Universally that person's acumen … ever irrevocably enjoined?' The Latin prose styles of Sallust and Tacitus rendered directly into English without any attempt to adapt them to English syntax and usage.

Parody 2 (lines 33–59): 'It is not why therefore … had been begun she felt'. The style of medieval Latin chronicles, with, once more, no attempt to turn them into normal English prose.

Parody 3 (lines 60–106): 'Before born babe bliss had … sorrowing one with other'. The mode of Anglo-Saxon alliterative prose, principally of Aelfric, heavily rhythmic; this is the style that recurs from time to time throughout the episode to indicate the movement of the oxen's hoofs. The first month of gestation begins at this point with the introduction of Bloom, the spermatozoon.

Parody 4 (lines 107–22): 'Therefore, everyman, look to that ... chiding her childless'. Style of Middle English prose homilies and of morality plays such as *Everyman*.

Parody 5 (lines 123–66): 'And whiles they spake ... Thanked be Almighty God'. Style of *Travels of Sir John Mandeville*, a medieval collection of traveller's tall tales; written in French and translated into English at the start of the fifteenth century. This marks the start of the second month of gestation.

Parody 6 (lines 167–276): 'This meanwhile this good ... murdered his goods with whores'. Style of Sir Thomas Malory's *Morte d'Arthur*, printed in 1485.

Parody 7 (lines 277–333): 'About that present time ... rest should reign'. Style of Elizabethan prose chronicles. Begins third month of gestation.

Parody 8 (lines 334–428): 'To be short this passage ... of a natural phenomenon'. A composite of several late-sixteenth-century and early-seventeenth-century prose styles, Milton, Sir Thomas Browne and Jeremy Taylor prominent among them.

Parody 9 (lines 429–73): 'But was Boasthard's ... bring brenningly biddeth'. The style of John Bunyan's *Pilgrim's Progress* (1675). Begins the fourth month of gestation.

Parody 10 (lines 474–528): 'So Thursday sixteenth ... queerities no telling how'. The style of late-seventeenth-century diarists, such as (especially) Samuel Pepys and John Evelyn. Begins fifth month of gestation.

Parody 11 (lines 529–81): 'With this came up ... sent the ale purling about'. The style of Daniel Defoe, pamphleteer and novelist (*c.* 1661–1731). Begins sixth month of gestation.

Parody 12 (lines 581–650): 'An Irish bull in an ... A man's a man for a' that'. The style of Jonathan Swift, especially *A Tale of a Tub*.

Parody 13 (lines 651–737): 'Our worthy acquaintance ... larum in the antechamber'. Style of Joseph Addison's and Henry Steele's *Tatler* and *Spectator* (1709–12). Begins seventh month of gestation.

Parody 14 (lines 738–98): 'Here the listener who ... of our store of knowledge'. Style of Laurence Sterne, especially his *Sentimental Journey through France and Italy* (1768).

Parody 15 (lines 799–844): 'Amid the general vacant hilarity ... on with a loving heart'. Style of Oliver Goldsmith (1728–74).

Parody 16 (lines 845–79): 'To revert to Mr Bloom ... the Supreme Being'. The style of eighteenth-century essayists, especially Edmund Burke and Samuel Johnson. Begins eighth month of gestation.

Parody 17 (lines 880–904): 'Accordingly he broke his mind ... feather laugh together'. The style of Richard Brinsley Sheridan (1751–1816), Irish-born dramatist and politician. The last two sentences may be a further parody of Samuel Johnson.

Parody 18 (lines 905–41): 'But with what fitness ... acid and in-operative'. The style of the unidentified eighteenth-century satirist, Junius.

Parody 19 (lines 942–1009): 'The news was imparted ... what God has joined'. Style of Edward Gibbon (1737–94), sceptic and rational-ist historian of the Roman empire.

Parody 20 (lines 1010–37): 'But Malachias' tale ... Murderer's ground'. The style of Horace Walpole's Gothic novel *The Castle of Otranto* (1764). Obviously, John Millington Synge is also parodied in this passage and Joseph Sheridan Le Fanu's *The House by the Church-yard* may also be involved.

Parody 21 (lines 1038–77): 'What is the age ... Leopold was for Rudolph'. The style of Charles Lamb (1775–1834), essayist.

Parody 22 (lines 1078–109): 'The voices blend and fuse ... the fore-head of Taurus'. The style of Thomas De Quincey (1785–1859), English Romantic writer.

Parody 23 (lines 1110–73): 'Francis was reminding ... from the second constellation'. Style of the *Imaginary Conversations* of Walter Savage Landor (1775–1864), English essayist. Begins ninth month of gestation.

Interlude (lines 1174–97): 'However, as a matter of fact ... about the place'. A paragraph that prefigures the style of the 'Eumaeus' episode, which is still to come. It is a gross insult to Thomas Babington, Lord Macaulay, whose style is parodied in the next paragraph, to suggest that he has anything to do with this passage. Bloom *has* in fact been wool-gathering; the style of 'Eumaeus', as we shall see, is perfectly fit-ted to such an activity.

Parody 24 (lines 1198–222): 'The debate which ensued ... yet to come'. The style of Thomas Babington, Lord Macaulay (1800–59), English historian and essayist.

Parody 25 (lines 1223–309): 'It had better be stated ... it was delivered'. The style of Thomas H. Huxley (1825–95), scientist and rationalist.

Parody 26 (lines 1310–43): 'Meanwhile the skill and patience ... faithful servant!'. The style of Charles Dickens, novelist, especially the more sentimental passages of *David Copperfield* (1849–50).

Parody 27 (lines 1344–55): 'There are sins ... silent, remote, reproachful'. The style of John Henry Cardinal Newman (1801–90).

Parody 28 (lines 1356–78): 'The stranger still regarded ... in her glad look'. The style of the aesthete Walter Pater (1839–94), especially his autobiographical reminiscence, *The Child in the House* (1894).

Parody 29 (lines 1379– 90): 'Mark this farther ... the utterance of the word'. The style of English sage and art critic John Ruskin (1819–1900).

Parody 30 (lines 1391–439): 'Burkes! ... *nunc est bibendum!*'. The style of Thomas Carlyle (1795–1881), historian, reformer, Victorian sage. Also marks the birth of the child in the text's embryonic development.

Parody 31 (lines 1440–591): 'All off for a buster ... Just you try it on'. The breakdown of style into a babel of conflicting voices; in Joyce's words in his letter to Budgen: 'a frightful jumble of Pidgin English, nigger English, Cockney, Irish, Bowery slang and broken doggerel.' This is the afterbirth.

COMMENTARY

'Oxen of the Sun' is by general agreement the most difficult episode of *Ulysses*. For many readers, the episode's extraordinary technique is just too much; it seems to come from out of the blue and to be there solely as an obstacle to reading. Just how difficult a reader finds it depends greatly on the degree to which the reader has taken on board the techniques of the preceding episodes. If one regards the expansionary passages of 'Cyclops', or the technique of the first part of

'Nausicaa', as just so many interferences with the development of the story, aspects to be ignored or skipped over while pursuing the adventures of Bloom, then this episode is indeed likely to prove impossible. If, though, these aspects of the preceding episodes have been given their full weight in the reading process, then 'Oxen' will not seem quite so formidable.

The previous two episodes have featured parasitic, secondary modes of writing, based on, or derived from, some of the dominant discourses of Edwardian Dublin: high-flown literary effusions, journalism, would-be 'translations' in the case of 'Cyclops'; sentimental 'romantic' fiction in the case of 'Nausicaa'. 'Oxen' takes the procedure just a step further, basing its many styles on the history of foregoing English prose.

The crucial difference here is that it is no longer possible to separate out what is being told from the telling. In the case of 'Cyclops' it would have been possible to skip the interpolations; in the case of 'Nausicaa' it would have been possible to treat the style of the first part as a semi-transparent screen (appropriately enough) through which it is quite possible to discern enough of the story to maintain the narrative momentum. With 'Oxen', these luxuries are no longer available. The 'story' has disappeared almost completely behind a screen far denser than any put up so far. It is, in fact, still going on, but it is almost invisible. The exercise I have performed above in attempting a summary is more artificial than at any other point in the book.

Part of the difficulty in reading this episode lies in the unfamiliarity, for most readers, of the passages being parodied. A parody works properly only if the style or passage which it is parodying is reasonably familiar; otherwise it will seem an empty exercise. Perhaps part of the point (some critics would certainly think so) is this very emptiness; 'Oxen' may be in part a comment on a culture where such prose has passed out of knowledge. An aspect of the problem is that prose is not studied or taught with anything like the same intensity as poetry; the dominance of fiction as the only recognised literary prose mode means that genres such as essay, satire, diary, travel, philosophical reflections, rhetoric, history, etc., are not even regarded as proper objects of literary study. And since it is precisely these modes that are principally parodied in 'Oxen', the inherent difficulty is compounded. The parodies themselves, indeed, sometimes lose touch with their apparent object of parody, and, as mentioned already, begin to intermingle phrases and words from different sources.

Various critical efforts have been made to account for the sheer oddness of 'Oxen'. Matters are in some ways complicated, not helped, by Joyce's own comments. Are we to take seriously his claim that the history of English prose is being presented as a parallel to the growth of the foetus in the womb? This is not to suggest that he is setting out to deceive, but it is to question the degree of seriousness to be attached to the enterprise called *Ulysses* from a certain point on. So disoriented have some critics become that they have resorted to the desperate measure of positing 'another' 'narrator' (all the words here have to be in quotation marks) who is recounting this episode. This is a figure (often called the Arranger) to whom the writing of the episode is, as it were, entrusted; he (assuming it's a he; 'it' might be more appropriate) finds the actual story being told something of a bore by now, and is far more interested in the special effects that his unparalleled verbal skills can produce. The 'official' subject, then, of each episode is merely a pretext, barely worth a glance before the Arranger takes off on another linguistic flight. (He is, for instance, the Noman of 'Cyclops'.)

This, as I have said, is a desperate measure, the product, perhaps, of a certain critical moment when 'authors' in general were out of favour, indeed by definition dead. I do not think it is helpful or necessary to drag in another narrative figure to try to account for things that apparently defy explanation in any other way. The issue really is whether *Ulysses* can be held together in one concept, or whether we have to surrender to its obviously fissiparous tendencies and accept that it is so diffuse we even have to posit different narrators to explain its diversity.

Let us try another way. In contrast to an implied further narrator, we can more safely say that each episode in some sense narrates itself, that the narration is in keeping with the subject matter of the episode, whatever that may be. Applying this principle to 'Oxen', it can be said that its ultimate 'subject matter' is birth, the physical process of giving life. This is a matter of acute anxiety at least to Stephen; we have seen this anxiety already back in 'Scylla and Charybdis', where much of his effort was concentrated on putting down natural mother-hood, and indeed natural fatherhood, in favour of a mystical estate, an apostolic succession. We can see much the same operation in pro-gress here, in an even wilder form, with attempted denigrations of the Virgin Mary, and a wholly traditional effort to exalt 'life', as an abstract principle, as against the messy process of actual motherhood, and, behind that, of actual begetting.

This anxiety is not just Stephen's, however. It is shared, to a greater or lesser degree, by all the male company gathered in the room in Hol-les Street Hospital – and it is strange enough indeed to have such a body of men gathered in this inevitably female institution. It manifests itself in various ways: in Mulligan's case there is a curious passage in which he actually turns himself into a woman (lines 810–16); at another point, he expresses as his sexual preference 'a nice clean old man'. Mul-ligan, as we have seen in Episode 1, is *the* epitome of conventional maleness: an athlete, a hardened man of the world, etc. At some point, this excess of maleness tips over into its opposite; under the pressure of the Holles Street experience, this is what seems to happen.

Bloom, similarly, manifests ambivalent traits, though these are less surprising in his case. His sympathy for and interest in the travails of women in labour seem excessive, almost prurient. It is as if he envied women their lot and would like to share it. In this book, of course, where nothing is impossible, he does indeed become a mother in the next episode.

More generally, the mostly young men in the hospital all manifest a preoccupation with the physical processes of childbirth that verges on the neurotic. We do not even need Freud (though we have him any-way) to tell us that we make jokes mainly about the things that frighten us: sex, death, in this case childbirth. This ingrained tendency is amply exemplified in the young men's endless quasi-comic circling around this one fearful activity.

In such circumstances, it is perhaps more natural than it may first appear that the chosen technique for the episode – the parodies – should be as far as possible removed from its actual content. The literary parodies form as heavy a cover story as could be imagined for what is actually going on. In this sense, the episode *is* disjunctive, but the disjunction is integral, if the slight paradox may be allowed. The episode's form is the text's own anxieties, projected on a massive screen, the screen of the history of English literature.

Ultimately, I think we have to live with the reality of the Homeric parallel. *Ulysses* translates the slaying of the sun god's oxen by Odysseus's men into (to quote Joyce's dangerous letter to Budgen) 'the crime committed against fertility by sterilizing the act of coition'. This requires assent to the proposition that the young men are indeed blasphemers against a sacred process; that the first cry of the 'new-born' Stephen (remember he is the embryo that Bloom fertilised) is 'Burke's!', the name of the nearest pub, whither the entire party decamps, rather as they do after the recitation of Taylor's speech in 'Aeolus'. As in 'Aeolus', the mountain labours and brings forth a pub, the acme of Irish civilisation.

This should not be quite the last word, however. Whatever the official purpose of the parodies, they remain hugely enjoyable in themselves, once a reader has got used to this very special experience they provide. As in 'Cyclops', once again linguistic energies carry the day. This is not to reinstate the Arranger; it is, though, to accept that the mode of this book is now predominantly comic, and that nothing is allowed to interfere with that primary impulse.

BIOGRAPHICAL

Line 74.   *A. Horne*: Dr Andrew J. Horne, joint master of Holles Street Hospital in 1904.

94.   *O'Hare Doctor*: a Dr O'Hare was on the staff of Holles Street Hospital in 1904. He died later that year.

190.   *Lynch*: Vincent Lynch, who is based on Vincent Cosgrave, a friend of Joyce in his time at University College Dublin and subsequently, until, in 1909, he claimed that he had been intimate with Nora Barnacle before she took up with Joyce. He drowned himself in the Thames in London in 1927.

SELECT GLOSSARY

Line 1.	Deshil: from Irish *deiseal*, turning to the right, clockwise.
1.	Eamus: Latin, let us go.
19.	lutulent: muddy, thick.
25.	inverecund: immodest.
67.	sejunct: separated.
80.	eft: archaic English, soon.
81.	swire ywimpled: archaic, throat covered with a wimple.
81.	levin: archaic, lightning.
82.	welkin: archaic, sky.
84.	rathe: archaic, quickly.
86.	stow: archaic, place.
88.	townhithe: hithe, archaic, port.
95.	grameful: archaic, full of grief.
98.	algate: archaic, although.
100.	housel: archaic, Eucharist.
105.	wanhope: archaic, sorrow.
114.	unneth: archaic, difficult.
125.	yclept: archaic, named.
126.	couth: archaic, polite.
134.	cautels: archaic, caution.
134.	avis: archaic, opinion.
137.	mandement: archaic, command.
151.	nie: archaic, deny.
161.	halp: archaic, helped.
162.	apertly: archaic, openly.
165.	nist: archaic, knew not.
168.	alther: archaic, of all.
201.	red: archaic, counselled.
202.	aresouns: archaic, questionings.
220.	rede: archaic, advice.
222.	let: archaic, hinder.
223.	eke: also.

231. leman: archaic, mistress.

241. orgulous: archaic, proudly.

245. an: archaic, if.

246. *effectu secuto*: Latin, 'one effect following on another'.

246. peradventure: archaic, by chance.

259. pardy: archaic, by God.

264. maugre: archaic, despite.

270. akeled: archaic, cold.

294. *Omnis caro ad te veniet*: Latin, 'All flesh shall come to you'.

295. aventried: archaic, took into her womb.

297. *omnipotentiam deiparae supplicem*: Latin, 'the omnipotence in petition of God's mother'.

303. *vergine ... figlio*: Italian, 'virgin mother, daughter of your son'. The opening line of Canto 33 of Dante's *Paradiso*.

304. Piscator: Latin, fisherman.

306–7. *Parceque ... Dieu!*: French, 'Because M. Léo Taxil told us that it was the holy pigeon who put her in that rotten position, belly of God!'

307–8. *Entweder ... oder*: German, either ... or.

315. Almany: archaic, Germany. (Also mentioned in Episode 9, 'Scylla and Charybdis'.)

321. gasteful: obsolete, wasteful.

326. chode: obsolete, past tense of 'to chide'.

327. chuff: archaic, a clown.

327–8. got in peasestraw: archaic, born on inferior straw, hence (figuratively) illegitimate.

328. losel: archaic, scoundrel.

329. dykedropt: archaic, born in a ditch.

340. intershowed: 'demonstrated (it) among them'.

347-8. *Ut novetur ... mysterium*: Latin, 'That the sexual mystery of the entire body be known.'

353. suadancy: persuasiveness.

366. *Orate ... memetipso*: Latin, 'Pray, brethren, for me myself'.

383.   foraneous: utterly remote.

383–4.   Assuefaction minorates atrocities: 'Becoming accustomed to atrocities lessens their effects'. An instance of the heavily Latinate prose of Sir Thomas Browne.

387.   *ubi* and *quomodo*: Latin, 'where and in what fashion'.

396.   ossifrage: the osprey.

396–7.   the ubicity of his tumulus: the whereabouts of his sepulchre.

401.   *Étienne, chanson*: French, 'Stephen, a song'.

551.   *Mort aux vaches*: French, literally 'Death to the cows'; in slang, 'Down with the police!'

705–10.   *Talis ac tanta ... magnopere anteponunt*: Latin, 'So much and so great is the depravity of this age, O citizens, that our matrons much prefer the lascivious titillations of any Gallic half-man to the weighty testicles and extraordinary erections of Roman centurions.'

728.   ovoblastic ... utricle: 'the gestation of the germ of the embryonic egg in the vesicle of the prostate gland'; in other words, male pregnancy.

776.   *marchand de capotes*: French, literally 'seller of cloaks'. In French slang, *capote* can mean condom.

777.   *livre*: French, 'a pound'.

780.   *avec lui*: French, 'with him'.

781.   *ventre biche*: a French oath, figuratively 'on my word'.

783.   *sans blague*: French, 'no lie'.

792.   *il y a deux choses*: French, 'there are two things'.

821.   *enceinte*: French, 'pregnant'.

850.   *mots*: French, 'words'.

889.   dundrearies: long side-whiskers without a beard.

951.   abigail: slang for lady's maid.

962.   acardiac: lacking a heart.

962.   *foetus in foetu*: medical Latin, 'foetus at birth'.

963.   aprosopia: incomplete development of face.

963.   agnathia: imperfect development of jaws.

973. *Sturzgeburt*: German, 'sudden birth'.

988. plasmic memory: in theosophy, the total memory of the soul's various incarnations.

1029–30. *Lex talionis*: Latin, the law of exact retribution.

1070. *(fiat!)*: Latin, 'let there be!'

1092. *Lacus Mortis*: Latin, 'The Lake of the Dead'.

1115. Bous Stephanoumenos: Greek, 'Bull soul of Stephen'.

1121. Stephaneferos: Greek, 'Stephen the garland bearer'.

1238. *Nisus formativus*: Latin, 'the formative level'.

1239. *succubitus felix*: Latin, 'the fertile one who lies under'.

1251. Kalipedia: Greek, the study of beauty.

1310. *accouchement*: French, 'delivery'.

1378. *(alles Vergängliche)*: German, 'all that is transitory'.

1408. *coelum*: Latin, 'heaven'.

1409. cessile: obsolete, 'yielding'.

1412. farraginous: rare, 'formed of mixed materials'.

1431–2. *Deine Kuh ... des Euters*: German, 'Thou art milking thy cow [named] Affliction. Now thou art drinking the sweet milk of her udder.'

1439. *Per deam ... bibendum!*: Latin, 'By the goddesses Partula [goddess of birth] and Pertunda [presided over loss of virginity] now we must drink!'

1445–6. *Benedicat vos ... et Filius*: Latin, 'May almighty God bless you, the Father and Son.'

1449. *En avant, mes enfants!*: French, 'Forward, my lads!'

1453. *Ma mère m'a mariée*: French, 'My mother married me [to a husband]'. Part of a bawdy song.

1457. *Silentium!*: Latin, 'Silence!'

1467. *übermensch*: German, 'superman'.

1494. *Les petites femmes*: French, 'The little women'.

1522. Horryvar, mong vioo: Distorted French from Lenehan, *Au revoir, mon vieux*: 'Goodbye, old man'.

1533–4. *Nos omnes ... posterioria nostria*: Latin, 'We will all drink green poison [absinthe] and the devil take the hindmost'.

1536. *Bonsoir la compagnie*: French, 'Good evening, all!'

1545. *à la vôtre!*: French, 'Your [health!]'

1574. *Laetabuntur in cubilibus suis*: Latin, 'Let them sing aloud upon their beds'. From Psalm 149.

1576. *Ut implerentur scripturae*: Latin, 'That the scriptures may be fulfilled'.

II
[15 · Circe]

Time: 12 midnight
Location: Bella Cohen's brothel, 82 Tyrone Street
(now Railway Street), in the red-light district of Dublin, between
Talbot Street and the present Sean MacDermott Street Lower.

SUMMARY

Note: Because of the length and confusing nature of the Nighttown episode, I have divided this summary into nine parts. These divisions are entirely artificial, and do not relate to any scheme of the author's.

Part 1 (lines 1–674): Arrival in Nighttown

We are at the Mabbot Street (now Corporation Street) entrance to Nighttown, the name Joyce gave to Dublin's brothel quarter, having derived it from the term for a Dublin newspaper's late shift. The scene is one of squalor and degradation. Cissy Caffrey and Edy Boardman, surprisingly enough, last seen on Sandymount Strand, appear to be part of it. Two British soldiers, Private Carr and Private Compton, make their way into the area. They are followed by a very drunk Stephen and by Lynch, who have journeyed by train from Westland Row to Amiens Street station. Stephen, despite or maybe because of his drunkenness, is attempting to make an obscure philosophical point about the primacy of gesture over any other form of expression.

Bloom is at the Talbot Street side of Nighttown. He has lost sight of Stephen and Lynch, whom he had followed (he had missed the stop and was carried on by the train to the next station). He has purchased bread and chocolate, but wants more to eat. He rushes into Olhausen's, the pork butchers, just as its shutters are coming down and emerges clutching a parcel containing a pig's crubeen in one hand, and a parcel holding a sheep's trotter in the other.

Bloom has rushed to keep up with the two young men and is now doubled up by a stitch. Darting to cross the road in order to keep Stephen in his sights, he is nearly knocked down by a corporation sand-strewer and receives a rude comment from the driver. In the first definite fantasy experience, Bloom is accosted by a sinister nameless figure who speaks in Irish and refers to 'the password'. Bloom decides he is a 'Gaelic league spy', sent by the citizen. Tommy and Jacky Caffrey run past.

Then, in the first fairly extended fantasy sequence, Bloom encounters first his father, Rudolph, and then his mother, Ellen, both of whom, despite the drawback of being dead, reproach him for wasting his substance among strangers. These are followed by a more alarming apparition, of someone who is very much alive, his wife Molly. She is in Eastern attire (Bloom has dreamt of her in Turkish slippers and breeches the night before) and is conveniently if improbably conveyed by a camel. Bloom naturally addresses her as 'Molly', and is told that the correct form of address is 'Mrs Marion' from now on, a foretaste of the huge humiliations Bloom will endure later on. She mocks him ('Poldy' as she habitually calls him) for his staid, 'stick in the mud' qualities and saunters off.

Bloom is accosted by a bawd, offering him a fresh maidenhead, and then, in brief fantasy, by two young women he has had sexual relations of a sort with, Bridie Kelly, the first prostitute he ever encountered, and Gerty MacDowell, who first tells him she hates him and then that she loves him. A more substantial apparition follows: Mrs Breen, sans husband. Mrs Breen first coyly reproaches him for being found in a quarter like this; Bloom pretends he is engaged in rescuing fallen women. Later, however, Mrs Breen becomes much more friendly; they even engage in mutual criticism of Molly and Bloom reproaches her for choosing to marry Denis Breen rather than him. Just as relations between them seem likely to get even warmer, Mrs Breen fades from his side.

Bloom forges on through Nighttown in quest of Stephen. From his reflections, recognisable as the 'Bloom style' to which we are accustomed, we learn that there was 'a scene' at Westland Row, presumably between Mulligan and Stephen. Privates Carr and Compton, meanwhile, are being brought to a bawdyhouse in Purdon Street (now disappeared) by a drunken navvy.

Bloom realises that he was foolish to buy the food in Olhausen's; he does not really want it, and taking it will only make him 'pigsticky'. He gives it discreetly to a dog that has been following him. As he does so, two rain-caped members of the watch (policemen) pass by.

Part 2 (lines 675–1267): Encounter with the Watch

In 'reality', the policemen just proceed past Bloom without comment (he is doing nothing wrong, after all); in Bloom's inner mental world, though, they spark a massive fantasy of crime, disgrace and punishment. Somehow his feeding of the dog, who amusingly changes species at every mention, is linked to cruelty to animals and Bloom is instantly on the defensive. A card he offers in proof of his identity turns out to read, as indeed it does, Henry Flower, not Leopold Bloom. Martha, his secret correspondent, is one of a number of people who come forward to accuse him.

The scene rapidly turns into a courtroom trial, complete with judge, jury and counsel. Philip Beaufoy, author of *Matcham's Masterstroke*, comes forward to accuse Bloom of plagiarism; Mary Driscoll, the servant-girl Bloom apparently tried to seduce, comes forward to testify against him. He is also accused of defecating in public into a plasterer's bucket. J. J. O'Molloy, barrister, acts as Bloom's counsel and defends him, citing hereditary weakness as a partial explanation of his misdeeds. However, three society ladies, Mrs Yelverton Barry, Mrs Bellingham and the Honourable Mrs Mervyn Talboys, accuse him of several indecent proposals and activities and threaten him with thrillingly sadistic punishments. Davy Stephens, the newspaper vendor, delivers a journal containing the names and addresses of all the cuckolds of Dublin, among whom Bloom is obviously one. Canon O'Hanlon and the other priests of 'Nausicaa' confirm it; the jury, which includes Noman, the narrator of 'Cyclops', are quite convinced. Bloom is sentenced to be hanged. At the last moment, however, the dog he has been feeding metamorphoses into Paddy Dignam, who confirms that Bloom was indeed at his funeral that morning, rather than planting a bomb as has been claimed. Dignam, in a strikingly grotesque passage, then retreats underground whence he had come. This seems to break the spell and 'All recedes.'

Part 3 (lines 1268–1957): Encounter with Zoe

Bloom presses on through the fog. He hears sad piano music coming from a lighted house and stops, suspecting that Stephen may be there. Zoe Higgins, an English prostitute, comes down the steps and tells him that this is Mrs Cohen's brothel, in Tyrone Street. Zoe puts her hand into Bloom's left trouser pocket and takes out his shrivelled potato, given to him by his mother to ward off bad fortune. Zoe takes it, so Bloom is deprived of his talisman. Zoe asks for a cigarette and Bloom lewdly replies that the mouth can be engaged in better things than smoking. Urged ironically by Zoe to 'make a stump speech of it', Bloom does exactly that and the episode glides into fantasy again. He launches into an impassioned oration proposing many of his pet projects, such as running a tramline from the cattle market to the river, and is acclaimed by the populace.

A vast procession of Ireland's dignitaries comes to honour Bloom. He is rapidly promoted from alderman to emperor-president and king-chairman of Ireland. The house in which he was born is to be adorned with a commemorative plaque and streets are to be renamed in his honour. At the height of his glory he proclaims 'the new Bloomusalem in the Nova Hibernia of the future.' He holds a 'Court of Conscience', administering justice and solving the problems brought to him by citizens. However, voices begin to be raised against him, notably that of Alexander J. Dowie, in something of a repeat of the previous fantasy, and Bloom calls medical evidence on his behalf. This is indeed surprising: it turns out that Bloom, 'a finished example of the new womanly man', is about to have a baby. He gives birth to no fewer than eight. Even this achievement does not save him from general opprobrium and by general request Lieutenant Myers of the Dublin Fire Brigade sets fire to Bloom. However, he dies a martyr's death, lamented by the Daughters of Erin.

Part 4 (lines 1958–2742): In the Brothel – Virag

Zoe brings Bloom into the brothel. In the main parlour are Stephen, Lynch, and two more prostitutes called Kitty Ricketts and Florry Talbot. Light comes from a chandelier lit by a stuttering gas jet; a moth is flying round and round it. The wallpaper pattern is of yew fronds and clear glades. Stephen is trying to expound to a sneering and sarcastic Lynch his theory of reconciliation of opposites and eternal return. A remark by Florry that 'They say the last day is coming this summer' leads to a prolonged mini-apocalypse, in which Elijah, in the guise of Alexander J. Dowie, obtains repentance and promises of

amendment from the three whores and Mananaun Mac Lir, merged
with George Russell, proclaims a theosophical epiphany.

The gas jet (an important determinant of the action in this episode)
fades again and Zoe adjusts it. Suddenly Lipoti Virag, Bloom's grandfather, emerges from the chimney flue and approaches Bloom. Virag's
preoccupation is entirely animal; he discusses the three whores in totally physical terms, as three objects of desire. He is in some sense
identified with the moth that is circling around the light. Stephen
meanwhile is having an internal dialogue, one half of him (Philip
Sober) telling him to ease up and save what money he has, the other
(Philip Drunk) encouraging him to carry on.

Mention by Zoe of a priest who had been in the brothel two nights
previously brings an anti-Christian rant from Virag, making scurril-
ous claims about Christ's parenthood – these have surfaced in various
forms throughout the day. Henry Flower, Bloom's alter-ego (Virag is
the Hungarian for 'flower'), appears, bringing a more romantic tone
to the proceedings. With a final jibe, Virag departs.

Florry suggests that Stephen must be a spoiled priest and Lynch
informs her that Stephen is a cardinal's son. At this point Stephen's
father, Simon, appears in the guise of a cardinal and recites some of
his favourite poetry. Bloom is alarmed at hearing a male voice in the
hallway outside and briefly wonders if it may be Boylan seeking additional satisfaction. He is relieved to hear the footsteps going down
the stairs. A 'firm heelclacking tread' is heard on the stairs and the
door opens.

Part 5 (lines 2742–3500): Bella

Bella Cohen, 'a massive whoremistress', enters. Once again, the episode slides into fantasy. Bella's fan starts speaking to Bloom and
instantly subjugates him. Bloom is compelled by Bella's ample foot
and bends down to lace up her boot. As he does so, he is fascinated by
Bella's heavy, dominant gaze. Bella metamorphoses into Bello, a harsh
male master. Bloom is completely subdued. Bello outlines a ferocious
programme of discipline and correction for Bloom, now meta-
morphosed into a maidservant. Many unkind aspersions are cast on

Bloom's manhood, and he is frequently reminded that a 'real man' is in possession in Eccles Street. Bloom (once again) is to be immolated on a suttee pyre.

The scene, however, shifts to a glade of yew trees (inspired by the yews and glades on the brothel room wallpaper). Bloom is confronted there by the nymph whose image hangs over his bed, the Calypso in the episode of that name. The nymph reproaches him with various sexual misdeeds, some of them committed in that very glade with the sound of Poulaphouca waterfall in the background, to which Bloom humbly confesses. However, as he half rises from his chair, one of his back trouser buttons snaps. This is an important moment, which a reader might well overlook, imagining it to be another part of the fantasy. In fact the snapping of Bloom's button is an epiphany that breaks the spell which Bella has cast on him and sets him free again.

Bloom then recovers his sang-froid and speaks to both Bella and the nymph with a contempt that is more than a match for theirs. The nymph proves to be a whited sepulchre; her plaster cast cracks and a cloud of stench emerges. Bella, too, is put in her place.

Part 6 (lines 3501–4004): Prelude to the Dance

Bloom retrieves his potato from Zoe, restoring to him his safeguard. It was the surrender of this precious item that left him so exposed to Bella's powers. Bella asks who is paying; Stephen offers to do so, but when there is a slight shortfall Bloom steps in and makes up the difference (Bloom contributes ten shillings and Stephen one pound). Stephen has trouble minding his money and Bloom offers to take care of it for him; indifferently, Stephen hands it over. Zoe starts to read the visitors' palms; something she reads on Stephen's palm alarms her, but on Bloom's advice she does not indicate what this is. She then reads Bloom's. She refers to 'henpecked husband' and whispers something to Florry. They both giggle, leading Bloom to believe that his cuckoldry has been discovered via his palm. This leads to an extended fantasy in which Bloom, an antlered flunkey, attends on Boylan as he arrives at Eccles Street to do his business with Molly. Bloom looks on through the keyhole while Boylan carries Molly around the bedroom.

Back in the real world, at Lynch's instigation, Stephen and Bloom jointly gaze into the mirror. Appropriately enough, the face of Shakespeare gazes back at them; he utters a few truisms and then metamorphoses into Martin Cunningham (who was supposed to resemble Shakespeare in appearance). Lynch mentions that Stephen has been in Paris, and he is urged by the whores to give them some 'parleyvoo'. Rather than speaking in French, Stephen does a mechanical, jerky English-French: this is French directly translated into English without grammatical modification, all about sinful Paris and its scandalous pleasures. He suddenly remembers his dream of the previous night, the street of harlots and the red carpet (in 'Proteus'), and realises this is the place, though without the red carpet. Stephen shouts his defiance to all who would break his spirit, and calls, like Icarus, on his father for aid. In response, his actual father, Simon Dedalus, arrives in the guise of a bird, as Daedalus of course did to Icarus. He makes encouraging noises, but is as little real help to Stephen as Daedalus could be to Icarus, who had flown too close to the sun.

The pastoral scene depicted on the wallpaper becomes a countryside through which a fox, which has buried its grandmother under a holly bush, is being pursued. This turns into a race, won by a riderless dark horse. Last of all is Garret Deasy, the schoolmaster, on Cock of the North.

Outside in the real Tyrone street, meanwhile, Privates Carr and Compton pass by, singing 'My Girl's a Yorkshire Girl'. This appeals to Zoe, who actually is a Yorkshire girl, and she calls for a dance.

Part 7 (lines 4005–313): The Dance

A couple of coins are inserted into the brothel's pianola; 'My Girl's a Yorkshire Girl' begins in waltz time. Stephen and Zoe waltz around. The dance, directed by Professor Maginni, dancing master, grows wilder and more frantic. The girls from Ponchielli's *Dance of the Hours* participate. Zoe drops out, being giddy, and Stephen continues with Florry, then with Kitty. All participate in the wild finale: Bloom with Bella, Kitty with Lynch, Florry with Zoe, and Stephen performing spectacular leaps and twirls on his own. At the climax the couples fall aside. Stephen halts suddenly, the room spins around him, he sees stars flying spaceward.

His mother appears to him, emaciated, in grave-clothes, with a torn bridal veil, her face worn and noseless, a ghastly apparition from beyond the grave. She gently reproaches him for his apostasy and prays earnestly for his repentance. She also, though, warns him to beware 'God's hand'. She prays God to have mercy on him. Stephen is beside himself with anguish and desperation at this manifestation; he rejects his mother's calls and engages in bitter recriminations with her. The others in the room notice his distressed condition, though of course they are not privy to this internal dialogue. In a frenzy, Stephen raises his ash-plant, and invoking the name of the sword of Wagner's hero, Siegfried, he strikes the chandelier. He then rushes out of the room. An angry Bella claims compensation for the damage to the light; Bloom rejects her demand for ten shillings and after some haggling gives her one shilling. He also claims mysterious knowledge of her son in Oxford (in fact he had heard one of the whores mention this), leaving Bella dumbfounded.

Part 8 (lines 4313–920): The Assault

Bloom rushes out of the brothel in pursuit of Stephen. He is pursued (in fantasy) by almost every character encountered in the book so far; they raise a hue and cry against him. At the corner of Beaver Street he comes upon a knot of people surrounding some quarrelling figures: Privates Carr and Compton on the one side, and Stephen on the other. Private Carr claims that Stephen has insulted his girlfriend, Cissy Caffrey; Stephen, vaguely aware that his hand is hurting him, is unclear of what exactly he is being accused of. Cissy says that the soldiers had left her to urinate and that Stephen had accosted her. The argument twists and turns, as these things do; Bloom attempts to drag Stephen away in vain. Stephen makes an unfortunate remark about the need to kill the priest and king in his head; this is interpreted by the soldiers as an insult to King Edward VII of England.

As the soldiers get more and more heated, and Stephen gets more and more vague in response, a number of emblematic figures gather around, prominent among them King Edward VII in person and Old Gummy Granny, representing Mother Ireland. The conflict takes on a symbolic import. The clash becomes apocalyptic; at its climax, a black mass is celebrated over the naked, swollen body of Mrs Purefoy. Lynch and Kitty have been hovering on the edges of the crowd which has gathered; appealed to by Bloom, Lynch merely walks away, followed by a cry of 'Judas' from Stephen. The soldiers' threats become more and more terrifying; eventually Private Carr rushes forward and strikes Stephen, who instantly falls to the ground, unconscious.

At this point, and not before time, the two constables of the watch arrive. The soldiers initially try to justify their action, but then become alarmed and take off. Bloom is left in the awkward position of trying to explain the situation to the policemen. Just then he spots Corny Kelleher on the fringes of the crowd (his presence in Nighttown had been referred to earlier). Corny, as has already been intimated, is on friendly terms with the police; he is able to smooth the matter over and placate the policemen. They depart, leaving Bloom with Kelleher, who says he has been leaving two commercial travellers down in Nighttown. Kelleher has a jaunting car but declines to bring the still unconscious Stephen home when he learns that the assault victim is living in Sandycove. He departs, leaving Bloom alone with Stephen.

Part 9 (lines 4921–67): The Recognition

Bloom stands irresolute, then tries addressing Stephen. He first calls him 'Mr Dedalus'. Receiving no response, he bends closer to the prostrate form and calls 'Stephen'. Stephen stirs, mutters about a black panther, murmurs some lines from Yeats's 'Who Goes with Fergus?' and sinks into unconsciousness again. Bloom, mishearing, thinks Stephen is referring to a girl called Ferguson, and reflects: 'Best thing could happen him'. He mutters some words from the Masonic oath. Against the wall a vision of Bloom's dead son Rudy appears to him: Rudy, now aged eleven, is smiling and reading a book, but does not see Bloom and does not address him.

CORRESPONDENCES

In Book 10 of *The Odyssey*, Odysseus describes how he landed on the island of the witch-goddess Circe, after his grim encounter with the Lestrygonians. A group, led by Eurylochus, sets out to explore the island. They reach Circe's hall, where all the party except Eurylochus are transformed by Circe into hogs. Eurylochus escapes to warn Odysseus, who sets off for Circe's hall alone. On the way, Odysseus is met by Hermes, the messenger of the gods and a god himself, who gives him a magical herb, moly, to guard him against Circe's magic. When Odysseus reaches the hall, Circe's spells fail to work against the power of the moly; threatened by Odysseus, she releases his men from the spell, and swears she will not harm him. Thereafter, Circe entertains Odysseus and his men so well that they remain on the island for a year. She also counsels him to seek advice from Tiresias in the underworld.

In the Gilbert schema, Circe, obviously enough, is Bella, the brothel keeper.

STYLE

The style of the 'Circe' episode is that of an extended drama, complete with stage directions, descriptions of characters' appearance and attire at first entry and apparent 'speeches' by characters prefixed by their names. This, however, is just an appearance; the episode is not really dramatic, in the sense of being stageable as written (it can be, and has been, performed on stage, but it requires considerable adaptation). In fact, the action is far too wild to be staged in its raw form; the changes of scene and character are bewilderingly rapid, apparently arbitrary and improvised and would impose impossible demands on any staging. Cinema can manage a lot better, and the episode is better considered as cinematic than as dramatic: it is a screenplay rather than a script.

The cinematic form emerged as the episode was being written – it was not pre-planned. (The same is true for the techniques of most of the other episodes; they were developed in the writing. Almost all began in what we have called the initial style, and then, as Joyce wrote on, certain special techniques emerged almost of their own accord.) It thus clearly came to seem to Joyce the most appropriate way to convey this material, and it is worth exploring why.

The technique is paradoxical: this is the Freudian episode, the one that most thoroughly explores the deepest recesses of the unconscious and the world of hidden desires. By definition it is therefore also the most diffuse, the most unpredictable in its twists and turns, the most arbitrary. Objects talk, the dead arise and appear, if not to many, at least to Stephen and Bloom, gender is changed as easily as a hairstyle. The focus sometimes narrows to a small moth flying around a lampshade, sometimes widens to almost cosmic dimensions. It seems strange, therefore, to impose on it the most rigid written format possible: the format of a stage play, with its fixed stage directions, its soliloquies, its exits and entrances, etc. However, the episode's technique is not really so strange; Freud frequently writes of dreams as scenes, slow enactments of some underlying obsessional moment; he refers to 'the primal scene' and highlights the acutely visual quality of dreams, the way that everything that is in the dreamer's unconscious has to have visual representation.

This is what the 'Circe' 'stage directions' do as well: they highlight the visual aspect of the brothel scenario. Things just happen, without explanation. Why should Bloom's grandfather turn up in the guise of an amateur sexologist? No explanation is proffered within the text at least. We do in fact get some access to the characters' inner world, via some of the 'soliloquies': when, for instance, Bloom pauses on his way through Nighttown and, under his speech prefix, we get: 'Wildgoose chase this. Disorderly houses' etc., this 'speech' or 'soliloquy' is the old Bloomian stream of consciousness at work again under a new guise. There are a number of such moments; Stephen, too, has his share, although as usual in the book, except for 'Wandering Rocks', these internal disclosures are confined to him and Bloom.

Yet even these passages are presented in a very externalised way; rather than giving us the sense of immediate access to an inner life, which was so striking a feature of the early episodes, the minds of Bloom and Stephen are here mediated by the figure of some anonymous film director or screenplay writer, who puts their names at the top of a passage before their feelings are evoked. The predominant effect of the episode's technique is of externality. The impersonal stage directions mean the reader is on the outside looking in, just as in dreams, too, the dreamer is spectator of a scene in which he or she may well also be a participant. So the externality of the dream-play technique becomes, paradoxically, the most appropriate form in which to represent this most internal of episodes. This is one more disjunction the reader has to live with.

COMMENTARY

'Circe' puts both the main characters of *Ulysses*, Stephen and Bloom, to their most severe tests; both come through, if only just. However, to refer to their experiences as 'tests', while it is in keeping with the Homeric paradigm, is a little misleading. In this most psychoanalytic of episodes, one of the basic principles of psychoanalysis needs to be kept in mind: the thing most feared, most reviled, is the thing most desired. This is explicitly stated by Bella at the start of Bloom's female transformation: 'What you longed for has come to pass'. The episode does not really enact Bloom's subjection by Bella, or Stephen's by his mother: it enacts their subjections by themselves. Bloom only fantasises this subjection – and it is worth bearing in mind that in psychoanalysis the word 'fantasy' can apply to something dreaded as much as to something desired.

The episode marks the triumph of one strand of the technique of *Ulysses*: it is now truly impossible to distinguish reality from fantasy. This operation has been growing progressively more difficult as the book has proceeded; here, the two are genuinely indistinguishable. The situation is particularly ironic because, as Hugh Kenner has pointed out, stage directions are one mode that seems ultra-objective: they can hardly afford not to designate exactly what is going on at any given time. Here this ostensibly reliable, objective, impersonal form is being used for very different ends. Although the mode of externality is largely maintained, every now and then these 'directions' abandon their objective function and seem to become part of the ongoing action: for instance, at the moment when the dance reaches its climax and the entire room seems to spin around, the 'stage direction' also spins around, mimicking the state of Stephen's head.

More worrying, however, is the fact that the stage directions simply cannot always be trusted. A good example is the appearance of Cissy Caffrey and Edy Boardman early on in the episode. (Cissy reappears much later as the soldiers' girlfriend and announces 'I'm only a shilling whore.') Are these really the same Cissy and Edy we encountered on Sandymount Strand in 'Nausicaa'? It seems most unlikely; their diction and behaviour seem to have altered too radically in the interim. (The subsequent appearances of Gerty MacDowell herself and of Baby Boardman are less problematic, being more obviously fantastic.)

A relevant comparison can be made with Stephen's imagining of his visit to his Aunt Sara back in Episode 3, 'Proteus'. A reader might initially believe that this was actually happening, but, with a little experience of the way *Ulysses* works, would soon understand that Stephen is merely envisaging the likely scenario that would occur should he actually make his visit.

A more tricky case is Mulligan's evocation of an encounter with Haines in the previous episode, 'Oxen of the Sun'. It really does look for all the world as if Haines has arrived in the room in Holles Street and is addressing the gathering. Again though, further experience of the episode's development will make it clear that this is merely a scene that Mulligan conjures up ('Malachias's tale'); it does not happen in the 'real time' of the 'Oxen of the Sun' episode.

In 'Circe', however, one has to give up. There is no way of distinguishing surely between fantasy and reality; the text can go in any direction whatever. And this is independent of the two principal characters: Nighttown is a hallucinatory world, a dangerous and contested psychic territory into which both venture, but which exists and has these properties independently of them.

How then do they fare? Bloom's surrender of his apotropaic potato exposes him to the ordeal of Bella's brothel; but well before that Bloom has already entered the realm of fantasy. The most striking thing about his two extended fantasies before his actual entry into Bella's brothel is their polarised nature. In the first one, generated in response to the watch, Bloom is reduced to a prisoner at the bar, sentenced to be hanged; only the intervention of Paddy Dignam, happily returned from the dead, saves him. In the second one, generated by Zoe's 'make a stump speech of it', Bloom is elevated to 'emperor-president' of Ireland. It is true that later his subjects turn against him (not even his spectacular feat in giving birth to eight children saves him) but he achieves a martyr's immolation, with the Daughters of Erin worshipping him. In this sense Bloom's fantasies follow the logic of dreams, where the dreamer is frequently placed either much higher or much lower than in real life. Desires and fears are being acted out.

These, however, are fairly conventional fantasies, even if staged with unparalleled exuberance and wit. Bloom's experience after he enters the brothel is a fantasy of a different order. Without going too far into the psychological undergrowth, it does seem to me that Bloom, having lost the potato give to him by his mother, is somehow exposed to the return of the person whom he has resolutely repressed throughout: his mother herself. And this figure returns with a vengeance, in the person of Bella/o. Bloom's own mother is a subdued, barely visible figure, who seems to exert no pressure whatever on her son; Bella, on the contrary, is enormously visible, exerting enormous literal and metaphorical pressure on her subject.

Bloom's transformation into a woman in the course of this dominatrix/victim fantasy is one of the most contested and controversial aspects of the book. Much has been made recently of Bloom's alleged androgynous qualities; it is certain that he presents a less macho image than the bulk of the male characters in the book. What this passage, and some other parts of the book, show us, I think, is the *constructed* nature of these gender definitions; as if gentleness were necessarily a female quality and toughness necessarily a masculine one. (Molly is clearly much tougher than Bloom; is she therefore more masculine? Few would say so.) Bloom's female metamorphosis in this scene is part of a scenario of subjection; Bloom is playing a role, a role in which certain gender stereotypes are involved, which are cultural and have nothing to do with actual gender at all. Reversal of reality is of the essence of this scenario; the reality that Bella is female and hence culturally subject to the masculine Bloom has to be inverted. Such are the strange ways of desire, but no particular judgment on either gender is necessarily involved.

Bloom recovers his sang-froid, rescued, bizarrely but in a very Joycean way, by the snapping of his back trouser button (what *Finnegans Wake* will call 'a culious epiphany'). One of the issues that preoccupied Joyce, as his letters to Budgen show, was what would correspond to the Homeric moly, the plant that Hermes gives Odysseus and which protects him against the wiles of Circe. He calls Hermes 'an accident of providence', a reasonable description of the snapping of Bloom's button, and mentions 'indifference due to masturbation' as among the reasons Bloom survives. Although he is soon plunged into another painful fantasy, attending as a flunkey while Boylan has sex with Molly, Bloom from this point on becomes more and more assertive, dealing with the angry Bella and rescuing Stephen after his encounter with the soldiers. This is one trial Ulysses clearly overcomes, despite the tribulations (all half desired) he undergoes.

Stephen's survival is more problematic. The most constant element of Bloom's fantasy humiliations is the sense of play that invests them; he always has a role which he acts out: flunkey, maidservant, politician, criminal, emperor, even mother. He goes through a dazzling kaleidoscope of transformations, constantly achieving new incarnations, new embodiments. This is what really saves him. Nothing similar happens to Stephen. He remains who he is, even as the room literally spins around him. This means that he has far less freedom from his obsessions than Bloom; he is unable to convert them into any kind of play. Thus when his mother appears to him, her appearance and the things she says are comic, in keeping with the general economy of this episode, where every fantasy manifestation is comic: 'Get Dilly to make you that boiled rice every night after your brain work.' (The apparition of the recently dead Paddy Dignam was equally humorous.) But there is nothing comic about Stephen's reaction. He remains just as anguished as he was in the opening episode.

In his encounter with the soldiers, similarly, Stephen remains Stephen, even though the entire ambience around him is fraught with fantasy and symbolic conflict. He would see any role as an imposition; and this limits him in a way that is not true for Bloom. This is probably what Joyce meant when he said that he found Bloom a more interesting character because Bloom could change, while Stephen's personality was fixed. It seems to me that neither the striking of the chandelier nor being assaulted by the soldiers 'does anything' for Stephen; what does do something for him, perhaps, is Bloom's attention, but that happens later, if it happens at all, and has to be inferred, rather than definitively known.

A particularly striking aspect of 'Circe' is its curiously mechanical quality. Homer's Circe changed men into animals; Joyce's equivalent seems to be the changing of men into machines. The 'organ' of the episode is the locomotor apparatus, the nervous system which ensures that headless chickens can still run around. Much of it is informed by an instinctive or mechanical drive that is independent of any rational control: Virag is an embodiment of such a force, while Stephen's performance as a jerky marionette during his Parisian impression also seems entirely mechanical. And of course the dance that leads to Stephen's vision of his mother, complete with mechanical pianola, turns all those involved into automatons. 'Circe' is itself a sort of textual machine, seeming to run under automatic pilot – or else to be out of control.

A point of equilibrium amid all the turmoil is reached when this witches' sabbath of an episode (as Joyce also described it) arrives at its climax in the Black Mass celebrated in the midst of Armageddon, the battle that will bring about the end of the world. As contending forces cancel each other out ('the O'Donoghue of the Glens against the Glens of the O'Donoghue') Father O'Flynn celebrates the Black Mass, which is, of course, a perfect inversion of the conventional Mass: the voice of the blessed cry 'Alleluia, for the Lord God omnipotent reigneth', while the voice of the damned simply say the same thing backwards. 'God' equals 'Dog'. This is the balance, or equilibrium, of paralysis; not the least of the achievements of Ulysses is to go past this nineteenth-century dead end.

BIOGRAPHICAL

Line 48.   *Private Compton, Private Carr*: both names are based on British consular officials with whom Joyce clashed during his time in Zurich; the story is told in Richard Ellmann's biography.

412.   *Tom and Sam Bohee*: black and white minstrels, like the Christy Minstrels; the Bohees appeared in Dublin in 1894.

565.   *Mrs Joe Gallaher*: a friend of the Joyce family, a daughter of the Major Powell who is a model for Molly's father, Major Tweedy.

571.   *Marcus Tertius Moses*: a Jewish tea merchant who lived in Delgany, Co. Wicklow.

703.   *Signor Maffei*: a character in the novel *Ruby Pride of the Ring*, which Bloom looks at in Episode 4. It is based on a real novel, although Signor Maffei is Joyce's improvement on the original's Signor Enrico.

761.   *Lesurques and Dubrosc*: a celebrated case of mistaken identity, in which Joseph Lesurques was executed in 1796 for robbing the Lyons mail. It later emerged that the perpetrator was Dubrosc, whom Lesurques strongly resembled. Dubrosc was guillotined in his turn. A play was based on the incident.

895.   *George Fottrell*: clerk of the crown and peace, Sessions House, Green Street.

1013.   *Mrs Yelverton Barry*: derives her name from Barry Yelverton, Baron Avonmore (1736–1805), politician, judge and orator.

1025.   *Mrs Bellingham*: probably linked to Edward Bellingham, fifth Baron Bellingham.

1122.   *Davy Stephens*: best-known Dublin newspaper delivery man; also appears in Episode 7, 'Aeolus'.

1162.   *recorder*: Sir Frederick Falkiner (1831–1908), recorder (chief judicial officer) of Dublin. Bloom spots him going into the Freemasons' Hall at the end of Episode 8, 'Lestrygonians.'

1173-4. *Long John Fanning*: based on Long John Clancy, sub-sheriff of Dublin in 1904. Fanning also appears in Episode 10, 'Wandering Rocks'.

1177. *Rumbold*: the hangman's name is based on Sir Horace Rumbold, the British Minister to Switzerland in 1918; he was involved in Joyce's quarrel with the British representatives in Zurich. Also mentioned in Episode 12, 'Cyclops'.

1279. *Zoe Higgins*: apparently fictional.

1285. *Mrs Mack*: a well-known brothel keeper, who had two establishments at 85 and 90 Tyrone Street.

1287. *Mrs Cohen*: Bella Cohen, less notorious than Mrs Mack, ran a brothel at 82 (not 81 as Zoe says) Tyrone Street. She was already out of the business by 1904.

1377-8. *Timothy Harrington*: an old Parnellite and lord mayor of Dublin from 1901 to 1903. A friend of the Joyce family, he wrote a letter of recommendation for Joyce on the writer's first departure for Paris in 1902.

1379-80. *Councillor Lorcan Sherlock*: deputy lord mayor in 1904; he became lord mayor from 1912 to 1914.

1655. *Chris Callinan*: a Dublin journalist, notorious for his malapropisms.

1711. *Father Farley*: probably Father Charles Farley S.J., St Francis Xavier's Church, Gardiner Street. Bloom remembers him in Episode 5, lines 332-3.

1714. *Mrs Riordan*: the 'Dante' of *A Portrait of the Artist as a Young Man*; the 'Cyclops' narrator mentions that she had stayed in the City Arms Hotel at the same time as Bloom and left him nothing in her will.

1726. *Hoppy Holohan*: mentioned in Episode 5, 'Lotus-Eaters'. He is also a character in the *Dubliners* story, 'A Mother'. He is based on a real person whom Joyce knew and whom he suspected of having had sexual relations with Nora Barnacle.

1740. *Theodore Purefoy*: fictional, but surname probably based on Richard Dancer Purefoy, former master of the Rotunda Lying-in Hospital.

1752. *Alexander J Dowie*: based on John Alexander Dowie (1847–1907), American revivalist preacher.

1818. *Mrs Thornton*: a midwife who lived at 19A Denzille Street. She delivered a number of the Joyce children, though not, apparently, James.

1906. *Mastiansky and Citron*: Julius Mastiansky, a grocer at 16 St Kevin's Parade, Portobello. He is apparently based on a P. Masliansky. J. Citron is recorded in *Thom's Directory* for 1904 as living at 17 St Kevin's Parade. The 'J.' is apparently a misprint for 'I.' (for Israel) Citron (1876–1951).

1910. *Mesias*: George R. Mesias, tailor, 5 Eden Quay.

1930. *Lieutenant Myers*: John J. Myers, commander of the City of Dublin Fire Brigade in 1904.

2050. *Kitty Ricketts*: apparently fictional.

2073–4. *Florry Talbot*: apparently fictional.

2304. *Lipoti Virag*: Bloom's grandfather; the name means in Hungarian 'Leopold Flower'.

3221–2. *M. Shulomowitz*: secretary of the Jewish library at 57 Lombard Street West.

3222. *Joseph Goldwater*: lived at 77 Lombard Street West.

3222. *Moses Herzog*: mentioned in Episode 12, 'Cyclops'. As previously noted, an 'M. Herzog' lived at 13 St Kevin's Parade, Portobello. Mentioned again at lines 4357–8.

3222–3. *Harris Rosenberg*: lived at 63 Lombard Street West.

3223. *M. Moisel*: lived at 20 Arbutus Place, near Lombard Street West.

3223. *J. Citron*: see note above, line 1906.

3223. *Minnie Watchman*: lived at 20 St Kevin's Parade.

3223. *P. Mastiansky*: see note above, line 1906.

3224. *Leopold Abramovitz*: properly Abraham Lipman Abramovitz, rabbi of the Dublin Jewish community, died 1907.

3326.   *Donald Turnbull*: lived at 53 Harcourt Street in 1904.

3326–7.   *Abraham Chatterton*: registrar of the Erasmus Smith High School in 1904.

3327.   *Owen Goldberg*: lived at 31 Harcourt Street in 1904.

3327.   *Jack Meredith*: John W. Meredith lived at 97 Haddington Road in 1904.

3328.   *Percy Apjohn*: fictional, although a Thomas Barnes Apjohn lived at 40 Brighton Square, Rathgar, next door to the house where Joyce was born.

3668.   *Father Dolan*: based on Father James Daly, prefect of studies at Clongowes during Joyce's time there. He appears in chapter 1 of *A Portrait of the Artist as a Young Man*.

4032.   *Professor Maginni*: already noted in Episode 10, 'Wandering Rocks'. His real name was Maginnis and he ran a dancing academy at 32 North Great George's Street.

4338.   *Mrs O'Dowd*: landlady of the City Arms Hotel, Prussia Street.

4341.   *sir Charles Cameron*: a distinguished Dublin doctor.

4342.   *red Murray*: Joyce's maternal uncle; worked for the *Freeman's Journal*; appears in Episode 7, 'Aeolus'.

4342–3.   *editor Brayden*: William Brayden, editor of the *Freedom's Journal*; appears in Episode 7, 'Aeolus'.

4343.   *T. M. Healy*: Parnell's principal opponent; later first governor general of the Irish Free State. Mentioned in Episode 7, 'Aeolus'.

4344.   *the reverend Tinned Salmon*: the Revd George Salmon, provost of Trinity College, 1888 to 1902.

4344.   *Professor Joly*: Charles Jasper Joly, director of Dunsink Observatory; mentioned in Episode 8, 'Lestrygonians'.

4348.   *Mrs Ellen M'Guinness*: pawnbroker, 38–39 Gardiner Street; mentioned in Episode 10, 'Wandering Rocks'.

4349.   *Mrs Joe Gallaher*: see note above, line 565.

4349.   *Jimmy Henry*: assistant town clerk; first appears in Episode 10, 'Wandering Rocks'.

4350.   *superintendent Laracy*: had been superintendent of the
          Hibernian Marine School, Grove Park, Rathmines.

4350.   *Crofton*: J. T. A. Crofton, worked in the Collector
          General of Rates office alongside John Stanislaus
          Joyce; mentioned in Episode 6, 'Hades', and appears in
          Episode 12, 'Cyclops' and in the *Dubliners* story, 'Ivy
          Day in the Committee Room'.

4351.   *Dan Dawson*: Dublin baker and minor politician;
          mentioned in Episodes 6 and 7.

4351.   *dental surgeon Bloom*: Marcus J. Bloom, 2 Clare
          Street, Dublin. Mentioned in Episode 10, 'Wandering
          Rocks' and Episode 12, 'Cyclops'. As Martin
          Cunningham confirms, the fictional Bloom has no
          relation to this real Bloom.

4354–5.   *Miss Dubedatandshedidbedad*: the Misses Du Bedat
          lived in Killiney.

4356–7.   *colonel Hayes*: Baxter Hayes, chief inspector of police
          for the Great Southern and Western Railway.

4357.   *Aaron Figatner*: diamond setter and jeweler, 26
          Wellington Quay. Bloom passes by his premises in
          Episode 11, 'Sirens'.

4358.   *Michael E Geraghty*: the customer who refused to pay
          Herzog in 'Cyclops'. An M. E. Geraghty lived at 29
          Arbour Hill.

4358.   *Inspector Troy*: the person the Noman narrator is
          chatting to at the start of 'Cyclops'.

4358.   *Mrs Galbraith*: mentioned by Molly later, in the
          'Penelope' episode. Apparently fictional.

4360–61. *Mrs Miriam Dandrade*: sold Bloom her underclothes
          in the Shelbourne Hotel, as he recalls in Episode 8,
          'Lestrygonians'. Mentioned by Bello during Bloom's
          subjection fantasy. Apparently fictional.

4612.   *Major Tweedy*: Major (or more likely Sergeant-Major)
          Brian Cooper Tweedy, of the Royal Irish Fusiliers,
          Molly's father. Apparently fictional, but he may have

some connection with Major Powell, father of Josie Powell, etc.

4684.   *Michael Davitt*: (1846–1906), organiser of the Land League and ally of Parnell.

4684.   *Justin M'Carthy*: (1830–1912), leader of the anti-Parnellite wing of the Irish Party.

4685.   *John Redmond*: (1856–1918), supporter of Parnell who became leader of the reunited Irish Party; supported Irish involvement in the first World War and subsequently was supplanted by Sinn Féin.

4685.   *John O'Leary*: (1830–1907), a Young Irelander and then a Fenian, he was deported in 1871, but allowed to return in 1885.

4695.   *The Reverend Mr Hugh C Haines Love*: combines Haines, the guest in the tower in Episode 1, based on Dermot Chenevix Trench, and the Revd Hugh C. Love, 'Father' Cowley's landlord in Episode 10, 'Wandering Rocks'. He was partly based on the Joyce family's landlord in Windsor Avenue.

SELECT GLOSSARY

Line 74.   *introit*: the entrance chant of the Mass.

77.   *Vidi ... Alleluia*: Latin, 'I saw water coming out of the temple on the right-hand side. Alleluia.' Part of the antiphon that accompanies the sprinkling of the altar with water during the Paschal ceremonies. Stephen continues with this antiphon down to line 98.

84.   *(altius aliquantulum) Et omnes ... ista*: Latin, '(with deep profundity) And all to whom that water came ...'.

98.   *(triumphaliter) Salvi ... sunt*: Latin, '(triumphantly) Are saved.'

122.   *la belle dame sans merci*: French, 'the beautiful woman
          without mercy'. A traditional phrase in Old French
          romances, the title of a poem by Keats.

122–3.   *ad deam ... meam*: Latin, 'to the goddess who gives
          joy to my youth'. A parody of the phrase in the introit
          of the Mass, spoken by the server, 'to God who gives
          joy to my youth'.

216.   *Bueñas noches ... esta?*: Spanish, 'Good evening, Miss
          White. What street is this?'

218.   *Sraid Mabbot*: Irish, 'Mabbot Street'.

220.   *Slan leath*: Irish, 'Health be with you' (goodbye).

257.   *Ja ... papachi*: German, 'Yes, I know, dear father.'

279.   *Goim nachez*: Yiddish, 'The proud pleasure of the
          Gentiles'.

289.   *Agnus Dei*: Latin, 'The Lamb of God'; in this case a
          medal bearing this image.

319.   Nebrakada! Femininum!: part of the invocation to
          obtain true love that Stephen had read back in Episode
          10, 'Wandering Rocks', line 849. In bastardised
          Spanish-Arabic, it may mean 'blessed femininity'.

351.   *Ti trema ... cuore?*: Italian, 'Does your heart tremble a
          little?' From Mozart's *Don Giovanni*.

355.   *Voglio*: Italian, 'I want'. From *La ci darem*, a duet in
          the same opera. Its proper pronunciation has been a
          source of anxiety to Bloom all day.

661.   *rencontres*: French, 'meetings, encounters'.

661–2.   *Chacun son goût*: French, 'Each to his taste'. Proverbial.

712.   *Leo ferox*: Latin, 'the fierce lion'.

722.   *Donnerwetter*: German, literally 'a thunderstorm',
          figuratively, 'damn'.

770.   Shitbroleeth: a mispronunciation of 'shibboleth', the
          password which the Ephraimites in the Bible (Judges
          12: 1–6) were unable to pronounce and so betrayed
          themselves.

916.   *pensums*: school tasks or lessons.

947.   *Prima facie*: legal Latin, 'at first glance', 'on the face of it'.

1020.   *La Cigale*: French, 'The Grasshopper', a comedy or a light opera.

1241.   Namine ... vobiscuits: distortions of Latin prayers used at Paddy Dignam's funeral earlier in the day. *Nomine*: 'in the name of ...'. Vobiscuits: *Vobiscum*: 'with you' (plural).

1333–4. *Schorach ... Hierushaloim*: Hebrew, 'I am dark but comely, O ye daughters of Jerusalem'. (From the Song of Solomon 1:5).

1369.   *Cui bono?*: Latin 'To whose benefit?', popularly, 'Of what use is it?'

1380.   *locum tenens*: Latin, 'holding the place', that is, a deputy.

1400.   *Mah Ttob Melek Israel*: Hebrew, 'How goodly are [thy tents] King of Israel', from the Book of Numbers 24:5.

1408.   *Kol Nidre*: Hebrew, 'All our vows', the title of a prayer said on Yom Kippur.

1444.   the curtana: a pointless sword carried before the sovereign at the coronation of the English sovereign.

1487–8. *Gaudium ... carneficem*: Latin, 'I bring you tidings of great joy. We have an executioner'. Parody of the formula used to announce the election of a Pope.

1499.   *Koh-i-Noor*: Persian, 'Mountain of Light'; the name of one of the largest known diamonds.

1507.   Selene: the Moon Goddess.

1530.   *Bonafide Sabaoth*: Latin cum Hebrew, 'True armies'.

1557.   *Morituri te salutant*: Latin, 'We who are about to die salute you'. The cry of the gladiators to the Roman emperor at the start of combat.

1623.   Aleph Beth Ghimel Daleth: the first four letters of the Hebrew alphabet.

1623.   Hagadah: Hebrew, the story of the exodus from Egypt.

1623.   Tephilim: Hebrew; tephilin (usual spelling) are little boxes containing verses from the Torah, which are strapped to the arm or forehead during morning prayers.

1623–4. Yom Kippur: Hebrew, the Day of Atonement.

1624.   Hanukah: the Feast of Dedication, marking the dedication of the new altar of the Temple in Jerusalem by Judas Maccabeus in 165 BC.

1624.   Roschaschana: Rosh Hashana, the Jewish New Year.

1624.   Beni Brith: Hebrew, 'Sons of the Covenant', a Jewish fraternity set up in New York in 1843.

1624.   Bar Mitzvah: Hebrew, 'Son of Command', the ceremony that marks a Jewish youth's coming of age.

1624.   Mazzoth: Hebrew, 'unleavened bread'.

1625.   Askenazim: the name for the Jews of middle and northern Europe.

1625.   Meshuggah: Yiddish, 'crazy'.

1625.   Talith: shawl worn by Jewish men during prayer.

1651–4. *Acid. nit. hydrochlor . . .ter in die*: Latin, 'dilute nitric acid and hydrochloric acid, 20 drops; bitters, five drops; extract of dandelion, 30 drops; distilled water, three times a day'.

1771–2. *sgeul i mbarr . . . gan capall*: Irish: literally, 'a story on the top of a stick [is like] a coach without horses'. Metaphorically, 'a pointless story [is like] a horseless coach'. This sounds like an Irish *seanfhocal,* but it is not.

1796.   *fetor judaicus*: Latin, 'Jewish stench'.

1827.   *Nasodoro*: Italian, 'Golden nose'.

1827.   *Chrysostomos*: Greek, 'Golden mouth'.

1827.   *Maindorèe*: French, 'Golden hand'.

1828.   *Silberselber*: German, 'Silver self'.

1828.   *Vifargent*: French, 'Quicksilver'.

1828.   *Panargyros*: Greek, 'All silver'.

1855.   *Leopoldi autem generatio*: Latin, 'This was the generation of Leopold'. Parodies Matthew 1:18, *Christi autem generatio*.

1868–9.   *et vocabitur . . . Emmanuel*: Latin, 'and his name shall be called Emmanuel [God with us]'. From Isaiah 7:14.

2089.   *Coela . . . Domini*: Latin, 'The heavens tell the glory of God'. An adaptation of the opening line of Psalm 19.

2093.   *Mais, nom de nom*: French, 'But, indeed'.

2094.   *Jetez . . . passe*: French, 'Sow the wild oats. Youth must pass.'

2121.   *Ecco!*: Italian, 'There!'

2159–60.   *Il vient! . . . primigène*: French, 'He comes! It is I! The man who laughs! The primal man!

2161.   *Sieurs et dames . . . jeux!*: French, 'Ladies and gentlemen, place your bets!'

2162.   *Les jeux sont faits!*: French, 'The bets are placed!'

2163.   *Rien va plus!*: French, literally, 'Nothing goes any more'; here, 'No more bets!'

2269.   yoghin: an adept in Yoga.

2269.   Occult pimander of Hermes Trismegistos: Occult Higher Being of Hermes the Thrice Great.

2270.   Punarjanam: 'A second birth' in theosophy.

2271.   Shakti: in Hinduism, the female energy in the universe.

2272.   Shiva: in Hinduism, the destroyer.

2288.   *pot*: French slang for a quick drink.

2304.   *basilicogrammate*: bastardised Greek: 'scribe of the king'.

2371–2.   *Argumentum ad feminam*: Latin, literally, 'argument to the woman'. A parody of the phrase 'argumentum ad hominem', meaning to discredit an argument by attacking the person who makes it.

2385.   *La causa è santa*: Italian, 'the cause is holy', from Meyerbeer's *Les Huguenots*.

2504.   *Ci rifletta. Lei rovina tutto*: Italian, 'Think it over. You ruin everything.'

2524.   *Zoe . . . agapo*: Greek, 'My life, I love you.' The refrain of Byron's *Maid of Athens*.

2553.   *Coactus volui*: Latin, 'Under compulsion, I desire.' A phrase uttered by Cashel Boyle O'Connor Fitzmaurice

Tisdall Farrell back in Episode 10, 'Wandering Rocks', line 1113.

2571–2. *Verfluchte Goim!*: Yiddish, 'Cursed Gentiles!'.

2583–5. *Qui vous a mis ... le sacré pigeon, Philippe*: French, 'Who has put you in that awkward position, Philip? It was the holy pigeon, Philip.' A variation on a dialogue which occurs in Episode 3, 'Proteus', lines 161–2.

2626. *Dreck!*: Yiddish, 'Rubbish!'

3228. *Shema ... Echad*: Hebrew, 'Hear, O Israel, the Lord Our God. The Lord is One.' A commonly recited Jewish prayer. Also cited in Episode 7, 'Aeolus', line 209.

3536. *Dans ce bordel ... état*: French, 'In this brothel where we keep our state.' Based on the refrain of Francois Villon's *Ballade de la grosse Margot*.

3546. *brevi manu*: Italian, 'short changed'.

3594. distrait: French, 'the distracted one', a phrase used about *Hamlet* back in Episode 9, 'Scylla and Charybdis', lines 118–20.

3640. *Dona nobis pacem:* Latin, 'Grant us peace', part of the *Agnus Dei* of the Mass.

3651–3. Hangende Hunger ... kaputt: German, 'Intense desire, questioning woman, finishes us all off'.

3865. *Et exaltabuntur cornua iusti*: Latin, 'And the horns of the righteous shall be exalted', from Psalms 75:10

3893. *dessous troublants*: French, 'disturbing underclothes'.

3894. *Ce pif qu'il a!*: French, literally, 'The nose he has'; figuratively, 'What a face he makes!'.

3896. *Vive le vampire!*: French, 'Long live the vampire!'.

3909. *pièce de Shakespeare*: French, 'play by Shakespeare'. Already used in Episode 9, 'Scylla and Charybdis', line 121.

3915. *double entente cordiale*: French, 'double cordial understanding'. 'Entente cordiale' is normally used in diplomacy; here it has a double meaning.

3915.   *mon loup*: French, literally 'my wolf'; figuratively 'my dear'.

3940.   *O merde alors!*: French, 'O shit then!'

4045–6.   *Tout le monde . . . place!*: French, 'Everyone move forward! Bow! Everyone to their place!'

4060.   *Carré . . . Balancé!*: French, 'Form a square! Advance by twos! Sway!'

4080.   *Avant huit! . . . Croisé!*: French, 'Eight [dancers] advance! Cross over! Nod! Exchange hands! Exchange sides!'

4090.   *Les tiroirs . . . Dos! dos!*: French, 'Form a middle rank! Women form a chain of hands! Form a basket! Back to back!'

4098.   *Boulangère! . . . Escargots!*: French, 'Bread-making!' (the hands form a kneading movement). In circles! Bridges [of hands]! Hobbyhorses! Twirls!'

4103.   *Dansez avec . . . Remerciez!*: French, 'Dance with your partners! Change partners! Present the little bouquet to your partner! Thank each other!'.

4120.   *Pas seul!*: French, 'Solo dance!'

4164–5.   Liliata . . . virginum . . . : Latin, 'May the lily-bedecked [throng] of glittering confessors . . . [May the chorus of rejoicing virgins] . . . An anthem first heard during the opening episode, 'Telemachus'.

4180.   *Epi oinopa ponton*: Homeric Greek, 'Over the wine-dark sea'. First uttered by Mulligan in Episode 1, 'Telemachus', line 78.

4227.   *Ah non, par exemple!*: French, 'Ah no, for sure!'

4228.   *Non serviam!*: Latin, 'I will not serve!'

4242.   *Nothung!*: the name of the sword of the hero Siegfried in Wagner's Ring cycle. In German, it means 'needful'.

4415.   *Enfin . . . oignons*: French, literally, 'Finally, those are your onions'; figuratively, 'this is your quarrel, not mine'.

4501.   *Bonjour! . . . dents jaunes*: French, 'Hello! The *old witch* with the *yellow teeth*.'

4508-9.   Werf those eykes . . . of gravy!: garbled German and
          Spanish, something like, 'Throw those disgusting ones
          to the ground at your feet, big grand pigs of
          johnyellows all covered in gravy!'

4576.   *ça se voit aussi à Paris*: French, 'This is also to be
          found in Paris'.

4591.   Soggarth Aroon: from Irish *Sagart a rún*, 'My beloved
          priest'. A standard catchphrase, and the title of a song
          by John Banim.

4618-9.   Mahar shalal hashbaz: Hebrew, 'Make haste to the
          prey'. Isaiah, 8:1

4621.   *Erin go bragh!*: Irish, 'Ireland forever!'.

4655-6.   White thy fambles, . . . dainty is: Elizabethan rogues'
          English, fambles, hands; gan, mouth; quarrons, body.
          This is first quoted in Episode 3, 'Proteus', lines 381-4.

4699.   *Introibo ad altarem diaboli*: Latin, 'I will go unto the
          altar of the devil'; a parody of the introit, the opening
          psalm that began the Latin Mass.

4730.   *Exit Judas . . . se suspendit*: Latin, 'Judas left. And
          went and hanged himself.' Based on words in St
          Matthew's gospel.

4737.   acushla: Irish, literally 'my pulse'; figuratively 'my
          love'.

III
[16 · Eumaeus]

Time: 1 a.m.
Location: the cabman's shelter at Butt Bridge, near the
Custom House

SUMMARY

Bloom gets Stephen back on his feet and tidies him up. Stephen expresses a desire for 'some beverage' (non-alcoholic) to drink and Bloom suggests repairing to the cabman's shelter at Butt Bridge. This is not far away, but Stephen's unsteady state, and their mutual tiredness, makes walking there rather difficult. Bloom decides to head to Amiens Street Station (now Connolly Station) in the hope of finding a carriage. They leave Tyrone Street via Beaver Street and head into Montgomery (now Foley) Street, reaching Amiens Street at the junction of the two streets. However, as no conveyance is plying for hire, the pair accept the necessity to walk to the shelter.

On the way, Bloom utters some cautionary words to Stephen about the dangers of dissipation with dissolute and exploitative companions. He also condemns the earlier 'desertion' of Stephen by all but one of his drinking buddies. '– And that one was Judas', Stephen replies.

Passing under the Loop Line bridge, Stephen notices a brazier burning before the box of a corporation watchman. He recognises the watchman as an old friend of his father's, called Gumley, and eventually remembers, as the reader may or may not eventually remember, that Gumley's present occupation had been mentioned much earlier in the day, in Episode 7, 'Aeolus'.

Stephen is greeted by an acquaintance called Corley. Corley is down on his luck and asks Stephen for a loan. Stephen, searching his pockets, finds his money is missing (he does not recollect having handed what was left of it to Bloom) but digs up a half-crown and gives it to Corley. Corley is also anxious to find a job and Stephen tells him that there will soon be a vacancy for a 'gentleman usher' (junior teacher) in a school in Dalkey (this of course is Stephen's own job, which he is going to resign). Teaching, however, is outside Corley's scope; he has noticed Bloom with Stephen and, having previously seen Bloom in Blazes Boylan's company in the Bleeding Horse in Camden Street, he asks Stephen to enquire of Bloom to enquire of Boylan, whom he knows to be a billsticker (or publicist), about the possibility of a job. (The episode's style is highly infectious.) Stephen, having rejoined Bloom, passes on this request and receives a predictably evasive answer; Bloom also expresses considerable scepticism about Corley's ostensible reason for needing a loan, namely to find a place to sleep for the night.

Bloom enquires about Stephen's own plans for the night; it becomes clear from this dialogue that there was indeed 'a scene' at Westland Row station involving Mulligan and Haines on one side, and Stephen on the other, and that following this event it will be virtually impossible for Stephen to return to the tower, even if he should want to. Bloom wonders if it is possible for Stephen to return instead to his 'father's house', but the mental image Stephen then conjures up of this abode makes it seem most uninviting. Bloom again issues warnings about Mulligan's unwholesome influence, but is unable to ascertain how Stephen views the situation.

They reach the cabman's shelter, and enter it while a group of Italians are having an animated argument about money round a nearby ice-cream car.

Bloom has previously mentioned to Stephen that the keeper of the shelter is rumoured to be Fitzharris, the member of the Invincibles also known as Skin-the-Goat. Their arrival attracts much curiosity from the occupants, a 'miscellaneous collection' of night-owls of various descriptions. Bloom orders coffee and a bun for each of them and these are duly supplied by the taciturn keeper.

Most of the inhabitants of the shelter have looked their fill at Bloom and Stephen, but one red-bearded man, who seems to be a sailor, continues to gaze. Bloom and Stephen have been discussing names and the sailor boldly butts in and asks Stephen what his name is. Stephen instantly tells him, disregarding a signal from Bloom that he should not do so. The sailor, rather remarkably, claims to know Simon Dedalus, Stephen's father; it turns out, however, that this is a different Simon Dedalus (the name is so common), a circus marksman.

Continuing on the theme of names, the sailor informs them that his name is D. B. Murphy, from Carrigaloe, in Queenstown (now Cobh). He claims to have a wife there whom he hasn't seen in seven years and Bloom can envisage the mariner's return to find another in his former place. The sailor tells them that he has arrived in Dublin that morning on the three-master *Rosevean*, coming from Bridgewater with a cargo of bricks. (This is the vessel that Stephen had seen sailing upriver at the end of Episode 3, 'Proteus'.) The sailor talks about his travels, and the many 'queer sights' he has seen.

Bloom, while not implicitly believing every word the sailor says, is nonetheless stimulated to recall his own wish to undertake a modest voyage 'by long sea' (around the English coast and up the Thames) to London sometime. He also has the idea of organising a concert tour of English seaside resorts. He further envisages the expansion of home tourism, wishing for greater access to such scenic areas as Wicklow and Donegal.

The sailor causes a distinct *frisson* among the company in the shelter by producing a 'dangerouslooking claspknife' to illustrate an anecdote about a killing in Trieste. Someone incautiously mentions the Invincibles (who of course used knives to kill Burke and Cavendish in the Phoenix Park) but the keeper of the shelter remains completely impassive. Bloom well remembers the killings, which caused a sensation at the time. An attempt by Bloom to prompt some reminiscences from the sailor about Gibraltar (where Molly comes from) falls completely flat and temporary silence descends.

Bloom muses very inconsequentially on the dangers and attractions of sea voyages; his main 'conclusion' is that someone has to do it, usually 'the other fellow', and the role of most people, himself included, is to support such events as Lifeboat Sunday.

The sailor begins to talk about his son in Cork, who has apparently followed in his father's footsteps and run away to sea. Scratching his chest (he believes there were lice in the vessel from which he has recently disembarked) he displays a tattoo of a young man's face with the figure 16 above it. The young man's name (he is now dead) was Antonio, and the sailor seems to have had a rather equivocal relationship with him.

A streetwalker looks in the door, causing great embarrassment to Bloom, who recognises her, having seen her already that day, and is afraid she will recognise him. To cover his confusion he picks up the late (pink) edition of the *Evening Telegraph*. Much to his relief the keeper makes her a 'rude sign' to be off. Bloom tells Stephen, perhaps pursuing his fatherly role, of the health risks attached to congress with this 'unfortunate creature'. Stephen replies indifferently that the real peril comes, not from her, but from those who would 'buy the soul.' Bloom, characteristically, would favour medical inspections and licensing of brothels.

The conversation, such as it is, meanders on to a discussion of the existence of the soul, with the term 'simple' as applied to the soul causing much confusion. Stephen intends the word in the scholastic sense (not containing any admixtures), while Bloom takes it up in the normal but utterly different sense of 'simple (uncomplicated) soul'. The two seem to diverge on the issue of the existence of God, but since Stephen is not seriously engaged in the conversation it is probably unwise to base too much on his apparent assertion of God's reality.

Surprisingly, perhaps, Bloom takes a dim view of temperance establishments such as the cabman's shelter; while admiring their philanthropic motives, he has a personal recollection of his wife being paid a pittance for her performance at one such premises. He is inclined to doubt D. B. Murphy's stories and has a suspicion that he may be an ex-convict. At the same time, and very characteristically, Bloom acknowledges that scenes such as the blood-chilling stabbing that the sailor has recounted do indeed sometimes occur. Some of it he is inclined to put down to national temperament, holding, for instance, that Italians are very given to such ghastly deeds. Stephen gives a general assent, citing the case of Dante and his impassioned love for Beatrice ('Miss Portinari').

Conversation in the shelter has meanwhile turned to shipwrecks, with a number of local cases being cited. The sailor goes outside to urinate and Bloom notices that while out there he takes a goodly swig of rum. (Alcoholic drink is of course barred in the shelter.) He then urinates noisily, disturbing a sleeping cabhorse and almost disturbing the sleeping Gumley.

Back in the shelter, the talk has turned to the decline of Irish shipping, and the difficulty in building up Ireland's maritime trade. The keeper, who, even if he is not Skin-the-Goat, is certainly an advanced nationalist, blames the British government for these problems and for many other Irish difficulties; he prophesies, however, that 'a day of reckoning' is approaching, and that the decline and fall of the British empire are close at hand. ('Her downfall would be Ireland,' he adds.) The mariner, who has now rejoined the company, voices great scepticism at this incredible claim, but the keeper holds steadfastly to his view, leading to some friction but no violence between them.

Bloom, too, doubts that the demise of the British empire is imminent: he is unimpressed by both parties to the debate. The keeper's language does remind him, however, of his earlier encounter that day with the citizen, and he proceeds to tell Stephen about it. They concur in deploring the violence that conflicting opinions, often very local and about very little, conduce to. Bloom, still stung by the citizen, proceeds to a general defence of Jews and advocates the importance of all working together for the good of Ireland. Stephen instantly opts out and, on Bloom pressing the point a little, declares that Ireland 'must be important because it belongs to me'. This remark greatly puzzles Bloom; he looks at the weary young man before him with concern, remembering many other promising youths who failed to fulfil their promise. He is also aware that his own behaviour has been uncharacteristic; his interest in Stephen has left him 'several shillings to the bad' but he reflects that he must be benefiting socially and intellectually from the unexpected acquaintance. He even thinks he could write a story, à la Philip Beaufoy, about the experience.

The final edition of the Evening Telegraph is lying on the table, and Bloom reads the account of Paddy Dignam's funeral, tickled to find Stephen Dedalus and C. P. McCoy, neither of whom was present, listed among the mourners, and nettled to find his own name given as L. Boom. Stephen inquires if Deasy's letter about foot-and-mouth has got in, and Bloom, to his surprise, finds it has. Bloom then reads the account of the Gold Cup race, still unaware that he had 'prophesied' the result to Bantam Lyons back in Episode 5, 'Lotus-Eaters'.

The conversation in the shelter has turned to Parnell; the widespread belief that he was not dead and would one day return, already voiced in Episode 6, 'Hades', is repeated by a cabman. Bloom does not believe it; he remembers being present when Parnell and his followers occupied the offices of an anti-Parnellite paper and recalls handing the 'Chief' back his hat when it was knocked off. Bloom's Parnellite credentials are solid.

The patrons of the shelter are all inclined to blame Mrs O'Shea for his downfall; Bloom ponders on the power of passion and the unpredictability of love. He mentions to Stephen his belief that Mrs O'Shea had Spanish blood and is surprised to be told that she was the king of Spain's daughter. (Stephen is thinking of a line in a poem by Padraic Colum.) Thus vaguely prompted, Bloom seizes the opportunity to produce a photograph of Molly and to enquire of Stephen if he thinks that she is a Spanish type. Bloom dwells on the charms of Molly's figure to Stephen in a manner which might well seem strange.

Returning to the Parnell–O'Shea imbroglio, Bloom reflects on the hypocrisy that attends comment on such cases in the public prints. He resents the remarks of the cabmen about the affair and the sense they project that they know all the whys and wherefores of it. His attention swings back to Stephen; he regrets that such a promising young man should waste his substance in Dublin's red-light district. The more immediate issue, though, is providing his young friend with something to eat. Bloom is astounded to find that Stephen has not dined all day; he wants to pursue the young man's acquaintance, perceiving a strange affinity between them (he believes that he as a young man shared the same radical political ideas as Stephen), but he is dubious about Molly's reception of this unexpected guest. He decides, however, to invite Stephen home to 'talk things over'. Bloom is hatching all sorts of schemes to profit by Stephen's acquaintance, many of them involving literature and music.

Bloom prudently pays, and the two leave the shelter, Stephen leaning on Bloom's arm. As they head northwards to Eccles Street they talk about music; Bloom again takes the opportunity to mention his wife and to laud her vocal powers. He tells of having heard Stephen's father sing Lionel's aria from Flotow's *Martha* that day and praises it to the skies. Stephen expresses his fondness for Elizabethan airs. They pause to avoid a horse pulling a corporation road-sweeper, and Bloom declares that his wife, a passionate lover of music, would be delighted to make Stephen's acquaintance. Stephen sings a snatch of an old German song, and Bloom instantly realises that the possessor of such a fine voice could have a very successful singing career. He resolves to issue a further hint to Stephen about Mulligan's untrustworthiness as a companion.

The horse contributes 'three smoking globes of turds' to the ground for its own road-sweeper to remove. The driver watches Stephen and Bloom as they walk up Lower Gardiner Street.

CORRESPONDENCES

In Book 13 of *The Odyssey*, Odysseus arrives in his own island, Ithaca. He has to go in disguise because the powerful suitors would kill him if they recognised him. Advised by Athena, he goes to the hut of the swineherd Eumaeus, one of the most loyal of all his field-hands. Eumaeus, even though he does not recognise his guest, treats Odysseus kindly and refuses to allow him go into the town to serve the suitors. In Book 16, Odysseus and Telemachus his son are reunited and they jointly plot the destruction of the suitors. Odysseus, again disguised by Athena as an old man, goes to the palace to carry out his revenge. On the way he is taunted, while unrecognised, by his goatherd Melánthios, who later attempts to aid the suitors. After the suitors' defeat, Melánthios is elaborately executed by Odysseus.

In the Gilbert schema, Eumaeus is Skin-the-Goat, the keeper of the cabman's shelter, Odysseus Pseudangelos (which can mean Odysseus Disguised as a Messenger or Odysseus the False Messenger) is the sailor D. B. Murphy; Melánthios is Corley.

STYLE

Of all Joyce's feats of style in *Ulysses*, 'Eumaeus' is the most extraordinary. Each stylistic variation in the later episodes of the book has presented a new challenge for the reader, a new textual system to come to terms with. Even though, with 'Circe', the adventures of Ulysses have formally come to an end, the reader's stylistic odyssey most certainly has not: the last three episodes are startlingly different, both from each other, and from anything preceding them, in stylistic terms. Odysseus may have returned to Ithaca, but there is no simple return to the initial style.

The most unexpected challenge for the reader, perhaps, is coming to terms with the narrator of 'Eumaeus'. This is one episode where it is, I think, appropriate to speak of a particular narrator who 'tells the story'. In his way (assuming it's a he, and it does seem that this person's principal context is the male Dublin world), this narrator is as distinctive a character as the anonymous narrator of 'Cyclops'. Of course, unlike the 'Cyclops' narrator, this one does not participate in the action, but in every other sense he is as all-pervading a presence.

This 'Eumaeus' narrator is a person whose only wish is to be helpful. He makes strenuous efforts to ensure the accuracy of all the information he conveys: if he thinks it may be wrong, he will tirelessly go back over it to try to get it right: 'No, it was the daughter of the mother in the wash kitchen that was fostersister to the heir of the house ...'. At the same time he is sadly aware of the possibility of error despite one's best efforts, and takes that into account as well: 'if the whole thing wasn't a complete fabrication from start to finish'. Similarly he feels a responsibility to history: narrating an incident involving Parnell he states: 'as a matter of strict history' with an obvious air of pride (the fact that the incident is entirely fictional is just one of the episode's ironies).

In his eagerness to be helpful, this narrator will quite often trip over words, and bring expressions together that logic might suggest should be kept apart: 'His questioner ... fell to woolgathering on the enormous dimensions of water about the globe ...'. There is so much information to convey, so many trains of thought to follow up. He is anxious to see both sides, or sometimes more, of a question; there is a good deal of 'on the other hand' and 'still' scattered about the text. Indeed, in his anxiety to be balanced and fair to all possible viewpoints, he will frequently drive a topic into the ground, leading to a *reductio ad absurdum* or an aporia that leaves a curious emptiness in its wake. In this respect 'Eumaeus' is the most Beckettian episode of the book: despite the narrator's eagerness to supply the facts, almost all the facts he supplies are open to question, most of all from himself.

Just like Homer, apparently, he has a great store of stock expressions to aid him in his task. Not all of these are entirely appropriate to the topic under discussion – Bloom's button, we learn, has 'gone the way of all buttons', something of a comedown from 'the way of all flesh' – but they are deployed with great earnestness and sometimes conjure up unexpected scenarios: 'ships of any sort, phantom or the reverse, on the stage usually fell a bit flat as also did trains'. At the same time, it would be a mistake to underestimate his level of culture (a caution that applies, *mutatis mutandis,* to almost all the characters of *Ulysses*): he is capable of quoting Latin tags from Virgil almost accurately (*haud ignarus*); he paraphrases a passage in *Paradise Lost*, probably without knowing it ('in every deep . . . a deeper depth'); he is, in his own way, something of a literary critic ('Albert William Quill wrote a fine piece of original verse of distinctive merit on the topic for the *Irish Times*').

Thus described, this narrator begins to bear a curious resemblance to Leopold Bloom himself: his values and attitudes, his worldview, his standard of education, the range of his knowledge, his general cast of mind, all seem very Bloomian. Reinforcing this impression is the fact that Bloom's is the only mind to which this narrator has direct access; all the other characters, Stephen included, are described externally, their states of mind inferred from their demeanours and actions. But Bloom's consciousness is as dominant in 'Eumaeus' as it last was in 'Lestrygonians'. (It is dominant for part of 'Nausicaa', but not for the entire episode, and although it is the most privileged consciousness in 'Sirens', a great deal more is happening there independently of him.) In this sense, among others, 'Eumaeus' is a homecoming, a return to Bloom, missing in stylistic action for so long.

Of course, Bloom's consciousness is not given to us in the interior monologue form with which we had become familiar: it is filtered through the narrator's rather special mode of discourse. Oddly, though, when Bloom speaks he speaks in exactly the same style as the narrator narrates: 'It is hard to lay down any hard and fast rules as to right and wrong but room for improvement all round there certainly is though every country, they say, our own distressful included, has the government it deserves'. That is Bloom talking, but there is nothing, stylistically, to distinguish this talk from the narrative surrounding it. All the other characters speak the way we would expect them to speak; only Bloom has this special idiom which does not correspond with his manner of speaking at any other time in the day. This continuity between Bloom's discourse and the narrator's is a powerful clue that the two are indeed closely intertwined and that Bloom's consciousness is a major determinant of this episode's style.

The concept of a 'Eumaeus' narrator who is in many respects very close to Bloom is preferable, as a way of accounting for the style of this episode, to the more conventional view that it represents the extreme tiredness of both Bloom and Stephen at this late hour of the night after a long and very active day. For one thing, the style is not tired; it is in fact extremely active, indeed tireless. Following its baroque twists and turns is one of the most challenging tasks a reader has to face. It is one of the most creative styles in the book, even if it often leads to an exhaustion of whatever topic comes under its purview. As the text itself very aptly puts it: 'the point was the least conspicuous point about it'.

It is also preferable to posit such a narrator than to argue that the style represents language set free, under the pressure of extreme tiredness, from any controlling consciousness. It is not clear why language should head in this particular direction, if set free, rather than any other. Ultimately, as Hugh Kenner says, the style of 'Eumaeus' continues the methodology of the 'Uncle Charles principle': Bloom's whole personality, not just the consciousness of a tired Bloom, is setting the tone for the style in which he himself is narrated.

COMMENTARY

In this episode, Bloom and Stephen are finally together. This is the point to which the book has been moving all day. Bloom's interest in Stephen has been palpable; Stephen, while showing no particular interest in Bloom, has certainly been exercised by speculations on fatherhood, clearly in a very personal way. Great things might therefore be legitimately expected by a reader; perhaps the book is going to have a point after all. Alas, to repeat the formula used above, 'the point was the least conspicuous point about it'. The great things do not manifest themselves. One of the reasons they do not is the fixity of Stephen's character; it is quite impossible for him to unbend to the point where he could actually relate to Bloom. The older man is very prepared to be friendly, but there is no reciprocation, nor could any be imagined.

The more interesting question is what motivates Bloom. His involvement, on the face of it, is fatherly; he is concerned about Stephen as a young man of promise who appears to have fallen among bad companions and as the son of a friend of his. All this is very commendable, but there are many other deserving cases that might equally attract Bloom's attention, and it is natural to suspect some self-interest in Bloom's concern. The oddness of Bloom's position emerges most clearly in his references to Molly. He is anxious to draw Stephen's attention to her, he tells Stephen that Molly would love to meet him (due to her interest in music, of course), he shows Stephen her picture, he even, apparently, refers to Molly's 'opulent curves' (though whether he actually says this is one of the many problems raised by the episode's narrative style: the phrase is taken from the novel Bloom has purchased that day, *Sweets of Sin*).

Bloom's activities strongly suggest that he would like to see Stephen replacing Boylan in Molly's affections. (Indeed, in the next episode, 'Ithaca', this intention becomes fairly explicit, as does Bloom's ultimate vision of a uniting of his daughter Milly and Stephen.) This idea would accord well with the Hamlet parallel: Stephen, as Bloom's spiritual son, would avenge the wrong done to his spiritual father, as the ghost of King Hamlet commissions his son to do – even if in this case the revenge would also entail another, but more acceptable, supplanting. However, Bloom's ambitious plan is never realised; it remains a perpetual possibility only in a world of speculation, an alternative ending that *Ulysses* does not pursue.

More certain is Bloom's sense of an affinity between them; what this is based on remains obscure. Mulligan, however, has already advanced one explanation for Bloom's interest that should not be ignored: homosexuality. (He does this at the end of the 'Scylla and

Charybdis' episode.) Is Bloom's interest more than fatherly? How would a young man feel at being invited back to someone's house by an older man he had just met? These questions are relevant; again, though, they cannot be taken any further than a certain point, since nothing happens in the text to shed any further light on them.

The main point is that the contact between Bloom and Stephen, such as it is, remains virtual, extremely tentative; many overtones can be read into it, but it is not going to give us dramatic meanings, either of a symbolic or a sexual nature. Critics have striven to find these, but they are reluctant to emerge. As is already clear, and as the next episode will confirm, nothing much happens when this unlikely duo meet. Stephen does in fact read a great deal into his encounter with Bloom, but he does so obliquely, implicitly, and it is best for us to approach the relationship obliquely and implicitly also.

The presence of the sailor D. B. Murphy in the episode is largely ironic. He is the closest figure *Ulysses* offers to a genuine mariner, a possible Odysseus. His role is made clear by his symbolic designation, Ulysses Pseudangelos, Ulysses the False Messenger. (The name comes from the title of a lost Greek play.) The sailor is a shadow Ulysses, a false portent. His presence indicates that literal correspondence – this character is a sailor; Ulysses was a sailor; therefore this character is Ulysses – is not the way this book works; Bloom is consciously referred to as a 'landlubber' in the course of this episode, but he is the true Ulysses of the tale. The sailor is given a bewildering, Homeric variety of appellations: 'friend Sinbad'; 'redoubtable specimen'; 'old tarpaulin'; 'the old seadog' etc. To him is assigned perhaps the most overtly Homeric phrase in the entire novel: 'draw the long bow', which is what Odysseus does just before he kills the suitors, but even that does not turn him into the true Ulysses.

In this episode of shifting and uncertain identities the keeper of the shelter (the Eumaeus representative) is another ambiguous figure. Is he Skin-the-Goat? Probably not, but the possibility that he might be, the curiously insistent focus on Parnell, and the heated discussion of the British empire's future, ground the episode in a strongly Irish, historical world which is part of the oblique homecoming that it celebrates. 'Eumaeus' is a very public episode; Bloom and Stephen, each alienated from their society in different ways, here at least demonstrate their involvement in it, reluctant or otherwise. As always, they are embedded in the discourse of the episode's narrator, and that discourse very much reflects a shared world.

The word 'shelter' in the term 'cabman's shelter' needs to be taken in a wide sense; it does offer shelter in every sense to Stephen and Bloom, even if just temporarily; towards the end Bloom does feel they had better not 'outstay their welcome'. In *The Odyssey*, Eumaeus is a loyal retainer who fails to recognise Odysseus on his return; this Eumaeus similarly fails to recognise *his* Odysseus on his arrival, but does at least accommodate him and provide for him within his means. Despite all the book's contortions, the Homeric parallel still holds good.

BIOGRAPHICAL/HISTORICAL

Line 129. *Corley*: a character in the story 'Two Gallants', in *Dubliners*. Corley is a far less imposing figure in this context than in his *Dubliners* appearance.

323–4. *Skin-the-Goat, Fitzharris, the invincible*: James Fitzharris, driver of the decoy cab in the Phoenix Park murders of 1882, was sentenced to life imprisonment but released in 1902. There is no reason to believe that he was keeper of the cabman's shelter, but it is possible that he minded stones for the corporation, as Gumley does in this episode.

945. *Pat Tobin*: secretary of the corporation's paving committee.

964. *that ship that ran bang against the only rock in Galway bay*: Mr Deasy has already referred to this unfortunate and true event in his letter to the papers re foot-and-mouth disease. See Episode 2, 'Nestor', line 326.

966. *Mr Worthington*: Robert Worthington, a Dublin railroad contractor, was one of the backers of the Galway harbour scheme.

968.   *Captain John Lever*: an English businessman who owned the ships involved in the failed Galway scheme.

996.   *Colonel Everard down there in Navan growing tobacco*: as the 'Eumaeus' narrator himself would say: a fact. The tobacco grower was Colonel N. T. Everard.

1298.   *Parnell*: the possibility of the return of Parnell was still bruited in 1904; it was already mentioned in Episode 6, 'Hades'.

1334–5.   The *United Ireland* newspaper was founded by Parnell in 1881 to promote his policies. In December 1890 it switched to the anti-Parnellite camp. The Parnellites, led by Parnell himself, occupied the building where the paper was printed and broke up the type.

1343.   *Roger Charles Tichborne*: a famous case of a false claimant to a title and fortune. The claimant, Arthur Orton, was eventually exposed, partly on the evidence of a schoolmate of Tichborne, Lord Bellew. Tichborne was drowned in the wreck of the ship, *Bella* in 1854. Orton was convicted of perjury in 1873.

1352.   Katherine O'Shea was indeed English, the daughter of Sir John Page Wood.

1503.   *O'Brienite*: William O'Brien (1852–1928), one of Parnell's principal opponents.

1583.   *Buckshot Foster*: epithet given to William E. Forster (not Foster), chief secretary for Ireland from 1880 to 1882, at the time of the land war.

1666–7.   *sir Anthony MacDonnell*: chief secretary for Ireland in 1904.

SELECT GLOSSARY

Line 54–5. *fidus Achates*: Latin, 'faithful Achates', the standard term Virgil gives to Aeneas's comrade in *The Aeneid*. Used sarcastically already about Buck Mulligan by Simon Dedalus in Episode 6, 'Hades'.

109.   *quondam*: Latin, 'former'.

118.   *qui vive*: French, literally 'who lives'; the standard term for sentry duty.

175.   *haud ignarus . . . disco*: Latin, 'scarcely ignorant of misfortunes, I have learned to succour others'; a slight variant of line 1:630 in Virgil's *Aeneid*.

314–19.   *Puttana . . . testa più*: Italian, 'Whore of a Madonna, he must give us the money! Am I not right? Broken arse!/Let's be clear. A half sovereign more . . ./That's what he says, however!/A half./Blackguard! His filthy dead [ancestors!]/But listen! Five more per person . . .'.

335.   *hoi polloi*: Greek, 'the common people'.

463.   *Gospodi pomilyou*: Old Church Slavonic, 'Lord have mercy on us'.

474.   *Choza de Indios*: Spanish, 'Hut of the Indians'.

489.   *Tarjeta Postal*: Spanish, 'postcard'.

534.   *tapis*: French, 'carpet'.

554.   *coup d'œil*: French, 'view'.

620.   *soi-disant*: French, 'so-called'.

759–60.   *corruptio per se . . . per accidens*: Latin, 'corruption through itself . . . corruption accidentally'. From Aquinas's account of the soul in the *Summa theologica*.

883.   *Roberto ruba roba sua*: Italian, 'Robert robbed his things'.

963.   *au fait*: French, 'in the swim'.

1091–3.   *Ex quibus . . . carnem*: Latin, from Romans 9:5: 'et ex quibus est Christus secundum carnem', 'and from whom [the race of the Jews] is Christ, according to the flesh'.

1138–40. *Ubi patria . . . vita bene*: Latin, 'Where my country [is, there is] the good life'. A Bloomian variant of the proverb: *Ubi bene, ibi patria*: 'Where the good life is, there is my country'. Bloom's 'translation' is impressionistic.

1161.   *faubourg Saint Patrice*: French, 'Saint Patrick's suburb', obviously Ireland.

1453–4.   puritanisme ... toi trop: French patois, 'puritanism ... then (Get a hard-on!) Bugger yourself all the way.' An obscure and doubtful passage.

1490.   decree *nisi*: a decree that will take effect unless (*nisi*) further cause is shown to prevent it.

1558.   *conditio sine qua non*: Latin, 'the indispensable condition', a stock phrase.

1637.   *passim*: Latin, 'throughout'.

1705–6.   *dolce far niente*: Italian, 'sweet idleness'.

1763–4.   *annos ... Doulandus*: Latin, 'I, [John] Dowland, used up my years in playing.' An epigraph about the lutenist and composer John Dowland (1563–1626) by his friend Henry Peachem.

1767.   *dux ... comes*: Latin, the theme or leader (*dux*) in the Farnabys' contrapuntal music; *comes* is the follower, or response.

1815–16.   *Von der Sirenen ... dichten*: German, 'From the craftiness (or art) of the Sirens,/poets make poems'.

1852.   *genus omne*: Latin, 'all their type'.

1884.   *Und alle Schiffe brücken*: German, 'And all ships bridge[?]'. Stephen may intend the word *brechen*, 'break', which would fit the context better, though the line does not really correspond to the end of Jeep's ballad in either version.

III
[17 · Ithaca]

Time: 2 a.m.
Location: Bloom's house at Number 7 Eccles Street

SUMMARY

Bloom and Stephen walk up Gardiner Street, turn left into Gardiner Place, then right into Temple Street, along Hardwicke Place, across Dorset Street and into Eccles Street. *En route* they talk about many matters, among them the reasons for Stephen's collapse in Nighttown. Bloom ascribes this event to lack of food, too much drink and vigorous dancing, Stephen to the reappearance of a cloud that had cast a shadow over the mornings of both, the one in Sandycove, the other in Eccles Street.

Bloom perceives a certain affinity between his views and those of Stephen on a number of issues, as well as some divergences. These liberal discussions remind Bloom of similar such wide-ranging debates he has held in his younger days with school friends and, later, with Molly and her father when he first knew Molly. He reflects with some melancholy on the dwindling opportunities for such converse that his life now allows him.

On arrival at Number 7 Eccles Street (at last) Bloom puts his hand in his pocket to obtain his key. To his chagrin he realises that he had left it in the trousers he had worn on the previous day, Wednesday. (He had put on the trousers he is now wearing specially for Dignam's funeral.)

Rather than disturb Molly, Bloom decides to climb over the area railing of his house, and lower himself with a slight fall into the area. Thence he enters the house via the area door, lights a candle in the kitchen, proceeds up to the hall and admits Stephen via the hall door.

They proceed carefully along the hall and down the stairs to the kitchen. There Bloom kneels down to light a fire, reminding Stephen of others, such as Brother Michael in the infirmary in Clongowes, who had lit fires for him at other times.

Bloom fills the kettle from the kitchen tap; we are treated to an elaborate account of the water's flow from its source in the Roundwood reservoir, followed by a long list of the qualities of water that Bloom, as 'waterlover', admires. He further proves his aquatic allegiance by washing his hands at the tap. Stephen, invited to do likewise, declines, citing his innate hydrophobia. Bloom finds this disturbing, but decides that water must be incompatible with genius. He is struck, however, by Stephen's confidence and by his 'equal and opposite power of abandonment and recuperation'.

The kettle eventually boils; Bloom reflects that he could also have used it to shave (he believes in the merits of shaving at night). On the dresser, among the familiar objects, he notices two betting tickets, each torn in two; he realises that these register the losing bets placed on Sceptre in the Gold Cup by Boylan for himself and Molly. Bloom by now understands that he had inadvertently given Bantam Lyons the winning horse (Throwaway), and he is satisfied that he had brought 'light to the gentiles', even if his prophecy had ultimately been ignored.

He serves cocoa to Stephen and to himself, using some of the cream reserved for Molly's breakfast. He also forgoes his special moustache cup in order to place himself on terms of equality with his guest. Bloom jocosely points out these marks of favour to his guest, who takes them very seriously. Together they consume 'Epps's massproduct, the creature cocoa'.

Bloom wrongly imagines from Stephen's silence that he is engaged in mental literary composition and this leads him to reflect on his own literary endeavours, such as a poem he had written for a competition in the *Shamrock*, a weekly journal, and a verse he had sent to Molly during their courtship.

He remembers the previous times he had met Stephen: one, already evoked in Episode 14, 'Oxen of the Sun', was in the garden of Mat Dillon's house in Roundtown (now Terenure), when Stephen was aged five; the other was in Breslin's Hotel, Bray, when Stephen was ten. A link they discover between them (Stephen has found his voice again) is the late Dante Riordan, the fierce opponent of Parnell in the Christmas dinner scene of *A Portrait of the Artist as a Young Man*, whom Bloom had also known when he had stayed in the City Arms Hotel during his employment in the nearby cattle market. (She has been mentioned already both in Episode 6, 'Hades' and Bloom's pecuniary interest in her has been alluded to maliciously in Episode 12, 'Cyclops'.)

Neither Bloom nor Stephen alludes openly to their racial

difference, but it is there as an unspoken presence between them. The episode goes on to compare their educational careers: Bloom's bent is principally towards the applied sciences; he is also particularly interested in the art of advertisement, which he rightly believes has yet to achieve its full potential in 1904.

In response to one idea for an ad suggested by Bloom, Stephen responds with a little scene of his own, in which a woman writes over and over on a writing pad 'Queen's Hotel, Queen's Hotel, Queen's Hotel. Queen's Ho . . .'. Bloom is naturally struck by the fact that this is the name of the hotel in Ennis in which his father committed suicide through taking poison on 27 June 1886, but puts the incident down to coincidence. Stephen's scene and the subsequent one he narrates, 'The Parable of the Plums', incline Bloom again to the view that there is considerable financial gain to be made from Stephen's literary talents. Bloom goes on, in a possibly significant linkage, to thoughts of how to divert his wife and keep her entertained; obviously Stephen might have a role in such a programme.

Prompted by the Mosaic allusions in 'The Parable of the Plums', Bloom mentions the eminence of Jewish thinkers such as Moses Maimonides; Stephen makes bold to mention Aristotle and Bloom repeats the legend that Aristotle had been taught by a rabbi. Stephen recites some Irish verse and writes a few Irish characters on a blank page of Sweets of Sin (Bloom carefully conceals the volume's cover); Bloom, reciprocally, recites some of the Song of Songs in Hebrew and writes down some Hebrew characters. The text goes on to enunciate some analogies between the two languages and races. Bloom chants some of the Zionist anthem, now the anthem of Israel.

At this crucial moment, each is deeply conscious of the reality of the other: Stephen hears in Bloom's chant 'the accumulation of the past'; Bloom sees in Stephen's youthful form 'the predestination of a future.'

Stephen, with sublime tactlessness, proceeds to a chant of his own: this is an anti-Semitic traditional ballad concerning the ritual killing of a young boy by a Jew's daughter. Naturally, the ballad arouses mixed feelings in Bloom; he thinks about his own daughter and testifies again to the concern and affection she engenders in him.

Bloom then proposes to Stephen that he pass the night in the room immediately beside the sleeping chamber of his host and hostess. Bloom secretly hopes that this improvised arrangement might be extended into something more permanent: he foresees, firstly, the removal of Molly's preoccupation with Boylan and ultimately, a 'reconciliatory union' between Stephen and Milly. Bloom's proposal is instantly, 'inexplicably', 'gratefully' declined. Bloom returns to Stephen the money which he had temporarily taken into his care. The two do, however, agree to meet again, and a number of venues are suggested for such further encounters. But these, as both know, are unlikely to take place. Bloom is all the more depressed by this knowledge since he wants to work for the betterment of human existence, certain unavoidable conditions, such as death, being allowed for, and contact with Stephen would (he thinks) conduce to such work. Stephen, however, affirms his own significance as 'a conscious rational animal' despite these ineluctable conditions, and Bloom substantially assents to this affirmation.

Stephen then departs, secretly intoning the psalm which celebrates the departure of the chosen people from the house of bondage. They leave the house by the back door; entering the garden, they gaze at the sky above them. Bloom, who is something of an amateur astronomer, reflects on the heavenly bodies, their antiquity, their remoteness, their vastness. Overawed, he narrows his speculations down to the moon, pondering the affinities between the moon and woman. Prompted, perhaps, by such speculations, he draws Stephen's attention to the semi-lighted window of the back bedroom, where Molly is at that moment reclining. Bloom takes pains to let Stephen know that Molly is there. Both then urinate while gazing at the lighted window, as a shooting star darts across the heavens.

Stephen leaves by the garden's back door; he and Bloom shake hands in parting, as the bells of St George's Church toll the time, just as they did the previous morning. Left alone, Bloom feels 'the cold of interstellar space' and remembers many companions who have died. He has previously stayed up all night to see the sunrise; on this occasion, however, he returns to the house, locking the scullery door behind him.

He goes up to the front room of the house on the hall floor and enters it. Instantly, he hits his head against the sideboard, which has been moved from its previous position beside the door to a point opposite the door. Several other items of furniture, including the piano, have also been shifted around in Bloom's absence. (The room also contains a furled Union Jack.) There is evidence from the position of the chairs and other matters of Boylan's presence with Molly there that day.

Bloom, suffering a light contusion on his right temple, lights a cone of incense and contemplates his features in the mirror. He also sees in the mirror the books on the shelves opposite, and these are duly catalogued. He sits down at the central table, admiring the statue of Narcissus on the table. Removing his shirt collar, he unbuttons his waistcoat, trousers, shirt and vest and removes his braces. The budget for Bloom's day is then supplied: its most salient, though not its only, omission is the expenditure of eleven shillings at Bella Cohen's brothel, and some of its figures, such as one shilling for a Fry's plain chocolate (at least as given in the Gabler edition), cannot be right. Bloom proceeds to unlace his boots; not surprisingly after a day spent largely walking, his feet are sore. He removes a protruding piece of big toe-nail and inhales its odour with satisfaction. The smell reminds him of other times when he had engaged in a similar exercise, especially as an aspiring pupil at Mrs Ellis's juvenile school; this brings back to him his ambitions of those days, ambitions which have now coalesced in the desire, given detailed expression here, to be the owner and occu-pier of a detached 'bungalowshaped two-storey dwellinghouse'. The appurtenances and amenities of this house are spelt out in elaborate detail; this is obviously Bloom's idea of the earthly paradise.

He sees himself as a resident magistrate, dispensing justice fairly and equitably, and imagines notices in the fashionable intelligence to the effect that 'Mr and Mrs Leopold Bloom have left Kingstown for England'.

Naturally, the question of how to afford such a dwelling and life-style has not escaped his attention: he thinks of such schemes as obtaining advance knowledge of the results of horse races (which, of course, he has already demonstrated), or the discovery of an object of great value. As the catalogue of schemes goes on, its scope becomes ever more vast, including such visionary projects as hydroelectric stations. While he knows that such plans are unlikely ever to be realised, he believes that contemplation of them is conducive to a good night's sleep and keeps evil influences at bay. His final and most cherished vision is of a single advertisement that would command universal attention and admiration.

Bloom opens the drawers of his writing-desk and their contents are disclosed: they include the three letters he has received from Martha, two condoms, two erotic postcards and a suppository for dealing with rectal complaints called The Wonderworker. Bloom adds his fourth letter from Martha to the collection, remembering as he does so the effect of his person and personality on other females in the course of the day, among them Mrs Breen, Nurse Callan and Gerty MacDowell. Another drawer contains various financial documents, showing that Bloom enjoys a modest but reasonably comfortable security. It also contains the suicide note of his father, Rudolph. Reading the inscription on this note, Bloom remembers with remorse the disrespect with which he treated many of his father's most cherished beliefs; he also recalls following as a child his father's itinerary between Szombathely in Hungary, whence he came, and Dublin.

He muses on the reversals of fortune that can occur, going now from the sublime of his detached two-storey dwelling to the depths of pauperism. One way of avoiding such a fate is to depart, and he speculates on a number of possible destinations, both in Ireland and abroad. Ultimately he sees himself as a cosmic wanderer, voyaging to the uttermost boundaries of space. He is not averse to leaving, feeling that he and Molly have little more to do with each other, but ultimately factors such as the lateness of the hour and the proximity of a warm bed with a warm human being in it compel him, inevitably, to stay. Before retiring he goes over in his mind the principal incidents of the day, each one compared to a Jewish ritual; he also remembers some 'imperfections' that marred his progress, such as his temporary failure to obtain a renewal of an advertisement. The table gives forth a loud crack just as he leaves the room.

He enters the bedroom and gets into bed, lying with his head at the foot of the bed, thus at Molly's feet. He feels the impression left by

Boylan's form on his side of the bed and reflects that Boylan, who may imagine he is unique, is but one of a series of men who have lusted after Molly. Bloom's feelings about Boylan are complex, composed of 'envy, jealousy, abnegation and equanimity'; they resolve themselves, though, into equanimity, ultimately having recourse, in this cosmic episode, to 'the apathy of the stars'. That is not quite the end of the matter, however: Bloom's 'final satisfaction' is at the thought of the ubiquity of female breasts and posteriors in all inhabited quarters of the globe. In consequence whereof, Bloom, now with 'an approximate erection', kisses Molly's bottom. This rouses Molly sufficiently to acknowledge Bloom's arrival and to inquire as to his day. Bloom gives her an account of his activities, with some substantial modifications: he omits the altercation in Barney Kiernan's, the scene with Gerty and of course the visit to Nighttown, pretending that he has attended the play *Leah* and had met Stephen at a supper in Wynn's Hotel afterwards. Stephen emerges as the main focus of the narration.

As Bloom speaks, both are aware of the limitations, physical and mental, on their intercourse. Full sexual intercourse has not taken place between them since shortly before the birth of their son Rudy in December 1893; and Bloom is conscious both that his mental intercourse with Molly has been circumscribed and that his freedom of movement has been subjected to increasing scrutiny since the coming to puberty of their daughter Milly.

The two are lying together in the bed, at opposite ends, being carried through space on the globe of the Earth. Bloom, weary, is at rest. He has travelled and as he drifts off to sleep, there is a sleepy list of his companions, all phonetic variants of Sinbad the Sailor. The story of Sinbad, by now identified with Bloom, concludes the episode; Bloom is carried off by sleep rather as Sinbad is carried off by the giant roc, the mythical bird of Arabia.

CORRESPONDENCES

Books 17–20 of *The Odyssey* relate Odysseus's confrontation with and slaughter of the suitors who had taken over his palace in Ithaca.

Odysseus enters the palace still disguised as a beggar; his remarks in the hall anger the most arrogant of the suitors, Antinous, who throws a stool at him, rather as Bloom is injured by the sideboard which has been moved in his absence. The next day, Penelope challenges the suitors to bend and string the longbow of her husband; whoever can do it will finally win her hand. All the suitors fail, but Odysseus strings it easily; Zeus accompanies this deed with a thunderclap, as the table in Bloom's house suddenly emits a loud crack just after Bloom has reviewed his day. Now the suitors know who they are dealing with, but they are penned into the hall by Odysseus and Telemachus (Stephen similarly locks the door after Bloom has admitted him to the house). The suitors are all duly slaughtered, Antinous and Eurymachus, the two boldest, being the first to go. Afterwards, Telemachus departs on an errand, rather as Stephen does, and Odysseus fumigates the house, as Bloom lights the cone of incense in his front parlour.

Odysseus reveals himself to Penelope very tentatively and she at first is slow to acknowledge him. It is only when he reveals his awareness of a detail of the construction of their marriage bed – that it is built around the trunk of an olive tree – a detail known only to the two of them and to a trusted slave, that she can believe he is truly her husband.

In the Gilbert schema, Eurymachus is Boylan (the other particularly aggressive suitor, Antinous, is Mulligan, already taken care of by Bloom in the previous episode). The bow of Odysseus is reason, and the slaughtered suitors are scruples.

STYLE

The style of 'Ithaca' is one of the most distinctive in the book. This is the quasi-objective episode, the one which provides the most detached narrative, and the style reflects this tendency. It is a catechism-type question and answer format, for the most part delivered in the most dry and colourless fashion imaginable. The 'techniques' of the last three episodes correspond to the techniques of the first three. Thus the previous episode, 'Eumaeus', is 'narrative (old)', as the first episode,

'Telemachus', is 'narrative (young)' and the fourth episode, 'Calypso', the one which introduces Bloom, is 'narrative (mature)'. Similarly, the technique of this episode is 'catechism (impersonal)', corresponding to the technique of the second episode, 'Nestor', which is 'catechism (personal)', referring to Stephen's questioning of the boys in the schoolroom and Deasy's later interrogations of Stephen.

The 'catechism (impersonal)' mode means that it is not possible to derive a personality from this anonymous duo, the questioner and the respondent, as it was possible to derive a personality from the narrator of 'Eumaeus'. The whole tendency is to abstraction, to a removal from the human sphere (literally, since a large part of the episode seems to be passed in outer space).

A large part of the effect, indeed, is of beings looking down from the heavens, from an enormous distance, on the affairs of humans, indifferent to the phenomena which they merely observe and report. The impression (false) is therefore of the utmost objectivity, the utmost reliability. Since these narrating entities are so detached from the action, it follows, must it not, that their testimonies and the information they provide are entirely unbiased, entirely trustworthy. In fact, it must not, and the ways in which it must not are one of the most fascinating things about the episode. The many omissions and distortions to which this narration is given will be examined in the commentary; but although the catechism is not reliable, the appearance, the simulacrum, of objectivity and detachment which it provides do set the tone for the episode.

The extreme formality and rigour of the technique can seem to impose a deadening uniformity on the prose, but, in fact, this is not the case. It is capable of a great deal of variation: it can be succinct ('Did either openly allude to their racial difference? Neither.'); it can be wildly prolix (Bloom's simple action in turning on a tap leads to an exhaustive and exhausting account of the water's source and flow, followed by an enormous list of the qualities of water that excite Bloom's wonder); it can be hilarious ('Was the clown Bloom's son? No. Had Bloom's coin returned? Never.'); it can be unexpectedly poetic ('The heaventree of stars hung with humid nightblue fruit'). Hugh Kenner's phrase 'an oddly cathedralised poetry' describes the effect very well.

Perhaps the style's greatest achievement, in this cosmic episode, is the poetic rendering of the vastness of the spaces within which Bloom, Stephen and Molly are deployed. Science and literature, the two tendencies represented respectively by Bloom and Stephen, are brought together, just as Bloom and Stephen are brought together in this episode. Most novelists would not risk having their central characters diminished in this way; they attempt to remain on the level of the microcosm and allow the reader to broaden the inference. Here, though, the effect of the style's poetry is not to diminish the characters but rather to expand their, and the book's, horizons to an almost infinite degree. Lying together at opposite ends of the bed, Bloom and Molly are both at rest and in motion – at rest relative to themselves and each other; in motion relative to the movement of the earth 'through everchanging tracks of neverchanging space'. The style succeeds in keeping both perspectives in balance.

COMMENTARY

'Ithaca' is the most deceptive episode of *Ulysses*. In this third and last part of the book, the Nostos, or homecoming, comprising the last three episodes, the pressure of the Homeric paradigm seems to me to intensify. One of the most striking features of Homer's epics, the one highlighted by Erich Auerbach in the celebrated opening chapter of *Mimesis*, is precisely their high lighting: their need to account for everything that happens, to leave nothing unexplained, nothing obscure and dark, nothing hidden in corners. The example he cites is the scar that Odysseus bears on his leg; even though this scar comes up at a crucial and extremely tense moment of the epic, the entire action is suspended while we are told in detail how Odysseus came to have this scar. This, as Auerbach says, is not a device to create suspense; it is a response to a pressure for full clarity, full disclosure in an eternal present.

Something of this tendency may underlie the peculiarities both of this episode and of its predecessor, 'Eumaeus'. In 'Eumaeus', as here, there is an earnest effort to impart information, to be perfectly clear and comprehensive. In 'Eumaeus', the effort is hampered by the restriction of the narrative to a single consciousness (Bloom's) and to a narrator with a penchant for linguistic infelicity which gets in the way of his efforts to tell the story; but nonetheless the basic tendency is to be helpful, to tell all, to throw as much light as possible on murky matters.

In 'Ithaca', the effort ought, on the face of it, to be more successful. This narrative is much better informed than that of 'Eumaeus'; an impressive mastery of facts, both minute and global, is manifested; and the narration has access, not only to the thoughts of Bloom, but occasionally to the thoughts of Stephen as well. And indeed we are given information in plenty, masses of it: we learn more 'objective' facts about Bloom (things like his height, his weight, his endowment policy) than we do at any other point of the day.

The information, though, is oddly disappointing. The narrative resembles that of 'Eumaeus' at least in this sense, that this one also shows no sense of discrimination, no sense of what might be important and what might not. We learn all about the progress of water from Roundwood reservoir to its emergence from Bloom's tap, but on a really crucial issue, such as why Stephen instantly declines Bloom's offer of a bed for the night, the text is completely silent.

Not only, though, is the narrative very selective in its information, it is also very unreliable. There is much misinformation among the copious quantities of facts that it rejoices in peddling. It is often hard to know whether these distortions are inadvertent or deliberate. One of the more startling is the omission from Bloom's budget – a document one would expect to be complete, since it is presented like an accountant's statement – of his expenditure of eleven shillings (ten shillings admission and one shilling for the damage to the lampshade) in Bella Cohen's brothel. It has been suggested that this is due to Bloom's internal repression of the entire experience. This explanation may well be correct; if so, it does indicate that the apparently objective, factual appearance of the information being conveyed in 'Ithaca' may often be misleading.

A second, serious instance of the confusion that the narration's apparent objectivity can generate concerns the famous list of Molly's lovers in lines 2133 to 2140. Because this list occurs in the context of Bloom's reflections on Boylan, and because Boylan himself appears in the list, it was for a long time thought that all these men were sexual partners of Molly in the same way that Boylan seems to be. But on correlating the list with Molly's own reflections on these people, and with some of the other evidence in the book, it becomes clear that almost all of them have had only the most tenuous relation with her; at most, they have lusted after her. Molly has not had twenty-five lovers. So what the text is *saying* has to be taken very carefully: a great deal of the time, what looks like objective information is actually the mind of Bloom, transmitted through this very special medium.

A final example of textual misinformation concerns the account that Bloom gives Molly of his day (lines 2251 to 2266). We are told that the account is modified both negatively and positively, meaning that Bloom omits some things that did happen and invents some things that did not occur. But among the things he narrates that the text implies are invented are *Sweets of Sin* (the novel he purchases in Episode 10, 'Wandering Rocks') and his leap over the area railings of his own house, both events that we know have 'really' happened. It seems that the word 'positive' has to be interpreted in a very special sense in this context: it may be that these two items are 'positive' in the sense that the purchase of *Sweets of Sin* may be pleasing to Molly and that Bloom's feat in getting over the railings may impress her.

In addition to these sources of uncertainty, quite a lot of the pseudo-scientific information proffered – the figures, etc – is inaccurate, plain wrong, but it is not always possible to tell if Joyce is aware of these errors. Therefore, it is very inadvisable to attempt to 'correct' them in the interests of greater accuracy. The erroneous information may well be part of the deceptive impression that this text is striving to present – pseudo-scientific, not truly scientific.

The arbitrary and unreliable nature of the episode's narration is especially frustrating because this is the moment of the book when Bloom and Stephen are in closest contact. This is the point the story has been tending towards all day, the ultimate meeting of the father and the son, their final commingling. Given this, it is not surprising that critics for many years have been flailing around to find hidden significance in the apparently banal encounter. The text, in its way, gives them plenty of support: a particularly tantalising morsel is the information that Bloom and Stephen share 'Epps's massproduct, the creature cocoa'. Surely this is a eucharistic allusion? Similarly, all sorts of symbolic resonances seem to hang around their joint urination in the garden, while gazing up at the light in Molly's window. This too has a highly 'symbolic' feel to it: the arc of Bloom's trajectory forms part of a Y, the first letter of the name of Yahweh; perhaps that is the point.

In fact, these hints are a deception. The text is no longer operating in this symbolic mode. Back in the very first episode, 'Telemachus', these eucharistic analogies really were operative; the book was then seriously deploying elaborate parallels and seriously setting up meaningful, weighty symbolic structures. But things have moved on from that: 'this is not the old sea, nor this the old seashore'. By this point in the book, textual play is dominant: meaning is not going to be conferred by symbolic structures. References to 'massproduct' are, I believe, deliberately teasing, suggesting a communion that nothing in the actual encounter justifies.

Similarly, we discover at lines 2044 to 2058 of this episode that a whole other set of parallels has been operative all along: Bloom's activities have corresponded not only to the Homeric and Shakespearean and other paradigms already described but are also symbolic of various Jewish rituals (rite of Melchisedek, etc.). The effect of this unexpected extra layer of symbolism is not to enhance meaning, but rather to empty it further; it appears that what Bloom does can be made to correspond to anything.

Another instance of the same procedure comes when Bloom is described as 'bearing in his arms the secret of the race', on his way to the Turkish baths in Leinster Street. 'The secret of the race' sounds like something very portentous and important (the secret of the Jewish race, the secret of the Irish race), but, in fact, it refers to the secret of the result of the Ascot Gold Cup race, a secret that Bloom actually possesses without knowing it. Once again, the expectation of major revelation, an overwhelming answer to an overwhelming question, is being undermined.

Given this mockery of the process of signification, it is surprising that critics still cling to meaning, to importance, to deep symbolic structures, when the text has abandoned all these long ago, in favour of a 'something else' which can perhaps best be described as serious play.

In any case, there is quite enough significance in what actually happens, without getting 'headaches among the overtones', as Samuel Beckett put it. Bloom and Stephen sit together in Bloom's kitchen; they sing the songs of their respective races; they find some mainly imaginary correspondences between the two peoples. As the 'Eumaeus' narrator has already put it: 'Though they didn't see eye to eye in everything a certain analogy there somehow was.' Stephen then chants a strange ballad which strongly implies that, for him, any further stay would be tantamount to suicide. The rapport between them has reached its limit, so, inexplicably but decisively, he duly leaves. Bloom and Stephen shake hands on parting; for Stephen to shake hands with someone is no small thing. What Stephen has made of this strange encounter is a matter for the overall reading of the book; Bloom realises that his hopes for a new life with Stephen are vain, but he remains wedded to the fantasy, as his frequent references to his young acquaintance in his narrative to Molly make clear, and as is confirmed in the next episode. Having repossessed his actual home, Bloom is granted a Utopian vision of Flowerville, his ideal home. Then, having dreamed about abandoning Ithaca and wandering to the uttermost limits of space, he opts instead to return to bed and Molly; whether to a new life with her or to the repetition of the same one remains to be seen.

BIOGRAPHICAL/HISTORICAL

Line 48.   *Owen Goldberg*: listed in *Thom's Directory* for 1904 as living at 31 Harcourt Street.

48.   *Cecil Turnbull*: probably based on Donald Turnbull, who lived at 53 Harcourt Street in 1904; he is named as Donald in the list of Bloom's schoolfriends in Episode 15, 'Circe', lines 3326–8.

51.   *Percy Apjohn*: mentioned already in Episode 8,
       'Lestrygonians'. Apparently fictional, though a Thomas
       Barnes Apjohn lived in Rutland House, Crumlin.

58.   *Julius (Juda) Mastiansky*: first mentioned in Episode 4,
       'Calypso'. Apparently based on P. Masliansky, of 16 St
       Kevin's Parade.

136.   *Brother Michael*: a character in *A Portrait of the Artist
       as a Young Man,* chapter 1, section 2. No precise
       original for Brother Michael has been traced.

140.   *Miss Kate Morkan*: features in the story 'The Dead', in
       Dubliners. Based on Joyce's grand-aunt, Mrs Lyons,
       who with her sister ran the Misses Flynn's music
       school at 15 Usher's Island.

141.   *his aunt Sara*: based on Joyce's aunt, Josephine
       Giltrap, married to William Murray; she has already
       been mentioned in Episode 3, 'Proteus'.

145.   *Father Butt*: based on Father Joseph Darlington, the
       dean of studies at University College Dublin during
       Joyce's time there, from 1898 to 1900. The college,
       oddly, is given the wrong address in this passage, being
       placed at 16 St Stephen's Green North, instead of at
       84A–87 St Stephen's Green South.

420.   *Michael Gunn*: manager of the Gaiety Theatre,
       Dublin, from 1871 to his death in 1901. First
       mentioned in Episode 11, 'Sirens', and several times
       thereafter.

424.   *Greenleaf Whittier*: the name of a minor American
       poet (1807–92); in fact the pantomime was written by
       Greenleaf Withers.

427.   *Nelly Bouverist*: combines the names of two 'principal
       girls' in pantomime, Kate Neverist and Nellie
       Bouverie.

467.   *Matthew Dillon*: an old friend of the Joyce family.
       One of his daughters, Mamie, who went to Spain, may
       have contributed something to the character of Molly
       Bloom

479. *Mrs Riordan (Dante)*: features in the early parts of *A Portrait,* based on Dante Conway, a distant relative of John Joyce, who stayed with the family for some time. She later moved out and (in fiction), stayed in the City Arms Hotel, Prussia Street, at the same time as Bloom and Molly. In this episode, the date of her departure is given as 29 December; this would be four days after the Christmas dinner scene of *A Portrait.*

485. *Joseph Cuffe*: presumably associated with Laurence Cuffe & Sons, cattle, corn and wool salesmen, 5 Smithfield, near the cattle market.

491. *Gavin Low*: livestock agent, 47–53 Prussia Street; first mentioned in Episode 14, 'Oxen of the Sun'.

537. *Hegarty*: the very Irish name of Bloom's fictional maternal grandmother confirms that he is not really Jewish, since Jewish descent is established through the female line.

627. *Francis Dennehy*: this chemist's shop allegedly in Church Street, Ennis, is fictional.

632. *James Cullen*: his existence and drapery premises in Main Street, Ennis, are similarly fictional. Indeed, no such street has ever existed in Ennis.

947. *Mrs Emily Sinico*: character in the story 'A Painful Case', in *Dubliners.*

1251. *Percy Apjohn*: see line 51.

1253. *Matthew F. Kane*: chief clerk in the Dublin state solicitor's office; a friend of John Joyce, he drowned in Dublin Bay on 10 July 1904. The character of Martin Cunningham is based on him.

1254. *Philip Moisel*: son of Nisan Moisel, lived in Heytesbury Street.

1254. *Michael Hart*: another friend of John Joyce, he provided most of the qualities for the character, Lenehan. He was dead by 1903.

1339. *Alderman John Hooper*: from Cork, he was the father of Paddy Hooper, a reporter on the *Freeman's Journal.*

1647.   *James Fintan Lalor*: (1807–49), radical land agitator.

1647–8:   *John Fisher Murray*: (1811–65), Young Irelander, political writer and satirist.

1648.   *John Mitchel*: (1815–75), advocate of physical force nationalism, he was exiled to Tasmania, but returned to Ireland in 1872.

1648.   *J. F. X. O'Brien*: (1828–1905), joined the Fenian Society in America, came to Ireland and was arrested for his part in the 1867 uprising. He became an MP and supported Parnell until the split. He held his seat until his death.

1656.   *the marquess of Ripon*: George Robinson (1827–1909), seen in Ireland as well disposed to Home Rule.

1656.   *John Morley*: (1838–1923), English politician, strongly supportive of Home Rule.

1782.   *Mr + Mrs M. Comerford*: lived at Neptune View, 11 Leslie Avenue, Dalkey.

2139–40.   *Alderman John Hooper*: see above, line 1339.

2140.   *Dr Francis Brady*: apparently fictional.

2140.   *Father Sebastian*: apparently fictional. Molly does not refer to him.

2171.   *George Mesias*: Bloom's tailor; in reality George R. Mesias, tailor, 5 Eden Quay. First mentioned in Episode 6, 'Hades'.

SELECT GLOSSARY

Line 727. *suil, sui ... cuin*: Irish, 'Walk, walk, walk, my love, walk in safety and walk in calm.' The first two lines of the ballad *Siúil a rún*.

729.   *kifeloch ... l'zamatejch*: Hebrew, 'Thy temple within thy hair is as a piece of pomegranate'. From Song of Solomon 4:3.

763–4.   *Kolod ... homijah*: Hebrew, 'As long as deep within the heart/The soul of Judea is stormy and strong.' The first lines of *Hatikvah* ('Hope'), a poem by Nephtali Herz Imber (1878), set to music by Zionist settler Samuel Cohen in the late 1890s, and now the anthem of Israel.

1030–31. *modus peregrinus . . . de populo barbaro*: Latin, 'mode of travelling abroad: on the departure of Israel from Egypt: the house of Jacob from people of a strange tongue.'

1230–31. *Liliata rutilantium . . . excipiat*: Latin, 'Bright with lilies/A throng surrounds/You of rejoicing virgins/A chorus shall receive.' Stephen is fitting the words of one of the prayers for the dying, which he has been reciting on and off all day (initially in Episode 1, lines 276–7), to the rhythm of the bells of St George's Church.

1383. *Soll und Haben*: German, 'Debt and Credit', a novel by Gustav Freytag (1816–95).

1611. *Semper paratus*: Latin, 'Always prepared'.

1885–6. *das Herz . . . Gott . . . dein . . .* : German, 'the heart . . . God . . . your'.

2044. breakfast (burnt offering): the burnt offering corresponds to morning prayer in ancient Jewish ritual.

2045. holy of holies: the innermost part of the Temple, entered by the high priest only on the Day of Atonement.

2045. rite of John: washing is part of the Jewish morning ritual. John the Baptist is also being referred to.

2046. rite of Samuel: a reference to Samuel's exorcism of witches, and to his burial.

2046–7. Urim and Thummim: Hebrew, 'Light' and 'Perfection', two symbols which the priest wears on his breastplate of judgment.

2047. rite of Melchisedek: Melchisedek is a senior priest of the Old Testament; he 'brought forth bread and wine' (Genesis 14:18).

2048. holy place: the inner part of a Jewish temple.

2049. Simchath Torah: Hebrew, 'Rejoice in the Law'; the last day of Sukkoth (the Feast of Tabernacles), when the reading of the Pentateuch is completed and the cycle begins again.

2050. Shira Shirim: Hebrew, 'Song of Songs', read on the Sabbath during Sukkoth.

2051. holocaust: Hebrew, literally 'a burnt offering, total sacrifice'; figuratively, the ceremony that commemorates the destruction of the Temple in Jerusalem by the Romans.

2053. wilderness: the wanderings of the Jews in the desert after their departure from Egypt, and the many periods of exile and dispersal the Jews have endured subsequently.

2053-4. rite of Onan: Onan spilled his seed on the ground, an act that so displeased the Lord that Onan died for it (Genesis 38:8-10); hence the term onanism.

2054. heave offering: a ceremonial peace offering, which is 'lifted up' (hence 'heave') by the priest.

2056. Armageddon: in Jewish tradition the site of the ultimate Messianic battle which will decide the fate of the world.

2058. atonement: Yom Kippur, the Jewish Day of Atonement, when the sins of the past year are expiated. It is the only day of the year when the high priest enters the Holy of Holies.

III

[18 · Penelope]

Time: None (clock time does not apply to this episode)
Location: the bedroom at Number 7 Eccles Street

SUMMARY

Note: 'Penelope' is written in eight enormously extended 'sentences', separated by paragraph markings. This summary will indicate the start of each sentence.

Sentence 1

Molly Bloom, lying in bed, sleepless, is under the impression that Bloom has asked to have his breakfast in bed the next day 'with a couple of eggs'. (Such a request is not recorded in the previous episode; this may be another instance of 'Ithaca' telling us everything except the really important thing. Alternatively, Molly may have heard Bloom mutter something about roc's eggs and bed and got the wrong impression.) She remembers the last time he requested breakfast in bed, which was when they were staying in the City Arms Hotel and he was pretending to be ill in order to 'make himself interesting' to Dante Riordan, who he hoped, wrongly, would leave him something in her will. This leads on to some sour reflections on Mrs Riordan, with whom Molly clearly had little in common.

Molly would not relish caring for an ill Bloom, but she does not believe he is actually ill; she believes his unexpected request and appetite arise because he 'came somewhere'; she is also sure it's not love, since he's not off his food. So she suspects (correctly) that Bloom has been in Nighttown and that the 'hotel story' and attendant details are lies. Bloom has referred to meeting Menton, presumably acting on the principle that one should put as much truth as possible into a fable to make it more plausible; this leads Molly on to contemptuous reminiscences of this solicitor (who figures in the alleged list of her lovers in the former episode).

Molly has noticed Bloom scribbling secretively in the front room and suspects (almost accurately) that he has something going with a young one he may have picked up somewhere. She remembers his carry-on with the maidservant, Mary, whom Molly had dismissed without compunction, partly for that reason and partly because she suspected her of pilfering oysters (Bloom's relations with Mary have been mentioned in both Episode 14, 'Oxen of the Sun', and Episode 15, 'Circe'). Molly remembers the last time Bloom came on her bottom (apparently this happens with some regularity): it was the night when she and Boylan first began to establish a rapport, as they walked along by the Tolka.

She knows that Bloom 'has an idea' about her relationship with Boylan, and that Bloom is staying out late deliberately to facilitate her. Molly feels that at least Boylan is a change; failing him, a 'nicelooking boy' would be welcome. She dislikes Bloom's idea of sex, which mainly seems to consist of asking her what man she is fantasising about at a particular time and then offering himself as a substitute, leaving Molly eventually to finish it off for herself, while Bloom comes off separately. Molly remembers with resentment being asked for the details of her sexual sins in confession, feeling she has 'already confessed it to God', though she did admire the priest's 'nice fat hand'. This leads her on to consider how pleasant it would be to be embraced by a priest in his vestments, 'with a smell of incense off him like the pope'.

She wonders if Boylan was satisfied with her; she didn't like the way he slapped her bottom on leaving, as if she were a horse or an ass. When her session with Boylan was over, Molly had fallen asleep until awoken by the loud crack of thunder which occurred in the 'Oxen of the Sun' episode. This led her to utter a quick Hail Mary, just in case; she fully believes in God, although with her own take on what religion is for (it's mainly for her). She believes the candle she lit in Whitefriars Street chapel for the month of May has 'brought its luck', in the person of Boylan, whose 'tremendous red big brute of a thing' has proved very satisfying; however, as she found when she made him ejaculate outside her, he hasn't that much spunk in him for the size of his member. So much the better, however, as it reduces the chances of her getting pregnant (Boylan sometimes comes inside her); she has no wish to end up like Mina Purefoy (the fertility goddess of 'Oxen of the Sun') with her multiple pregnancies and multiple children. She toys with the idea of having another child, but not with Boylan; 'Poldy [Bloom] has more spunk in him,' she reflects.

She knows Bloom has met Josie Powell (Breen), on whom he had a small crush in younger days; this, and the thought of Molly herself and Boylan together, may have 'set him off' on the path of sexual gratification. Molly remembers in detail the relations between her, Bloom and Josie in the early days of her courtship with Bloom; Josie was jealous of the two of them, and this encouraged Molly to tease her a little. At the same time, Molly 'had the devil's own job' to get Bloom to actually propose to her, though she also admired his restraint. She wonders about Josie's life now with her reputedly mad husband; bad and all as Poldy is, he has some redeeming features as compared to Denis Breen. Molly prides herself on her tolerance of Bloom's eccentricities; she is not like the notorious Mrs Maybrick, who poisoned her husband. Nevertheless, Molly fully understands the power of passion, and consoles herself with the thought that 'they' would not hang a woman (in fact, 'they' did not hang Mrs Maybrick).

Sentence 2

Boylan had noticed Molly even before they were introduced; they had spotted each other in the Dublin Bakery Company. Apparently the shape of her feet had particularly appealed to her lover. Molly remembers having made Bloom ejaculate with her foot on one occasion; she then recalls the more passionate phases of Bloom's courtship and her own slightly awkward position, caught between the need to appear not to understand the things that Bloom was saying and writing, and her wish to have him say and write more. Thoughts of these matters make Molly impatient for next Monday, when Boylan has another assignation with her. She remembers her anxiety and impatience before Boylan's arrival on this day. The concert tour to Belfast on the following Thursday is also an inviting prospect: Molly is glad Bloom won't be along, since it coincides with the anniversary of his father's death (we had already learned this in Episode 6, 'Hades'). She is glad, however, not so much because Bloom's presence would interfere with her activities with Boylan; rather, it's because Boylan would become aware that she and Bloom do maintain some kind of sexual congress. Molly has apparently told Boylan that nothing of the kind happens between her and her husband. As Molly sagely observes, 'its all very well a husband but you cant fool a lover'.

Moreover, various mishaps seem to attend Bloom on his travels, as they do Odysseus: Molly recalls an incident in Maryborough (now Portlaoise) where Bloom walked down the platform still eating his soup, pursued by an importunate waiter. Molly wonders if Boylan will want to 'do it in the train' – she speculates idly about eloping with Boylan and never returning from Belfast. The concert engagement is a big thing for her; she has not sung in public for a year, and is angrily aware that she is not in favour with the nationalist element that now dominates such events in Dublin; Molly's British army background and foreign origin (she was born in Gibraltar) are held against her. She suspects Bloom may have had a hand in setting up this tour and reflects bitterly on the damage done by politics and war, with particular reference to the Boer War, where an earlier lover of hers, Lieutenant Stanley Gardner, died. However, she loves military pageantry and parades; she remembers the great military exercises in Gibraltar and the displays in the Phoenix Park.

She hopes to get a present or two, such as a kimono, from Boylan while on the tour; since he is unmarried, and unlikely to marry, she might as well get what she can from him. Boylan's enjoyment of his afternoon was greatly disturbed, however, by the discovery that Sceptre, on which he had bet some £20 in total, was well beaten by the outsider Throwaway in the Gold Cup (this historical event has resonated through the story all day). Boylan blames Lenehan for this disaster, and Molly recalls Lenehan as 'that sponger' (he also appears in the alleged list of her lovers in the previous episode).

Molly is determined, in any case, that if her affair with Boylan is going to last, she will need some fine new undergarments, and that Bloom will have to come up with the wherewithal for these. At thirty-three, she feels that she does not have much youthful beauty left to her, and doubts if she will be able to emulate Lily Langtry, reckoned a beauty up to the age of forty-five. Bloom, she feels, ought to give up his work for the *Freeman's Journal* and obtain some salaried office position. Molly recalls her efforts to salvage Bloom's job at Cuffe's cattle merchants, from which Bloom had been fired for (apparently) 'giving lip to a grazier' (this is mentioned in Episode 12, 'Cyclops'). Molly did not succeed in getting Bloom his job back, but she certainly earned some admiring glances from Joe Cuffe (also mentioned in the list of her 'lovers').

Sentence 3

Molly, recalling Cuffe's admiration of her bosom, feels that Boylan's sucking on her breasts has made them firmer; she feels that woman's beauty is aesthetically far more pleasing than male appurtenances; nor does she care for male exhibitionism. She remembers a young student, Penrose, trying to catch a glimpse of her as she washed in Lombard Street West (he, too, is on the list). Memory of Boylan's attention to her breasts reawakens her lust; she feels unable to wait till Monday for his next visit.

Sentence 4

A train whistles in the distance; Molly pities the life of train drivers 'in those roasting engines'. The day has been an unusually warm one by Dublin standards, and Molly remembers the heat in Gibraltar before the 'levanter', the strong east wind, came on. She contemptuously contrasts 'their 3 Rock mountain' in Dublin with Gibraltar's massive Rock. She recalls her friend Hester Stanhope, wife of a friend of her father's, and remembers how attentive Hester's husband was to her at such events as the bullfights at La Linea (a town just over the border in Spain, already mentioned in the previous episode). She speculates idly about what an affair with him might have been like, while admitting it would have been disloyal to Hester. (However, Molly would know when to stop.) Her thoughts drift back to Gibraltar, remembering the dullness of the days there, especially after Hester's departure. There was no 'nice fellow' to make eyes at, and she reflects with bitterness on men's slowness to pick up a signal, even a very obvious one: 'where does their great intelligence come in Id like to know'. Life, it seems, is equally dull in Dublin, with no visitors or letters; but there is at least Boylan to liven things up, though his love letters seem to leave a lot to be desired.

Sentence 5

Molly does not herself enjoy writing letters, but she enjoys receiving them. The letter she got from Harry Mulvey, a lieutenant of the Royal Dublin Fusiliers based in Gibraltar, was her first love letter; she remembers her excitement on getting it and reading it. She goes on to recall her assignation with Mulvey 'under the Moorish wall' and her first sexual experience with him high up on the Rock of Gibraltar. Mulvey departed Gibraltar, promising to write, but like much else in Molly's life, he has gone without trace. She remembers her excitement after her experiences with Mulvey, and her sorrow at his departure. Ultimately she was bored with Gibraltar; only the visit of United States President Ulysses S. Grant and the towing into harbour of the mysteriously abandoned ship *Marie Celeste* livened things up.

Molly hears another train in the distance; the noise of its whistle reminds her of her song, 'Love's Old Sweet Song', that she has been rehearsing with Boylan, when not otherwise engaged. She again refers contemptuously to the new breed of nationalist-influenced singer, and is determined to show them up as paltry performers. Feeling the need to fart, Molly moves herself in the bed in order to release wind as quietly as possible; she has no wish to awaken Bloom for another session of 'slobbering'.

Sentence 6

The lamp in the room is left on low all night; Molly is nervous without some light. She hopes that Bloom is not going to make a habit of taking up with medical students and coming in so late, followed by orders for breakfast that now go beyond eggs and tea to encompass 'Findon haddy' (a haddock) and hot buttered toast. Thought of food leads her to wonder what she will have for dinner tomorrow; she thinks she will get some fish for a change. She would also like to go for a picnic, envisaging a possible *ménage à quatre* involving herself, Boylan, Bloom and Mrs Fleming, the cleaning lady. She would also like a trip to the seaside, but has unpleasant memories of going out in a rowing-boat with Bloom; Molly was so scared by Bloom's performance that she would have dearly liked to 'flagellate' him (a word she has learned from one of the semi-erotic novels Bloom has bought her). Nonetheless, the smell of the sea excited her, bringing back Gibraltar to her memory.

She frequently finds Bloom's presence a nuisance, but on the other hand she does not like being alone in the house at night, so she decides she will 'have to put up with it'. He does have his uses, as on the night Molly thought she heard a burglar in the kitchen. Bloom had many ambitious schemes on moving into this large house, but Molly is used to Bloom and his schemes: he had similarly promised her the sun, moon and stars prior to their marriage, but she had prudently discounted these; Molly knew her man.

Now Milly is absent, Molly is even more alone in the house; she suspects that Bloom dispatched Milly to Mullingar deliberately to get her out of the way while Boylan was in the vicinity. Molly has been conscious of Milly's observant presence lately and is glad she is not now on the premises. Her daughter's growing independence is a source of conflicting emotions for Molly: she is both glad and sorry to see the inevitable separation between them under way.

Molly is not happy at Bloom's bringing Stephen down into the kitchen where, at times at least, her underclothes are on display: the Blooms' cleaning woman, Mrs Fleming, is not the most efficient and is in any case leaving to look after her sick husband, who beats her. At this point Molly's reflections are interrupted by the arrival of her period, proof, at least, that Boylan had not made her pregnant. Remembering various awkward moments when this has come on her, she gets out of bed to avail of the chamber pot and of cloths she has in a press.

Sentence 7

This emission from her insides reminds Molly, still sitting on the pot, of her visit to a 'dry old stick' of a gynaecologist. The visit was apparently occasioned by a complaint brought on by frequent masturbation due to the stimulating nature of Bloom's letters in the days of their courtship. She ponders on their lives together now: Bloom's frequent changes of job and of address, the sense that no real social or financial advance is ever being made—and, to crown it all, the sudden demand for breakfast in bed in the morning.

Returning to bed, Molly still has her suspicions about Bloom's activities during the day just past; she believes he was with 'some little bitch'. She has no time for the company in which Bloom found himself during the day; she is convinced they are all out to get what they can from each other, leading her to vow: 'well theyre not going to get my husband again into their clutches'. She does admit, however, that Simon Dedalus has a fine voice. This leads her on to wonder what his son is like, and what Bloom is up to in suggesting a greater intimacy between her and Stephen. She realises with great excitement that Stephen's arrival had been forecast in the cards she laid out that morning. Molly is fond of poetry (she thought Bloom was a poet initially). Inevitably, thoughts of poetry bring her back to Gibraltar and to song, the medium in which much of her soul finds expression. She happily envisages a romantic future with Stephen, until she remembers that there is still the problem of Bloom to be dealt with.

Sentence 8

Thought of Stephen increases her dissatisfaction with Boylan; she recalls with greater anger his slapping her bottom on his departure the previous day. Nonetheless, sexual attraction is domineering and ubiquitous; Molly does not see why it occasions such jealousy and turmoil. She herself, in fantasy at least, would not mind trying it with anyone she could get 'if the fellow you want isnt there'.

However, her thoughts return to Stephen: she envies parents who 'have a fine son like that'. Molly has none; and she shares, in a more considered way, Bloom's grief at this loss. She has her own tenderness for dead Rudy, less overt than Bloom's, but real nonetheless.

She still hopes that Stephen might stay, and sketches out an idyllic future for them; far from bringing Bloom his breakfast in bed, she now envisages Bloom bringing up breakfast for both her and Stephen in their separate beds. Trying again to get to sleep, she turns the lamp down lower. She plans to get up early in the morning to go over to the markets and buy some nice food. But she also wants to excite Bloom, to allow him come off on her bottom if he wants, and then she would expect to get at least £1 or 30 shillings from him to enable her to buy underclothes. However, her period is an unfortunate obstacle to this plan. Still, she does hope Stephen will turn up at 7 Eccles Street; if he does, she would like to have flowers in the house; she would 'love to have the whole place swimming in roses'.

This mention of roses awakens her sense of marvel at nature and its works; she can't imagine that anyone could doubt the existence of God given the stupendous phenomena of the natural world. It would be as feasible to deny God's existence as to try to stop the sun rising the next day. The mention of the sun brings back to her Bloom's words on that fateful day when he finally proposed to her, following a long kiss, as they lay together on Howth Head: 'the sun shines for you he said.' Molly did not answer immediately (a female privilege); instead, her mind went back to a world that Bloom never knew, the world of the Gibraltar of her youth. She remembered the scenes there, the heat, the people, the sea, the streets. She also remembers Mulvey, her first love, who kissed her under the Moorish wall. All of this went through her mind before she answered Bloom, with whom Mulvey has been partly mixed up; but she finally did reply to Bloom, and the book ends with her momentous yes.

CORRESPONDENCES

In *The Odyssey*, Penelope, the wife of Odysseus, is subjected to the unremitting attentions of the suitors during her husband's prolonged absence. Faced with such pressure, she resorted to various devices to keep them at bay: one such strategy was to ask for time to complete a tapestry, or web, she was weaving as a shroud for Odysseus's elderly father before she decides which suitor to accept. Each night, however, Penelope secretly unwove the shroud she had woven by day, thus ensuring that the work would never be completed. Although the suitors eventually realised they were being duped, Penelope gained three years' grace as a result of her stratagem. Penelope is a byword for patience and endurance.

After the slaughter of the suitors, Penelope is woken by the nurse, Euryclea, and told what has happened. At first she does not believe it: in fact she is remarkably stubborn in her disbelief. She accepts that the person who has killed the suitors is indeed Odysseus only when he turns out to know a detail of the construction of their bed that is known to no one else.

In the Gilbert schema, Penelope (Molly) is the earth; the Web that she weaves is movement (presumably the motion of the earth both on its axis and through space, since Molly herself is virtually motionless).

STYLE

A reader who has got this far on the stylistic obstacle course of *Ulysses* may well feel that there can be no surprises left. Nevertheless, the style of 'Penelope' will still come as something of a shock. The absence of all punctuation (save for one enigmatic full stop at the end of 'sentence' five); the absence of apostrophe marks in words such as 'don't' or 'can't'; the absence of all quotation marks or initial capitals or italics to indicate quotations (mainly from songs): all these make for an initially disconcerting reading experience. After a while, though, a reader does begin to get the hang of how this episode works, and thereby gains access to an experience of interiority virtually without parallel in literature.

The context of the episode is clear enough: this is Molly lying in bed, reflecting on the day and on what Bloom has told her; and the style is that of her own unspeaking consciousness as thoughts and feelings go through her mind. The normal appurtenances of reading – punctuation, apostrophes, italics, etc – are dispensed with in order to render the character's consciousness with unprecedented directness. This is the way Molly thinks; this is the way Molly's thoughts are given.

The reader's task is to try to follow that mind in its meanderings, and Molly's is a very meandering mind indeed. However, it is by no means an impossible task: soon enough the reader begins to supply the missing punctuation, to make the breaks that the sense demands, to accommodate sudden changes in person and number and to fill in the gaps that Molly's easily diverted mental progress can leave in its wake. When Molly is musing on Mrs Maybrick, who murdered her husband, and the text runs 'wasnt she the downright villain to go and do a thing like that', the reader is in a position to supply the missing question mark after 'that' and the apostrophe in 'wasnt'.

Again, when Molly is reflecting on Bloom's supposed infatuation with the unsatisfactory maidservant, Mary, and the text reads 'but I told her what I thought of her suggesting me to go out to be alone with her', the reader realises that 'her' and 'suggesting' do not refer to the same person despite their proximity, the 'her' being Mary and the 'suggesting' being done by Bloom.

Remembering her first love, Harry Mulvey, whom she met in Gibraltar, Molly reflects: 'he went to India he was to write the voyages those men have to make to the ends of the world and back'. The reader quickly perceives that the necessary break is between 'write' and 'the voyages': it is not that Mulvey 'was to write the voyages' but rather that he was to write to Molly; 'the voyages' marks another, though related, turn in Molly's thought processes.

Very temporarily, the reader will interpret the passage as 'write the voyages'; this is part of the process of reading 'Penelope', a process of weaving backwards and forwards, of revision and reinterpretation that is one of the most involving and exciting that literature has to offer. And it is appropriate to hold in mind, however temporarily, the possibility that 'write the voyages' is the correct reading; 'writing the voyages' is what Homer, and Joyce after him, does.

The necessary breaking up of the flow of 'Penelope' into relatively coherent and logical units is secondary to the experience of the multiple possibilities that Molly's mode of expression gives rise to. The reader has no choice but to engage, initially at least, with these possibilities in order to make sense of this text. Making sense is what we do, but 'Penelope' really works at a level prior to the logical and coherent dimension.

In addition to the micro-structures of meaning that the reader discovers while engaging with 'Penelope', there are also larger structures holding the episode together. Joyce, in a letter to Budgen, said that the episode's 'four cardinal points [are] the female breasts, arse, womb and cunt expressed by the words *because, bottom* (in all senses bottom button, bottom of the class, bottom of the sea, bottom of his heart), *woman, yes.*'

These words, because, bottom, woman and yes, do provide a non-grammatical framework for the episode. The 'yeses' signal a pause, a moment of self-confirmation, before the flow resumes again. They, and to a lesser extent the 'becauses', are markers that help the reader also to draw breath before plunging into the next verbal maelstrom.

The eight 'sentences' do not obey the rules of formal grammar, but they are nonetheless not without structure. The first sentence, for instance, begins with the word 'Yes'. This 'yes' is a 'yes' of confirmation: Molly is reiterating to herself her conviction that Bloom has come off somewhere as the explanation for his demand for breakfast in bed. (Thus we are eavesdropping on Molly's reflections in midstream; they have begun before we start to overhear them.) Although she then appears to wander off into thoughts of Mrs Riordan and other matters, her mind remains focused on her husband: her fourth 'yes' brings her back to Bloom and his unusual request: 'yes he came somewhere Im sure by his appetite'. Many lines and many 'yeses' later she comes back to Bloom and his possible activities on the day before: 'yes because he couldnt possibly do without it that long'. As this long 'sentence' goes on Molly keeps returning to her theory about Bloom's behaviour, still worrying at it and not quite sure she has it right: 'I suppose it was meeting Josie Powell and the funeral and thinking about me and Boylan set him off'. So certain underlying preoccupations (later on they include Boylan and Stephen Dedalus) do recur and do underpin the apparently plotless sweep of the episode.

The technique of 'Penelope' is described in the Gilbert schema as 'monologue (female)' and the episode is often referred to as 'Molly's monologue'. This is a little misleading, insofar as the word 'monologue' implies a speaking voice. There is of course no such voice: the interiority of 'Penelope' is far deeper than that, and far more powerful. The episode offers a uniquely intimate experience of consciousness, all the more potent for the fact that the consciousness in question is a strongly libidinal one.

COMMENTARY

One of the great merits of the 'Penelope' episode of *Ulysses* is that it produces very personal responses from readers. For quite a number (I am happy to include myself in their ranks) it is the most inspired, the greatest, of Joyce's achievements; for others, however, the episode is problematical on several levels. For quite some time, the issue was obscenity; it is very easy now to be blasé about this, but to deny to 'Penelope' its power to shock is to deny something of its overall effect. Molly *is* obscene at times; this is a necessary part of her consciousness, a part that has to be taken on board, as it were, for the episode to express or exert its full potential. One certainly does not want anybody closing the book in disgust, still less calling for it to be banned, but something is also lost if a world-weary superiority blinds a reader to the full force of what Molly is expressing.

It is necessary to acknowledge fully the power of Molly's libidinal world, because if one does not, it can operate subliminally, skewing one's perceptions of her as a person. This is what appears to have happened in the early readings of Molly: critics were so taken aback at the pervasive, generalised nature of Molly's desire that they decided she had to be a slut. Support for this view was found in the famous list of lovers in the 'Ithaca' episode, a list which, as we have already seen, is actually very misleading. Starting from that premise, critics could either deplore Molly, seeing her as the final confirmation of the animal-like, waste-land-like nature of the Dublin depicted throughout the book, or celebrate her as an Earth Goddess, giving herself to all men indifferently. (This apparently was one of the job specifications for an Earth Goddess.) Deplored or celebrated, the underlying assumption was the same: Molly was completely promiscuous, sexually rapacious and sexually indifferent in her choice of partners.

Actually reading 'Penelope', however, we find that this premise is far from being well founded. Many, perhaps most, of the men who enter Molly's mind are spoken of in terms of contempt: Menton (an alleged lover) is 'that big babbyface', Lenehan (another) is 'that sponger', Val Dillon, (a third) is 'that big heathen' with 'his dirty eyes'. It is clear from the context that all three have made approaches of a sort to Molly and that this is the furthest extent of their involvement with her.

Molly, therefore, has been misread, monstrously misread. The idea that a generalised imaginative, sexual longing could coexist with a strong aversion in particular sexual instances seems to have been too much for critics to take. Her attitude to men, and her social attitudes generally, are nuanced, refined, discriminating. If these are not words that we normally associate with Molly, perhaps the reason is that we are so fixated on her sexual dimension that other aspects of her character are rendered obscure to us. She is well able to appreciate the difference between Stephen and Boylan, for instance; even if her fantasies about a relationship with Stephen are likely to remain in the realm of the imaginary, they are predicated on a real distinction.

Not only does Molly think herself fully the equal of the various men she ponders in the course of her sleepless night, she is very much their superior. Most of them, not just her alleged lovers, she despises: here she is on Arthur Griffith, a person Bloom rightly sees as 'very intelligent' and 'the coming man': 'Griffiths is he well he doesnt look it thats all I can say'. That the basis of Molly's judgment of Griffith, whom she also misnames, is a little cursory matters less than the strength of the decision being made.

She is by a considerable distance the strongest character in the book, so much so that she almost unbalances the rest of the work. Molly unweaves at night the tapestry that has been woven during the day: the characters are picked apart, their personalities mercilessly dissected by a person who outdoes them all. She even outdoes her author—and this is perhaps the best response to understandable feminist doubts about the appropriation of a woman's consciousness, even a woman's body, by a male author. That Joyce did feel he had created a character who in some sense surpassed him is indicated by one or two incidents that occurred shortly after the book was written: Joyce wrote a parody of the song 'Molly Brannigan' in which the mythical, superhuman qualities are even more strongly emphasised than in the text itself, and the author himself is a sadly, if humorously, diminished figure, clinging 'like a child to the clouds that are your petticoats'. Joyce also had a dream, of which there are two different versions, but in both of which Molly declares her independence from her creator, and indeed threatens him with death. All of this is important evidence of the degree to which Molly has outpaced her maker.

As 'Penelope' proceeds, a definite evolution in Molly's consciousness takes place: early on, she expresses a mild resentment at Boylan's slapping her bottom as he left the house, in an over-familiar way (another instance of the nuanced nature of Molly's discriminations: just because Boylan has sex with her, it does not mean that he has the right to treat her in this fashion). At the start of the very last sentence of 'Penelope', Molly's distaste for Boylan's action has sharpened emphatically: 'no thats no way for him has he no manners nor no refinement nor no nothing in his nature'. Bloom's introduction of Stephen as a possible protégé has had its effect; Molly's thoughts have turned to this preferable other. Even though this will be a virtual relationship, it does reorient Molly's fantasies in a different direction. Oddly, there is a parallel here with a work with which *Ulysses* has nothing else in common, namely Edward Albee's *Who's Afraid of Virginia Woolf?*, where a couple invent a son in order to cope with the gaps and difficulties in their lives.

Molly's last thoughts are with Bloom, not Stephen or Boylan, as she remembers that momentous day when he formally proposed to her. *Ulysses* does end on an affirmative note, but it is a note that is tied irrevocably to the past. The book, rather than offering a vision of the future (what does happen the next morning? The question is unanswerable), redeems itself and the people in it by plunging into the past, to the fortunate fall that is Molly's consent to life itself. The end of *Ulysses* confirms that Joyce's response to the paralysis he initially diagnosed as the condition of Dublin was not to escape from it, but rather to go further into it, to realise all its dimensions, especially its circularity.

More important than these considerations, however, is the extraordinary power of the book's closing pages, and it is appropriate to close with an examination of one of the sources of this power. One of the marvellous things about Molly is the musical echoes that continually permeate her musings: without any break a line from a song will float through her mind, prompted by a word, a phrase, a memory. Of course, there is nothing in the text to indicate that she is recalling a song, no italics, no quotation marks, but very often the different diction is a clear sign that a song is being quoted. Molly remembers getting her first love letter from Harry Mulvey in Gibraltar many years before; she went around the house in a state of great excitement singing 'shall I wear a white rose', probably with an eye to her attire on the thrilling day when she would 'walk out' with Mulvey. The words are from a song, 'Shall I Wear a White Rose', by H. S. Clarke and E. B. Farmer, one of many such songs that float through Molly's mind.

Towards the end of 'Penelope', as Molly fantasises about the possibility of Stephen turning up the next day and wonders what to wear, she remembers the song again and repeats the line in this new context. At the very end of 'Penelope', Molly remembers her youth in Gibraltar, where, like the Andalusian girls, she put a rose in her hair. This time she completes the quotation, adding another line from the song, 'or shall I wear a red'. The effect of this completion is the effect of all great art, much harder to describe than to experience. It is, though, a moment of closure, a moment, too, in which the power of quotation and citation, operative throughout the book, achieves its fullest expression. Mulvey, Stephen and Bloom are linked through this line from a very ordinary song; the motif of roses (quite a prominent one in the book) comes to full bloom in Molly's last song.

BIOGRAPHICAL

Line 4.   *Mrs Riordan*: first mentioned in Episode 6, 'Hades'. Stephen's relative Dante Riordan of *A Portrait*, whom Bloom and Molly later got to know in the City Arms Hotel.

38.   *Menton*: John Henry Menton, solicitor; appears in Episode 6, 'Hades'.

56.   *Mary*: Mary Driscoll, the scullery maid; appears in fantasy in Episode 15, 'Circe'.

169.   *Josie Powell*: wife of Denis Breen; appears first in
         Episode 8, 'Lestrygonians'. Based on the daughter-in-
         law of Major Powell, a model for Molly's father,
         Major Tweedy.

185.   *Floey*: one of Mat Dillon's daughters. Mat Dillon was
         an old friend of the Joyce family. One of his daughters
         had gone to Spain and was considered a 'Spanish type'.

234.   *Mrs Maybrick*: Florence Maybrick was found guilty of
         murdering her husband by poisoning him in 1889. She
         was sentenced to death but this was commuted to life
         imprisonment. She was released in January 1904.

344.   *the 2 Dedalus girls*: Katey and Boody Dedalus (based
         on two of Joyce's sisters) who appear in Episode 10,
         'Wandering Rocks'.

376.   *Kathleen Kearney*: appears as a character in the story
         'A Mother', in *Dubliners*.

378.   *Lord Roberts*: Sir Frederick Roberts (1832–1914) a
         leading British general popularly known as 'Bobs'.
         Also mentioned in Episode 14, 'Oxen of the Sun'.

386.   *Griffiths*: actually Arthur Griffith, first mentioned in
         Episode 3, 'Proteus'.

394–5.   *oom Paul . . . Krugers*: Stephanus Johannes Paulus
         Kruger (1825–1904), the leading Boer statesman,
         popularly known as 'Oom [uncle] Paul'.

429.   *Val Dillon*: Valentine Dillon, lord mayor of Dublin,
         1894–5; he died in 1904. First mentioned in Episode 8,
         'Lestrygonians'.

443.   *Lewers*: Mrs R. G. Lewers, ladies' outfitters, 67
         Grafton Street.

451.   *ORourkes*: Larry O'Rourke's pub, at 74 Dorset Street
         Upper, on the corner of Eccles Street. Bloom passes it
         in Episode 4, 'Calypso', and exchanges a word with
         Larry O'Rourke.

481.   *Mrs Langtry*: Lillie Langtry (1852–1929), the most
         famous mistress of the Prince of Wales, later King
         Edward VII.

500–1.	'*HRH he was in Gibraltar the year I was born*': the Prince of Wales visited Gibraltar in 1859 and 1876, but not in 1870, the year of Molly's birth.
510.	*Mr Cuffes*: Joe Cuffe's cattle merchant's, at Smithfield, where Bloom worked briefly; first mentioned in Episode 6, 'Hades'.
516–17.	*Todd and Burns*: Todd, Burns and Co., Ltd, drapers, silk merchants, etc., Jervis Street and Mary Street.
517.	*Lees*: Edward Lee, draper and silk mercer, Mary Street and Abbey Street.
553.	*the Comerfords party*: Mr and Mrs M. Comerford, Neptune View, 11 Leslie Avenue, Dalkey. Mentioned in Episode 17, 'Ithaca'.
573.	*Citrons Penrose*: Citron is mentioned in Episode 4, 'Calypso' and Penrose in Episode 8, 'Lestrygonians'.
576.	*doctor Brady*: mentioned in Episode 15, 'Circe'.
617.	*Concone*: Giuseppe Concone (1801–61), an Italian vocal teacher who devised popular singing exercises.
650.	'*Thomas in the shadow of Ashlydyat*': *The Shadow of Ashlydyat* is a novel by Mrs Henry Wood (1814–87). Thomas Godolphin is the hero of the novel.
682.	*general Ulysses Grant*: US president from 1869 to 1877. He did visit Gibraltar on 17 November 1878.
683.	*old Sprague*: Horatio Sprague was US consul in Gibraltar from the 1870s to his death in 1902.
684.	*the son*: Sprague's son, John Louis, was vice-consul until his death in 1886.
690–1.	*sir Garnet Wolseley*: Dublin-born British general (1833–1913), who fought in Africa.
720.	*Floey Dillon*: one of the daughters of Mat Dillon, Bloom's (and Simon Dedalus's) friend.
783.	*Oharas tower*: a tower on a high point on the Rock of Gibraltar, named after a General O'Hara, military governor of Gibraltar in the late eighteenth century.
848.	*Lunita Laredo*: Molly's mother. Very little is said about this woman, whom Molly apparently never

knew. Molly later refers to her as 'jewess looking' at line 1184. If she was indeed Jewish, this would technically make Molly Jewish also, while Bloom, whose mother was a gentile, is not.

944. *Buckleys*: John Buckley, victualler, 48 Dorset Street Upper. Mentioned by Bloom in Episode 4, 'Calypso'.

965. *Burke*: Andrew 'Pisser' Burke, mentioned as staying in the City Arms Hotel in Episode 12, 'Cyclops'. The unlovely sobriquet 'Pisser' was originally applied to a certain Pisser Duffy, with whom Joyce's brother Stanislaus had a fight in Drumcondra.

1006. *Skerrys academy*: George E. Skerry and Co, civil service, commercial and university tutors, St Stephen's Green and Harcourt Street. The Harcourt Street branch featured shorthand, typing and commercial college.

1023–4. *Tom Devans*: a friend of the Joyce family on whom the character Mr Power (first appears in Episode 6, 'Hades') was based.

1042. *Beerbohm Tree*: English actor-manager (1853–1917). Beerbohm Tree produced and played in a production of *Trilby* at the Gaiety Theatre in October 1895.

1052. *Conny Connolly*: probably linked to Connie Connolly, sister of Joyce's school friends, Vincent and Albrecht Connolly.

1055. *Martin Harvey*: Sir John Martin-Harvey (1862–1944), actor and theatrical producer, a frequent visitor to Dublin; also mentioned in Episode 13, 'Nausicaa'.

1068. *Mrs Joe Gallaher*: a friend of the Joyce family; daughter of a Major Powell, on whom Major Tweedy, Molly's father, is partly based.

1111. *Michael Gunn*: manager of the Gaiety Theatre from 1871 until his death in 1901. Also mentioned in Episode 11, 'Sirens'.

1111–12. *Mrs Kendal and her husband*: Mr and Mrs William Hunter Kendal, stage names of English actor-manager William Grimston and his wife Madge.

1113. *Drimmies*: David Drimmie & Sons, Life Assurance agents, 41 Sackville Street Lower. John Stanislaus Joyce's monthly pension cheque was channelled through this office for many years.

1153. *Dr Collins*: a Dr J. H. Collins practised at 65 Pembroke Road in 1904, but Joyce also knew an American Dr Joseph Collins in Paris. This Dr Collins later wrote on Joyce in a book called *A Doctor Looks at Literature*.

1213. *old Cohen*: there was a David Cohen, boot and shoe seller, at Engineer Lane, Gibraltar, in 1889 (the relevant time), but whether this is the person referred to is not clear.

1214. *Lord Napier*: Field Marshal Robert Napier (1810–90) was governor of Gibraltar from 1876 to 1883.

1220. *'worse and worse says Warden Daly'*: this saying and the person referred to have not been traced. It also turns up in *Finnegans Wake*. There was a Warden Daly who was a Methodist minister in nineteenth-century Galway.

1228. *the little man*: Arthur Griffith; see line 386.

1257. *Hornblower*: the porter at the Lincoln Place entrance to Trinity College. Bloom salutes him at the end of Episode 5, 'Lotus-Eaters'.

1264. *Tom Kernan*: friend of Bloom's. The incident Molly mentions is the opening of the story 'Grace' in *Dubliners*.

1342. *Billy Prescotts*: William T. C. Prescott, cleaners, head office at 8 Abbey Street Lower. The firm lasted well into the 1970s.

1343. *Keyess*: Alexander Keyes, grocer, 5–6 Ballsbridge. Bloom tries to place an advertisement from Keyes in Episode 7, 'Aeolus'.

1414–16. *Bloomfield laundry ... model laundry*: Model Laundry, owned by Bloomfield Steam Laundry Company Ltd, Edmondstown, Rathfarnham.

1463–4.   *Delapaz Delagracia*: these are fairly standard Spanish names in Gibraltar.

1464.   *father Vilaplana*: Father J. Vilaplana was a priest working in the Cathedral of St Mary the Crowned in Gibraltar, though apparently not until 1912.

1465.   *Rosales y Oreilly*: the name is perfectly possible; a James O'Reilly lived in the street mentioned in 1890.

1466.   *Mrs Opisso*: Mrs Catherine Opisso, milliner and dressmaker, Governor's Street, Gibraltar.

1475.   *Valera*: Juan Valera (1824–1905), Spanish novelist.

1482.   *Abrines*: R. and J. Abrines, bakers, Main Street, Gibraltar.

1497.   *Walpoles*: Walpole Brothers, drapers, Suffolk Street, Dublin.

1548.   *Lambes*: Miss Alicia Lambe, fruiterer and florist, 33 Sackville Street Upper.

1548.   *Findlaters*: Alexander Findlater & Co. Ltd, general grocers, 29–32 Sackville Street Upper, with many branches around Dublin. Mentioned by Bloom in Episode 4, 'Calypso'.

1554.   *Liptons*: grocers, 59–61 Dame Street, also with many Dublin branches. Part of a large British chain.

SELECT GLOSSARY

Note: Some of Molly's colloquial and Hiberno-English terms are very hard to interpret. An attempt is made here but certainty is not guaranteed.

Line 195.   plabbery: defined in Diarmuid O Muirithe's *Anglo-Irish Dictionary* as indistinct soft talk.

204.   glauming: 'grasping', 'clutching'.

214.   grigged: 'teased'.

290.   skeezing: 'spying'.

306.   O Maria Santisima: Italian, 'O Most Holy Mary'.

307.   dreeping: Donegal dialect form of 'dripping'.

441.   Manola: a Spanish street song.

507.   plottering: probably a variant of 'pottering', which
       sounds appropriate; perhaps combines 'pottering' and
       'plotting'.

512.   mirada: Spanish, 'look'.

520.   mathering: unknown; I am unconvinced by Gifford's
       suggestion of Irish dialect, 'mothering'.

557.   meadero: Spanish, 'urinal'.

673.   taittering: apparently English dialect 'tilting', but it
       does not fit the context, which sounds more like
       'trembling'.

687.   jellibees: Molly's version of 'jellabas', the loose hooded
       cloak worn by Arab men.

720.   pisto madrileno: tomatoes and red peppers in Madrid
       style.

751.   horquilla: Spanish, 'hairpin'.

756.   carabineros: Spanish, 'carbine-carrying soldier'.

774.   de la Flora: Spanish, 'of the flower'.

779.   pesetas and the perragordas: small Spanish coins.

802.   embarazada: Spanish, 'pregnant'.

822.   block: slang for sexual intercourse.

844.   brig: slang for 'to steal'.

865.   peau dEspagne: French, 'skin of Spain', a perfume.

879.   skitting: laughing, but it seems here to be linked to
       'skipping'.

919.   sierra nevada: Spanish, 'snowy range', the highest
       mountain range in Spain, about 130 miles from
       Gibraltar.

936.   lecking: variant of 'licking'.

952.   ruck of Mary Ann coalboxes: obscure, but Molly
       seems to be referring to 'common' over-dressed
       women, dressed more for the music hall than for a
       holiday outing.

1141. scout: slang for 'eject liquid forcibly'. Probably derived
       from 'skite' (see Dolan).

1174.   strap: Hiberno-English for a bold girl.

1185.   sloothering: Hiberno-English, 'cajoling', 'coaxing'.

1187.   blather: Hiberno-English, 'nonsensical talk'.

1188.   strool: probably derived from Irish *srúill*, a river or a current, which fits the context. Not in Dolan.

1189.   O beau pays de la Touraine: French, 'O beautiful country of la Touraine', an aria at the beginning of Act 3 of Meyerbeer's *Les Huguenots*.

1251.   wethen: Short for 'well then'.

1345.   ruck: a crowd of 'common' people.

1394.   coronado: Spanish, 'tonsured'; Molly probably intends *cornudo*, 'horned', 'cuckolded'.

1471-2.   como esta usted . . . y usted: Spanish, 'How are you? Very well, thanks, and you?'

1483.   criada: 'maid'.

1486-7.   dos huevos estrellados senor: Spanish, 'two fried eggs, sir'.

1507-8.   mi fa pieta . . . son piu forte: Italian, 'I'm sorry for Massetto! . . . Quick, I am no longer strong'; from Mozart's *Don Giovanni*.

1595.   posadas: Spanish, 'inns' or 'town houses'.

1597.   serene: the Spanish *sereno*, the call of the night police as they make their rounds.

Ulysses: *An Afterword*

THE 'FIRST' *ULYSSES*

In September 1906, Joyce wrote from Rome to his brother Stanislaus that he was planning a new story for *Dubliners*; it was to deal with a man called Mr Alfred Hunter. We now know a lot more about Hunter and his wife than we did even twenty years ago. We know he was an advertisement canvasser, like Bloom, and that his wife was called Marion, like Bloom's. We already knew that she was rumoured to be unfaithful, like Bloom's wife. Quite a few aspects of Hunter's life seem to resemble Bloom's. On the other hand, we know that he had no Jewish blood and that the legend that he rescued and looked after Joyce after an altercation rests on very shaky foundations. Joyce, though, may have believed that Hunter was Jewish. Perhaps the very fact that he was rumoured to be Jewish was enough. The new story was to be called 'Ulysses'. The story, as Joyce wrote to Stanislaus on 6 February 1907, 'never got any forrader than the title', but it is a fact of the first importance that the title 'Ulysses' was floating around in Joyce's mind from as early as 1906. It is more than likely that if the story had been written, Hunter would have been a Bloom-type figure; it is even possible that the central incident of the real *Ulysses,* Bloom's rescue of Stephen after he is assaulted by the soldiers, might have formed the centre of the proposed *Dubliners* story, despite its dubious foundation in reality.

It is clear that some sort of parallel between the story of Hunter and the story of *The Odyssey* must have been envisaged even in 1906; the parallel is in no sense an afterthought, added on to a pre-existing structure to give it weight or profundity, even though many details of the correspondences were worked out later. It is also clear – and very touching to know – that this once ultra-obscure Dubliner, Alfred H. Hunter, was the catalyst for the greatest work of literature of the twentieth century.

It is impossible to know how Joyce intended to incorporate or allegorise or boil down *The Odyssey* in the confines of a short story: given the things that have been read into some of the actual *Dubliners* stories, however, he would probably have managed. It is likely, though, that he soon realised that in order to 'do justice' to the already envisaged parallel between the story of his ordinary Dubliner and *The Odyssey*, a much larger canvas was needed. Indeed, a diary entry by his brother Stanislaus in November 1907 indicates that James had already realised that the concept was too big for a short story: it was now to be 'a short book', 'a Dublin *Peer Gynt*, implying some kind of wandering and return as its principal motif.

Joyce had always been greatly attracted to Homer's hero: as he told Frank Budgen, Odysseus (the name is Romanised to Ulysses) possessed a far greater range of human qualities than did those born bruisers Hector and Achilles. Odysseus was a tactician, a strategist, a reluctant warrior, a husband, a father, a lover of music, an exile; all these traits are replicated in Joyce's hero, Leopold Bloom. Given the amount that Joyce could see in the figure of Odysseus alone, it is not surprising that the parallel he envisaged had to operate on a grand scale.

Moreover, Joyce's thoughts, as the *Dubliners* collection neared completion, seem already to have been running in a strongly mythical, allegorical direction, an area for which the 'classical' short story is unsuited. (Another proposed title for an unwritten *Dubliners* story at the time was 'The Last Supper'.) But it remains a fascinating fact that the vast novel which was published in 1922 had its roots in an unwritten short story. Traces, at least, of this original conception (perhaps Bloom's rescue of Stephen and their return to Bloom's home, as mentioned above) may be found in the multi-layered work that actually was produced. The relatively humble origins of Joyce's masterpiece may suggest, for instance, that the *Ulysses* we have is an immense detour, an immense distraction, from a basically simple underlying story or situation.

THE LINATI LETTER

Joyce made relatively few helpful statements about *Ulysses* both as he was writing it and afterwards: as he grew older he became more and more reticent about his work. Quite a number of these statements are reported by other people; there is no suggestion that they are made up, but obviously memory can be deceptive in these matters, so a certain amount of caution has to be exercised. The most helpful comment he made was in a letter in Italian to the Italian critic Carlo Linati on 21 September 1920. In it, Joyce states of *Ulysses*:

> It is the epic of two races (Israel-Ireland) and at the same time the cycle of the human body as well as a little story of a day (life) ... It is also a kind of encyclopaedia. My intention is not only to render the myth *sub specie temporis nostri* but also to allow each adventure (that is, every hour, every organ, every art being interconnected and interrelated in the somatic scheme of the whole) to condition and even to create its own technique. Each adventure is so to speak one person even though it is composed of persons – as Aquinas relates of the heavenly hosts.

Every phrase in this short passage is illuminating, both in terms of theme and technique. The 'epic of two races' concerns the highly tentative relations between Stephen and Bloom, and Bloom's own equivocal position in Dublin as an Irish Jew. Possible parallels between the two races are frequently implied, and are made explicit in the 'Ithaca' episode. Underlying the high comedy of the 'Cyclops' (public house) episode is the awareness that the Irish drinkers, who might be expected to feel an analogy with Bloom as persecuted Jew, instead align themselves with their English oppressors, wishing merely to exchange places with them. The British empire would, if possible, be replaced by an Irish empire: that is the only liberation these people can envisage. Bloom becomes a scapegoat, reviled for his victimhood. Later, however, in the 'Ithaca' episode, he and Stephen do explore some genuine affinities between the two races and create some sort of rapport. This is one of the few positive developments that *Ulysses* allows itself, though even this is somewhat put in question by Stephen's innate suspicion, as evinced in the distinctly inappropriate ballad he later chooses to sing.

The use of the word 'epic', rather than 'novel', shows the scale on which Joyce had conceived his work and provides a strong clue as to the way in which it is to be read. Conventional novelistic expectations with regard to character, plot, plausibility, etc., may be unhelpful, even a hindrance, when something on the scale of *Ulysses* is involved.

The encyclopaedic nature of the book is very evident: it describes itself as an 'all-including chronicle'. This encyclopaedic quality is one that readers often have great difficulty with: the long lists of people and places in 'Cyclops' (the pub episode); the exhaustive instances of English prose in 'Oxen of the Sun' (the maternity hospital); above all the endless enumeration of facts and details in the 'Ithaca' episode can seem pointless and boring. Once again, the novelistic context is the wrong one for appreciating these elements of the book: such lists have their place in epics, and are used in *Ulysses* as a form of epic parody (this is similarly their function in Rabelais, who was also very fond of them); in 'Ithaca' they form part of the episode's strange poetry. There is a tradition of literary encyclopaedias; *Ulysses* is unusual only in presenting such an encyclopaedia in the parodic form of a novel.

Even more important are Joyce's references to the cycle of the human body and to the little story of a day corresponding to a life. This points to one of the crucial aspects of *Ulysses*: that it is conceived as a total form which transcends the individual people in it. In some way, the book *Ulysses* is a person, a person who contains all the people who appear in it as characters. This is the point of the various organs of the body assigned to the various episodes: collectively, these organs and these episodes constitute a whole body, which is itself the book. The book is then itself the cycle of this body, its changes and functions, as it goes through a day, a day which is itself an epitome of the cycle of a life.

This conception is again likely to encounter some reader resistance.

It can seem as if the actual characters in the book, even Bloom and Molly, are being devalued by this insistence on a larger totality that encompasses them. But Joyce is in this respect, as in some others, almost a medieval writer, interested in larger units, and in larger forms, than the personal. The problem again arises from certain standard expectations of fiction, which began in the late seventeenth century as the classic form of bourgeois self-expression, placing the individual, and the individual's concerns, at the centre of society. Joyce is more like Dante or Blake or Rabelais than any other novelist in his focus on larger literary forms, indeed on literature itself as a total form. Bloom never loses his humanity, but even he is caught up in something that encompasses him.

The reference to 'each adventure' (or episode) being allowed 'to condition and even to create its own technique' is also a vital clue to the method of *Ulysses*. It is this that accounts for the bewildering variety of styles deployed throughout the book. Each episode is conceived as a total environment (just as the whole book is in a larger framework); the literary representation then modifies according to the circumstances of this new environment. Again, this is something larger than the consciousnesses of the individual characters; it will not just be explained by the state of mind of Bloom or Stephen at a given time. The setting, the time of day, the particular art being featured: all will have their effect on the literary representation. Not only is it larger than any individual character; it is also larger than an individual author. It is often unhelpful to think of James Joyce as the direct author of this material at all; as mentioned before, the writing has been entrusted to the presiding genius of each episode. Each one writes itself.

Once more, this implies a degree of impersonality – authorial, this time – with which readers might well be uncomfortable. However, it does not mean that the writing is being done by a machine. It might be better to think of some larger social entity – the collective voice of Dublin, even – as the repository of these various techniques, which the novel draws on. This is not unlike the situation of Homer, who may well be a social construct himself.

'ONE THINKS OF HOMER'

While it is impossible really to know what might be in a writer's mind when embarking on a major work such as *Ulysses* (the writer himself may not know), it seems likely that Joyce saw the Homeric epic as a way of uniting two strands of his work that had hitherto been separate: the 'Stephen Dedalus' strand and the *Dubliners* strand. The 'Stephen Dedalus' strand covers *Chamber Music*, the abortive novel *Stephen Hero*, *Exiles* and *A Portrait of the Artist as a Young Man*; the *Dubliners* strand covers *Dubliners* and some of the epiphanies that Joyce had been writing earlier. The 'Stephen Dedalus' strand was intense, highly subjective, elaborate, over-wrought in every sense. It dealt almost exclusively with a personal world and the hero is in radical opposition to the social world in which he finds himself. The *Dubliners* strand was detached, ironic, observant, deploying 'scrupulous meanness' as its main mode. The characters do not struggle against or oppose their society; instead, they are presented as trapped within it, unable to break free of the pervasive paralysis. The two modes in which Joyce was working correspond to the two main literary means of expression in the late nineteenth century: naturalism and impressionism, intense objectivity, as in Zola and Hardy, or intense subjectivity, as in the Symbolists or in 'decadent' novelists such as Huysmans and Wilde.

Joyce's tendency, which was ever integrative, was to bring these modes together in one work. *Ulysses* 'objectivises' the subjective tradition by placing consciousness, including the consciousness of Stephen Dedalus, in a social framework and providing it with social links; Stephen, it turns out, is also a Dubliner, and not just in name. At the same time, *Ulysses* 'subjectivises' the social world of Dublin by endowing its people with an inner life whose intensity matches that of the more aristocratic possessors of privileged consciousness who were the favoured vehicles of the Symbolists and their epigones. *Ulysses* is in this respect a marvellously democratic book. If you delve into anyone's inner life, it seems to say, you get something just as rich and strange as the world of Mallarmé.

Not only are the people in it fully the equal of the more advanced Symbolist poets; they are also the equal of the heroes and villains of the 'vast expanse' of the Homeric world. For a crucial point about *Ulysses* is that Homer is not being used to put Dublin down: the Homeric parallels are not there, as some early readers thought, to show up the lives of these Dubliners as debased and inferior, wanting in heroism, etc. No, these lives are in their own way just as heroic, just as adventurous. The Joycean view of history is not of an inevitable decline, *à la* most of his fellow Modernists, still less of an ongoing perfectibility, *à la* most of the eighteenth century and some of the more optimistic elements of the nineteenth century; rather it is cyclical, based on an eternal recurrence. It is here that much of the power of *Ulysses* lies.

The attitude is very different from that of T. S. Eliot and Ezra Pound, where the modern age really is being compared with antiquity – very much to the former's disadvantage.

JOYCE THE MODERNIST

This brings us to the vexed issue of Joyce's relation to Modernism. Classifying writers is a natural and inevitable process; no writer's work exists in such isolation that it is without relation to the tendencies and currents (both literary and extra-literary) of the writer's time. Even the most ostensibly apolitical writers, like Joyce, are expressing something of the spirit of their age when they express themselves. Modernism is the term applied to the radical new developments in the arts that began in the 1890s and reached full flowering in the early 1920s (*Ulysses* was published in 1922). In literature, the term has two meanings: a set of techniques and a set of attitudes.

The techniques feature discontinuities, subjectivity, an abandonment of linear developmental logic, abrupt transitions, more intense and direct experience of consciousness than any previously attempted. This consciousness was fragmentary, episodic, uninterested in logical and coherent connections. Temporal narrative sequence was disrupted in favour of a more fluid conception of time. Indeed, the entire dimensions of time and space, and the relations between them, were being reconceived, as they were simultaneously in science by Einstein. In this sense, Joyce is the ultra-Modernist, the Modernist of Modernists, the one who pushed such techniques, especially internalisation, further than anyone else. Nor is it just a matter of technique: Joyce is a Modernist also in terms of character. Bloom is not a stable, fixed character in the manner of the classical novelists: as the 'Circe' episode in particular demonstrates, his personality is fluid, he can assume various identities, he can even switch genders. He is much more like a character from Shakespearean comedy than from the nineteenth-century novelistic tradition.

As a set of attitudes, literary Modernism was identified with a belief in hierarchy and order, in large-scale assertions of will to power, in a return to mythical roots for a renewal of a degenerate society. The fragmentary consciousness it features is an unhappy one, a consciousness adrift and trapped in a rootless, Godless society, longing for coherence and searching for a vehicle (religion, fascism) through which to bring it about. Literary Modernism was a reaction – a highly complex reaction – to the social and personal fissures induced by the huge technological changes that marked the start of the twentieth century.

In so far as Modernism is identified with such attitudes, then Joyce is not a Modernist at all. His book is emphatically not about 'the immense panorama of futility and anarchy which is contemporary history', to cite Eliot's attempt to describe *Ulysses*. Hence, the term 'Joyce's Modernism' has to be very carefully construed: yes, he is a Modernist master in the technical sense; no, he is not a Modernist at all in the thematic sense.

FATHER AND SON

Ulysses does more than just bring the 'Stephen Dedalus' strand and the *Dubliners* strand of its author's work together in juxtaposition. It gradually integrates them as the work proceeds. The stories of Stephen

Dedalus and Leopold Bloom start off as quite separate, unrelated. But various subtle correspondences are soon established between them. The first is the allusion by Mulligan's friend at the Forty Foot to the 'photo girl' that Bannon has met in Mullingar; although the reader does not know it then, this is Milly Bloom. Many other narrative threads link Bloom and Stephen throughout the day: their paths cross at several points, and of course Bloom is intensely aware of and interested in Stephen, while Stephen seems barely conscious of the older man's presence. But there is a far more profound connection between them than mere narrative echoes.

Towards the end of the third episode, 'Proteus', Stephen reflects: 'Dead breaths I living breathe, tread dead dust, devour a urinous offal from all dead.' On the next page, at the start of the first episode involving Bloom, we read that Bloom liked 'grilled mutton kidneys which gave to his palate a fine tang of faintly scented urine.' Stephen's metaphorical consumption of a 'urinous offal' is matched by Bloom's literal one. In 'Proteus' also, Stephen remembers his dream of the previous night, in which a man whom he meets on a 'street of harlots' invites him into a dwelling and holds a melon against his face. This prefigures Stephen's eventual meeting with Bloom in the 'Circe' episode. The linkages go even further back, however: Haines dreams of a black panther; at the end of the library episode, Bloom is described as walking with the 'step of a pard'. Later he is called a 'Black wary hecat'. Bloom is then the black panther of which Haines dreamed. These secret correspondences go on throughout the day.

Bloom gradually takes on mythical aspects, and not merely in his Homeric dimension. For Stephen, Bloom is even a possible killer; this seems to be the point of the curious ballad that Stephen chooses to sing while a guest in Bloom's kitchen. One can see, then, why at best any rapport between the two is provisional, and why Stephen declines Bloom's invitation to remain for the night. This issue complicates the theme of paternity which is often seen as the essence of the novel: Bloom's 'fatherhood' of Stephen will remain very virtual, and indeed is rejected by his putative son. The novel's differing perspectives are difficult for readers to keep in mind simultaneously: Bloom, for

Stephen, is the black panther, the darkness shining in the brightness, Christ, or any number of possibilities, though mostly negative ones; for Bloom, he is just Bloom; for the reader, he is Ulysses.

Stephen's attitude to Bloom shows why Joyce lost interest in the young artist: all Stephen's positions are fixed. In any given situation, you know how he is going to behave and react. Bloom is different; Bloom has powers of development that continually intrigue his creator.

NIGHT AND DAY

As mentioned in the commentary on 'Ithaca', the Homeric world is one of exceptional brightness: everything is strongly illuminated, no relevant detail is kept in shadow. Nothing is left unexplained. This sunny, highly lit quality makes *The Odyssey* particularly suitable as the framework for a 'day book', a book, like *Ulysses*, that takes place over a whole day and is partly about a day. Day and its values – clarity, precision, freshness – dominate especially the earlier parts of the book. Later, of course, things get more complicated. But even from the start, there is a counter-tendency to this upholding of the qualities of daylight. Both Stephen and Bloom are dressed in black – the one in mourning for his mother, the other out of respect for Paddy Dignam. Very early on, in the 'Nestor' episode, Stephen, thinking of the Moors and their contribution to civilisation, reflects on 'a darkness shining in brightness'. He thereby reverses the opening of St John's gospel, which speaks of Christ as a light shining in the darkness which the darkness could not comprehend. This is again a foreshadowing of Bloom the black panther.

So in some way the two main characters of *Ulysses* are working against the novel's official agenda, working against the clarity and order of the schema, and opening up 'another' *Ulysses*, a *Ulysses* that is much 'darker' and more affective than the world of daylight which surrounds them. This role is emphasised by their respective alienation from the society around them, their position as outsiders, at odds with the prevailing ideologies of their day. Stephen's distancing is clear enough; in the case of Bloom, too, the tide of history is not with his rationalist, practical approach to social problems (running a tramline from the cattle market to the quays). All Bloom's schemes of civic regeneration are going to run into the rock of the 'hearts with one purpose alone', that will dominate Irish history for much of the coming century.

Ulysses, then, is an ambiguous day-book: some of its deeper impulses seem to be straining against its ostensible programme, the elaborate programme of parallels and correspondences outlined in the famous schema. And of course Molly's final nocturnal episode, part of a long tradition of night meditations, such as Sir Thomas Browne's *The Garden of Cyrus*, undoes the strict categories of the day's discriminations in favour of a seamless merging which ultimately engulfs the whole book in the abysm of the past: 'and O that awful deepdown torrent'.

ULYSSES IN PROGRESS

The title of this section is identical with that of Michael Groden's classic book on the writing of *Ulysses*, which deals with the same issue from a textual angle. It concerns what many readers seem to find the central problem of the book, the issue that remains after one has absorbed the Homeric parallels; faced the challenge of the many styles; taken on board the different bodily organs, colours, etc., appertaining to each episode; struggled with many recondite words and phrases; learned to correlate elements from widely different parts of the book, and performed many other readerly feats: what makes this book hang together? What unifies it in its bewildering diversity? Can the centre hold?

It is not that organisation is lacking; if anything, the book is over-organised. When the novel appeared in 1922, the initial impression was one of chaos, 'a slice of life', a disorganised stream of consciousness. After a while, though, it emerged that *Ulysses* is structured with extreme care; anything less arbitrary or random it would be hard to imagine. But structure is not the same as unity, the 'organic form' that the Romantics prized as the highest attribute of a work of art.

This, though, may be the problem: perhaps 'unity' of that sort is not what *Ulysses* is about, or for. The issue really concerns the dramatic change, or turn, that occurs in the book about midway through it. Up to the 'Sirens' episode, the book has been largely a serious work about two men both of whom are in difficult situations.

The Stephen Dedalus we meet at the beginning of *Ulysses* is a very different person from the soaring, confident figure who was going forth to encounter the reality of experience at the end of *A Portrait of the Artist as a Young Man*. This is a defeated, aimless Stephen, unable to get past the guilt and remorse occasioned by his mother's death. He drifts around Dublin all day, spending the money he has earned and retreating further and further into drink. 'Bitterness' is not a term one associates with the earlier Stephen, who is essentially confident and arrogant; it is the keynote of the Stephen of *Ulysses*.

Bloom is not anguished in the way that Stephen is, but his own situation is also very difficult. Principally, there is the hurt of Molly's affair with Boylan and the absence of satisfactory sexual relations that underlies it. Bloom spends much of the day trying to avoid his own awareness of this painful reality but he does not succeed. In addition to this, though, there are the actual circumstances of Bloom's social and commercial life, which are just as constricted as those of any character in *Dubliners*. The fact that Bloom is something of a freethinker makes little difference: Mr James Duffy in 'A Painful Case' is also something of a freethinker, and little good it does him.

A novel which features an extended visit to a cemetery as one of its principal early episodes does not seem likely to conduce to gaiety, and in general, up to the 'Wandering Rocks' episode, the tone of *Ulysses* is that of a hugely expanded *Dubliners* short story.

It is all the more surprising, therefore, when, from the 'Sirens' episode on, the book begins to take on a different tonality: things that had been very serious begin to seem merely occasions for fun. 'Sirens' is, I believe, the crucial episode in this respect. It ought to be the most serious of them all, since it marks the time when Boylan arrives at Eccles Street for his assignation with Molly. Bloom even sees Boylan depart from the Ormond Hotel for this fateful encounter. But the seriousness of the situation disappears under a stylistic overlay of musical parallels, jokes, allusions, songs and many other diversions. By the next episode, 'Cyclops', the change is well advanced: as mentioned in the commentary on that episode, the death of Paddy Dignam, which weighed heavily on the earlier part of the book (the effect of his death on his son had been movingly portrayed in the 'Wandering Rocks' episode) is now a standing joke, an occasion for much comedy.

If *Ulysses* is about anything, it is about this change of tone, more than it is about paternity, or androgyny, or colonialism, or Irish freedom, or many another thematic word one could summon up. There is rather more to it than just a change of style, for the novel has already been stylistically quite diverse before we get to 'Sirens'. The 'Aeolus' and the 'Scylla and Charybdis' episodes in particular show very distinctive stylistic traits. Indeed, the headlines in the 'Aeolus' episode are a foretaste of the tonal shift, but the actual 'Aeolus' narrative retains the seriousness that characterises all the early part of the book. No, the difference from 'Sirens' on is more a change of register, of attitude. It is a kind of liberation, a liberation into style. Bloom's situation, and Stephen's, does not radically change in the course of the day; but something does change in the writing of the book. Against all the odds, it transpires that we have been reading a comic work. Nothing would have seemed less likely judging by the tone of the opening episodes. In the static world of Joycean Dublin, a difference has occurred – and that is in itself a remarkable fact, flying in the face of the entire aesthetic credo enunciated in *A Portrait* and embodied in *Dubliners*.

Ultimately, then, Joyce is an Aristotelian, not a Platonic novelist. Despite the 'spatial form' that *Ulysses* is often held to embody, it is a movement, an 'actuality of the possible as possible'. The conditions of possibility of that movement are obscure, but they have something to do with Bloom's infinite adaptability, his ability to metamorphose into whatever shape seems appropriate, while still remaining

Leopold Bloom. Bloom, an entelechy, is still Bloom 'under everchanging forms'. Poised between two very clearly defined characters, Stephen and Molly, Bloom's fluidity is his, and the book's, salvation. It is this, ultimately, and not the Homeric parallels, or the stream of consciousness technique, that provides the key to *Ulysses*.

The movement of *Ulysses*, however, is cyclical, not progressive; it is the story of one day, and there is some sense that once Molly has unwoven the book's tangled tapestry at the end, it will weave itself together again the next day. The characters will move through the same or other predestined patterns, repeating paradigms of which they know nothing. It is as if the movement of *Ulysses*, rather than being a liberation from the paralysis portrayed in *Dubliners*, actually represents a deeper experience of it, a conversion of paralysis into eternal recurrence – the only movement possible for Joyce. This is a movement that definitively aligns *Ulysses* with Eastern philosophies rather than Western, goal-oriented religions. The Eastern affinities of the book were first proposed by Stuart Gilbert in a very early study. They have received rather a bad press, partly because of the excessively solemn tone in which Gilbert propounded them and partly because Joyce takes good care to have the claims of theosophy and the Eastern interests of the day frequently mocked in the novel itself by both Stephen and Mulligan. But it is in this area – eternal recurrence, reincarnation, metempsychosis – that the drift of *Ulysses* lies.

But behind and beneath all that lies the reality of Dublin. When Bloom and Stephen gaze up at the heavenly bodies, they do so not from just anywhere, but from a very specific location: the back garden of Bloom's house at Number 7 Eccles Street. For Joyce, Dublin's reality was primarily linguistic: that is why his departure from the city made so little difference: he carried its language, which was its world, with him. When one of the jarvies in the cabman's shelter says to the sailor: 'You seen queer sights, don't be talking', or one of the street urchins outside Davy Byrne's shouts at Bloom: 'Eh, mister! Your fly is open, mister!', we know we are in the hands of a writer to whom Dublin's street argot is second nature. But more than that, many other Dublin discourses are also available, not all of them unique to the city, but all of them certainly operative in it. Joyce's identification with the city was total; it was his muse, his interior paramour. Perhaps the apostrophe in the term 'Joyce's Dublin' could be read as not just a possessive: the Dublin of Joyce, but also as standing for a missing letter: Joyce is Dublin. The same would hold true for Dublin's Joyce.

Joyce's *1921 Schema for* Ulysses

Title	Scene	Hour	Organ
1. Telemachus	The Tower	8 a.m.	
2. Nestor	The School	10 a.m.	
3. Proteus	The Strand	11 a.m.	
4. Calypso	The House	8 a.m.	Kidney
5. Lotus-Eaters	The Bath	10 a.m.	Genitals
6. Hades	The Graveyard	11 a.m.	Heart
7. Aeolus	The Newspaper	12 noon	Lungs
8. Lestrygonians	The Lunch	1 p.m.	Esophagus
9. Scylla and Charybdis	The Library	2 p.m.	Brain
10. Wandering Rocks	The Streets	3 p.m.	Blood
11. Sirens	The Concert Room	4 p.m.	Ear
12. Cyclops	The Tavern	5 p.m.	Muscle
13. Nausicaa	The Rocks	8 p.m.	Eye, Nose
14. Oxen of the Sun	The Hospital	10 p.m.	Womb
15. Circe	The Brothel	12 midnight	Locomotor apparatus
16. Eumaeus	The Shelter	1 a.m.	Nerves
17. Ithaca	The House	2 a.m.	Skeleton
18. Penelope	The Bed		Flesh

The schema reproduced here first appeared in 1921 and was later printed in Stuart Gilbert's *James Joyce's 'Ulysses': A Study* in 1930.

Art	Colour	Symbol	Technic
Theology	White, gold	Heir	Narrative (young)
History	Brown	Horse	Catechism (personal)
Philology	Green	Tide	Monologue (male)
Economics	Orange	Nymph	Narrative (mature)
Botany, Chemistry		Eucharist	Narcissism
Religion	White, black	Caretaker	Incubism
Rhetoric	Red	Editor	Enthymemic
Architecture		Constables	Peristaltic
Literature		Stratford, London	Dialectic
Mechanics		Citizens	Labyrinth
Music		Barmaids	Fuga per canonem
Politics		Fenian	Gigantism
Painting	Grey, blue	Virgin	Tumescence, detumescence
Medicine	White	Mothers	Embryonic development
Magic		Whore	Hallucination
Navigation		Sailors	Narrative (old)
Science		Comets	Catechism (impersonal)
		Earth	Monologue (female)

Epilogue: Ulysses *at 100*

From Monster to Monument to Mobile

Perceptions of *Ulysses* have varied greatly in the 100 years since it first appeared. Even before its publication on 2 February 1922 it was already pretty notorious, owing to the obscenity prosecution of the New York-based *Little Review* following its serialisation of the book. The prosecution was successful, leading to the effective banning of Joyce's work in the US for many years subsequently.

Thus *Ulysses* was scandalous from even before day one: *The Sporting Times* (also known as 'The Pink 'Un') had the famous headline, very soon after the book's publication, 'The Scandal of *Ulysses*' (a phrase which was to be used again subsequently in different contexts). The book appeared as something monstrous, monstrous in its sheer bulk, monstrous in its sexual frankness, monstrous in its complexity and alleged unreadability. In causing such a shock, in creating such a stir, *Ulysses* was playing its part in a central aspect of Modernism: the shock of the new, as it has been well called, the wholly unexpected arrival of a 'rough beast', radically different from the literature that had preceded it and, on the face of it, radically different from *any* preceding literature. Was it literature at all? Novelty and shock value go hand in hand, and both are crucial to the Modernist ethos.

Contemporary reviews reflect this sense of outrage, of readers facing a challenge of unprecedented dimensions. Joseph Brooker's *Joyce and His Critics* (listed in the Bibliography) captures well the disorientation, the near anxiety, that Joyce's work occasioned. Kevin Birmingham's *The Most Dangerous Book* and Joseph Hassett's *The Ulysses Trials*, also listed, are similarly useful recent reminders of what *Ulysses* 'did to people' on its first appearance.

Brooker is particularly sharp on the contemporary reaction to the book's sexual material. Leaving aside 'The Pink 'Un', Brooker describes a kind of visceral reaction on the part of reviewers as sophisticated as H. G. Wells, which is telling in relation to the sheer challenge *Ulysses* posed to accustomed habits of reading. Today, when the work has 'classic' status, we are no longer, of course, 'shocked' by these things, but something is also lost in our tamed acceptance of, say, all of Molly's fantasies. Or is it rather, as I suspect, that this shock, this visceral reaction, is in fact still there, but – the new prudery – now covered over in the interests of appearing a fully paid-up member of the classic *Ulysses* club?

In some respects, this 'monstrous *Ulysses*' phase lasted quite a long time. The book was not legally on sale in the US until 1934 and in the UK until 1936. But, in other respects, its 'rogue' status was already being steadily undermined from within the Modernist camp itself. As already explained in the Afterword section, the book was taken up by some influential Anglo-American Modernists, notably Ezra Pound and T. S. Eliot. Thus the process of monumentalisation had begun. The academic prestige of Eliot in particular meant that the cause was soon being championed in English departments in both the US and the UK.

Progress was not uniform: there was still considerable resistance in academic circles up to the 1940s or early 1950s in the US and, even more, the UK (and in Ireland up to the 1960s at least), but slowly, and with a certain inevitability, *Ulysses* became accepted as a classic text, a monument. Its one-day time-frame, its schemas, now much better known, its Homeric echoes, its careful structure, all lent it this statuesque air, a kind of impregnable fortress of high Modernist writing.

Importantly, it was *difficult*; one had to work to understand it, and this gave it a certain respectability which meant that some of its more 'basic' qualities – its Irishness, say – could be contextualised and sanitised. (This was all the easier since Irish critics of and commentators on the book were not exactly to the fore in this era.) Under the influence of the then-fashionable theory of 'spatial form', *Ulysses* seemed timeless, an object in space like a work of art, impervious to change or to instability.

It is difficult to say when exactly this sense of Joyce's work as a monument more unchangeable than bronze began to alter. Perhaps the catalyst was the revelation, in the early 1980s, that the text of the book was in some respects seriously faulty. This was something of a surprise (I won't say 'shock'). If the book was a bronze statue, it seemed to have feet of clay. However, assurances were given: all would be well. Under the editorship of Hans Walter Gabler of the University of Munich and his team, the problems would be ironed out and the text would be established in a permanent and authoritative form.

That, though, is not what happened. After this edition appeared in 1984, it soon came under vigorous attack for both its methodology and its practical textual changes. This is now ancient history, and there is no need to revisit it: the attacks were greatly overdone, though making one or two valid points. In fact, the text produced by Gabler and Co. remains the best available – it is the one used in this volume – but any sense that it is 'definitive' has been tacitly but totally abandoned. So this inherent textual instability is certainly a factor in altering our sense of *Ulysses*'s monumental permanence.

Another factor in making *Ulysses* seem less of a timeless creation is the increased critical emphasis on history and its outworkings in the book. The rise of post-colonialist studies, which has gone hand in hand with an increased focus on the text's Irishness, has served to take the text out of eternity and place it back in a specific time and place, the time and place in which it is set. It is telling that Emer Nolan's *James Joyce and Nationalism*, which is in this vein and appeared in 1995, was the first monograph on Joyce published by an Irish academic based in Ireland. All this work also helped to make *Ulysses* part of 'the living stream', rather than 'a stone in the midst of all'.

The final factor that has changed the status of *Ulysses* again over more recent years is the new attention being paid to textual matters – not, any longer, with a view to an edition, definitive or otherwise, but rather the text for its own sake. This renewed attention has been greatly stimulated by the acquisition of many more manuscripts of the work than had previously been known to exist by the National Library of Ireland in 2002. What has emerged from this examination is how radically unstable and arbitrary much of this seemingly immutable text is.

The book by Luca Crispi listed in the Bibliography is exemplary in this regard. It presents a Joyce who is changing his mind constantly, adding phrases, moving phrases around, altering chronology in response to new conceptions, to give just a few examples. Sometimes he will move a phrase originally written to describe a particular person so that it now applies to someone else. Crispi shows how the 'characters' of Leopold and Molly Bloom are constructed out of scraps and fragments, 'a thing of shreds and patches', composite figures whose component parts are constantly shifting.

Similarly, the recent finding that, in the various parodies of the 'Oxen of the Sun' episode, Joyce used many words and phrases taken from other writers than the one being parodied also serves to destabilise the presumed fixities of the text, even though I do not agree that this renders the parodies entirely random and unattributable (see discussion of style in 'Oxen' episode).

As Michael Groden points out in the essay in *Ulysses in Focus*, from which I derived the phrase 'from monument to mobile', not only is *Ulysses* changed over time by the different responses of different readers, 'reinserting *Ulysses* into the history of its writing gives it an altered past as well.' More and more it seems that the book's publication date of 2 February 1922 – Joyce's fortieth birthday – was an entirely arbitrary cut-off point to bring a term to a labour that was properly interminable.

'Mobile', in the sense in which Groden uses it, refers to the kind of sculpture in which the parts are suspended in air and constantly move, most associated with Alexander Calder. It is an apt figure for what has happened to *Ulysses* over the past 100 years: we can certainly say that it is multi-faceted, continually catching new shifts of light, and inexhaustible to interpretation.

Select Bibliography

Adams, Robert M., *Surface and Symbol: The Consistency of James Joyce's 'Ulysses'* (Oxford University Press, 1967)

Birmingham, Kevin, *The Most Dangerous Book: The Battle for James Joyce's 'Ulysses'* (Head of Zeus, 2014)

Brooker, Joseph, *Joyce's Critics: Transitions in Reading and Culture* (University of Wisconsin Press, 2004)

Budgen, Frank, *James Joyce and the Making of 'Ulysses'* (1934; reissued Oxford University Press, 1972)

Bulson, Eric, *Ulysses by Numbers* (Columbia University Press, 2020)

Corser, Sophie, *The Reader's Joyce: 'Ulysses', Authorship, and the Authority of the Reader* (Edinburgh University Press, 2022)

Crispi, Luca, *Joyce's Creative Process and the Construction of Characters in 'Ulysses': Becoming the Blooms* (Oxford University Press, 2015)

Deming, Robert H., ed., *James Joyce: The Critical Heritage* (2 vols, Routledge and Kegan Paul, 1970)

Duffy, Enda, *The Subaltern 'Ulysses'* (University of Minnesota Press, 1994)

Eliot, T. S., 'Ulysses, Order and Myth', in Frank Kermode, ed., *Selected prose of T. S. Eliot* (Faber and Faber, 1975)

Ellmann, Richard, *James Joyce* (revised edition, Oxford University Press, 1982)

—*'Ulysses' on the Liffey* (Faber and Faber, 1972)

—ed., *Selected letters of James Joyce* (Faber and Faber, 1975)

Flynn, Catherine, ed., *The Cambridge Centenary Ulysses: The 1922 Text with Essays and Notes* (Cambridge University Press, 2022)

Gibson, Andrew, *Joyce's Revenge: History, Politics and Aesthetics in 'Ulysses'* (Oxford University Press, 2002)

Gilbert, Stuart, *James Joyce's 'Ulysses': A Study* (1930; reissued Faber and Faber, 1952)

Groden, Michael, *'Ulysses' in Progress* (Princeton University Press, 1977)

—'*Ulysses' in Focus: Genetic, Textual, and Personal Views* (University Press of Florida, 2010)

—*The Necessary Fiction: Life with James Joyce's 'Ulysses'* (Edward Everett Root, 2019)

Hassett, Joseph M., *The Ulysses Trials* (Lilliput Press, 2018)

Hayman, David, *'Ulysses': The Mechanics of Meaning* (revised edition, University of Wisconsin Press, 1982)

Igoe, Vivien, *The Real People of Joyce's 'Ulysses': A Biographical Guide* (University Colllege Dublin Press, 2016)

Kenner, Hugh, *Dublin's Joyce* (1956; reissued Columbia University Press, 1987)

—*Joyce's Voices* (Faber and Faber, 1974)

—'*Ulysses'* (1980; revised edition, Johns Hopkins University Press, 1987)

Kiberd, Declan, *'Ulysses' and Us: The Art of Everyday Living* (Faber and Faber, 2009)

Latham, Sean, ed., *The Cambridge Companion to 'Ulysses'* (Cambridge University Press, 2014)

Lawrence, Karen, *The Odyssey of Style in 'Ulysses'* (Princeton University Press, 1981)

Nolan, Emer, *James Joyce and Nationalism* (Routledge, 1995)

Norris, Margot, *Virgin and Veteran Readings of 'Ulysses'* (Palgrave Macmillan, 2011)

Seidel, Michael, *Epic Geography: James Joyce's 'Ulysses'* (Princeton University Press, 1976)

Senn, Fritz, *Joyce's Dislocutions: Essays on Reading as Translation* (Johns Hopkins University Press, 1984)

—*Inductive Scrutinies: Focus on Joyce* (Lilliput Press, 1995)

Slote, Sam, Marc A. Mamigonian and John Turner, *Annotations to James Joyce's 'Ulysses'* (Oxford University Press, 2021)